MARTIN LUTHER KING, JR.
AND THE CIVIL RIGHTS MOVEMENT

Edited by David J. Garrow

A CARLSON PUBLISHING SERIES

The Sit-In Movement of 1960

Martin Oppenheimer

PREFACE BY DAVID J. GARROW

CARLSON
Publishing Inc

BROOKLYN, NEW YORK, 1989

Library of Congress Cataloging-in Publication Data

Oppenheimer, Martin
    The sit-in movement of 1960 / Martin Oppenheimer.
        p. cm. — (Martin Luther King, Jr. and the Civil Rights
Movement ; 16)
    Originally presented as the author's thesis (Ph.D.)—University
of Pennsylvania, 1963.
    Bibliography: p.
    Includes index.
    1. Afro-Americans—Civil rights—History—20th century. 2. Afro
-Americans—Civil rights—Southern States—History—20th century.
3. Civil rights demonstrations—United States—History—20th
century. 4. Civil rights demonstrations—Southern States-
-History—20th century. 5. Southern States—Race relations.
6. Afro-Americans—History—1877-1964. I. Title. II. Series.
E185.61.067   1989   89-9868   323.1'196073075—dc20
ISBN 0-926019-10-4 (alk. paper)

Typographic design: Julian Waters

Typeface: Bitstream ITC Galliard

The index to this book was created using NL Cindex, a scholarly indexing program
from the Newberry Library.

For a complete listing of the volumes in this series, please see the back of this book.

Printed on acid-free, 250-year-life paper.

Manufactured in the United States of America.

Contents

List of Tables
and Graphs

TABLES

GRAPH

Series Editor's Preface

Martin Oppenheimer's 1963 dissertation on the student sit-in movement of 1960 has long been an important resource and reference tool for scholarly students of the southern civil rights struggle, and I am very pleased that Carlson Publishing's series of volumes on *Martin Luther King, Jr., and the Civil Rights Movement* will now be able to make it available to a considerably wider audience.

As Oppenheimer himself notes in his 1989 preface, his disciplinary affiliation with sociology required that he organize and analyze his study of the sit-ins in ways that sometimes diverge from traditional historiography, but Oppenheimer's work still remains, over twenty-five years later, the richest and most detailed study, published or unpublished, that we yet have on what in retrospect was clearly the breakthrough year for the southern civil rights movement, 1960.

The greatest values of Oppenheimer's volume lay both in the very detailed and original account of the sit-ins own spread that is contained in sections D and E of part III and in the important and largely unique studies of ten different communities—Charlotte, Nashville, Atlanta, Jacksonville, Rock Hill (South Carolina), Columbia, Tallahassee, Montgomery, Orangeburg, and Lawrenceville (Virginia)—that are presented in part IV. The landmark initial events in Greensboro, North Carolina, have been nicely chronicled in William Chafe's *Civilities and Civil Rights* (Oxford University Press, 1980), but no latter-day comprehensive study of the south-wide sit-ins has yet supplanted Oppenheimer's almost contemporaneous work as a detailed and dependable record of how quickly this new manifestation of black student activism burgeoned all across the South. Both in tracking the chronological and geographic spread of the sit-ins, and in analyzing both the attitudes of the participants and the dynamics of their interactions with local white authorities, Oppenheimer makes an invaluable contribution to the overall historiography of the black freedom struggle in the South. When the day comes that a truly comprehensive and broad-gauged history of the entire southern movement is prepared, Oppenheimer's volume will be a major building-block in such an effort; in the meantime all scholars and students with an interest in how the sit-ins of 1960 and their youthful sponsors sparked the crucial intensification of the southern struggle will find that *The Sit-In Movement of 1960* is the most valuable place to begin.

David J. Garrow

Preface 1989

What was considered sociology twenty-five years ago has become history. The history of the civil rights movement has recently become an object of fascination, part of a wider interest in all of the movements of the sixties. Unfortunately, the media often portray history as nothing but personalities and movements, nothing but arguments about style. This message must be overcome and supplanted with a sensibility that the present is derivative, and is in turn mutable, and that movements were, and are, about real issues.

The real issues of the sixties persist. In the case of the present series, the issue is one of racial conflict within the United States. An understanding of the persistence of the conflict and, hopefully, the development of sound strategies to come to terms with it, demands far more than a romanticized, Hollywood version of what the civil rights movement (and its opponents) were all about.

Social scientists know that generations and decades are socially-derived categories, and that "beginnings" are arbitrary. Still, the sit-ins of 1960 have come to be acknowledged by many as the opening event of "the movements of the sixties." In my view the sixties actually began on December 1, 1955 with the Montgomery Bus Boycott, and ended only in 1975 with the collapse of the Saigon regime. Be that as it may, it is hardly debatable that the sit-ins constituted a major breakthrough.

The sit-in movement activated masses of people, particularly college students, resulted in the integration of a range of public facilities in the South, and opened the way to the Freedom Rides, Mississippi Summer, Selma and many other events. Veterans of the black student movement have gone on to play major roles in politics and in the wider society. Many white Northern students who had been mobilized in support of the sit-ins and later civil rights work became active in the anti-war movement after 1965; they too have gone on to play important roles in other reform efforts. Many women participants became leaders in the feminist movement. Although no revolution (political, economic, racial, or psychic) has taken place, the face of American politics and society more generally has been unalterably changed due to the movements of the sixties, many of which can trace their genesis to February 1, 1960 in Greensboro, North Carolina.

The sit-ins "broke out" just as I was casting about for a dissertation topic through which I could continue to pursue my interest in social movements, especially "Negro" movements. Of course social scientists do not come to the study of a subject arbitrarily. This is probably more true of the study of social movements than of nearly any other area. We study movements either because we sympathize with their objectives (and hope that our work will, perhaps, be of assistance to them) or because we are antagonists (and hope that we can, somehow, aid in their downfall or in the prevention of something similar in the future: my M.A. Thesis was on the Hitler Movement).

I understood equal rights for minorities, and the struggle for them to be an inherent part of being Jewish and integral to being a socialist. Taking sides, however, was frowned upon by most of my sociology professors in the fifties: it was not "objective." Neutrality was deemed to be the correct stance. Moreover, my scheme of studying communities by undertaking a field trip was questioned on practical grounds. "It can't be done," I was told by a historian who would later be a leading chronicler of the movement. I was nevertheless able to complete the work (without grants or assistantships) thanks to a tolerant adviser. "They hate you here," he told me. "Just finish it and get out." This context is part of the reason for the sometimes awkward sociological edifice of this dissertation.

Yet sociology is not without its uses in historical narrative. It provides tools with which to organize data coherently and ways in which to analyze. Data rarely "speak for themselves." In those terms the present dissertation holds up pretty well. Some of the language is outdated: one notes the use, throughout, of the terms "Negro" and "his" (denoting an unawareness of the considerable contribution of women to the movement). Although one senses a materialist framework, especially in the discussion of the role of urbanization in the development of political consciousness, it is all too brief and insufficiently explicit. A good deal of subsequent work by many others is now available to illuminate those issues in far more detail. In particular, the now extensive literature on the economic modernization of the South provides a solid underpinning for a better understanding of the social changes leading to the civil rights explosion of the early sixties. [See, for example, Frances Fox Piven and Richard A. Cloward, *Poor People's Movements*, 1977, Chapter 4; Doug McAdam, *Political Process and the Development of Black*

Insurgency, 1930-1970, 1982, Chapters 5 and 6; and Gavin Wright, *Old South, New South: Revolutions in the Southern Economy Since the Civil War*, 1987.]

Sociological theory about social movements has also evolved. The field of sociology, perhaps because of its much advertised "objectivity," often ignores important political and cultural movements when they develop, coming to study them only years later. This was clearly the case with the Hitler Movement. The sixties movements, as McAdam points out, were no exceptions, and real discussion and debate about their sociology (that is, how their dynamics as movements can be best understood) has come only recently. [A thorough discussion of these issues can be found in McAdam, 1982, Introduction through Chapter 4; see also Aldon D. Morris, *The Origins of the Civil Rights Movement*, 1984, Chapter 11.]

The effect of national and local power structures (that is, what McAdam calls the social-control response) on the development and outcome of movements ought to be an important dimension of the study of movements; this dissertation brings that in at the community level, and there now exists a considerable body of literature about national power structures. [Recent examples are G. William Domhoff, *Who Rules America Now?*, 1983; Domhoff, *The Powers That Be*, 1978; Michael Parenti, *Power and the Powerless*, 1978; Alan Wolfe, *The Seamy Side of Democracy*, 1973; and Wolfe, *The Limits of Legitimacy*, 1977] but there is still very little social scientific material available on the responses of national power structures to social movements. [An exception is Piven and Cloward's *Regulating the Poor*, 1971.] There are the "official" responses, e.g. *The Report of the President's Commission on Campus Unrest* (1971) and the like, but these are little more than superficial rhetoric, not sociological or historical analyses. This appears to be an area where we must still let "the facts speak (sometimes scream) for themselves." [See Ward Churchill & Jim Vander Wall, *Agents of Repression: The FBI's Secret Wars Against the Black Panther Party and the American Indian Movement*, 1988; David J. Garrow, *The FBI and Martin Luther King Jr.*, 1981, etc.] However, the relationship of national power structures to specific policy as carried out by government agencies remains murky, at least insofar as the civil rights movements is concerned.

There is not a great deal of work published since 1963 on the sit-ins themselves. Howard Zinn's *SNCC* (1964) has but a short chapter. Miles Wolff's *How It All Began* (1970), a journalistic account, is limited to Greensboro. Rev. King's role is discussed briefly in David L. Lewis' *King*

(1970) as well as in most subsequent work on King. Anthony Orum's monograph *Black Students in Protest: A Study of the Origins of the Black Student Movement* (1972), a revision of his dissertation, is a study of the participants. An essential historical work is August Meier and Elliott Rudwick's *CORE: A Study in the Civil Rights Movement, 1942-1968* (1973). All works on SNCC necessarily have some material on the sit-ins, as do studies of the movement in particular cities such as Atlanta. A comprehensive follow-up study of the participants (including the original Greensboro four and/or the original SNCC members) remains to be done.

Many who participated in the movements of the sixties, especially the early sixties, now look back on that period as a rare golden moment that gave meaning to their lives. The analogy to a previous generation's feelings about the Spanish Civil War, or the labor movement of the 1930s, is inescapable. The sad part is not that their movements achieved less than had been hoped for, but that the larger portion of their lives since that period has been so bereft of meaning. To the extent that meaning comes from active participation in efforts to end oppression and extend democracy, the events of the coming decade may well provide the opportunity for many veterans of the sixties once again to find meaning in their lives. The retelling of the story of their earlier efforts may help in that process.

Martin Oppenheimer
January, 1989

The Sit-In Movement of 1960

ONE

Introduction

The purpose of this dissertation is to present the origins, development, structure and results of the Sit-In Movement of Negro students in the Southern part of the United States, with emphasis on the year 1960. This exposition of the first year of what has become known as the Southern Negro Student Movement is to take place with the framework of the theories of social movement (discussing the movement as a whole, or from the macrocosmic viewpoint); and intergroup social conflict (viewing specific community-level developments from the microcosmic approach). The historical, social, political and economic factors that may have contributed to the rise of the movement, and which may have affected its overall development, will also be discussed.

The dissertation may conveniently be divided into four general parts: (1) A general discussion of the concept of social movement and the development of a series of propositions or hypotheses related to the "life-cycle" approach to the study of social movement. (2) The testing of this series of hypotheses through an examination of the historical development of the Sit-In Movement. (3) A general discussion of the dynamics of social conflict leading to the development of a series of propositions or hypotheses related to intergroup and intragroup functioning in conflict situations. (4) The testing of this series of hypotheses through an examination of a series of cases of communities in various parts of the South undergoing the stress of a student sit-in movement of one kind or another.

Insofar as source-material for this study is concerned, it is not possible to carry on a methodologically-tight study of a social movement in process on an area-wide scale. This is true primarily because trained observers were on hand only in a small number of cases (work by such observers has been utilized here). It was possible for this writer to be on hand as an observer at a number of conferences, but not during the main part of the sit-in activity during 1960. This writer visited and studied at close hand fourteen communities in which activity of varying kinds had taken place, but this was a full year after the initial wave of the Movement, and in many cases the

1

original participants were no longer available for interviews. In addition, the amount of time available for field study was limited, so that in no case did the writer stay in a community for longer than five days. Adverse opinions and hostility to the study of such a movement by the social scientists in a locality contributed in some instances to the shortness of the stay.

The sources of data for those sections dealing with the testing of hypotheses (the history of the Movement and the case studies of communities) can be summarized in the following manner: (1) Primary data such as interviews, access to some correspondence, files, publicity releases, reports (in some cases confidential), of a number of individuals and organizations. (2) Secondary data including accounts in the public press, accounts of observers published as theses, unpublished manuscripts, and publications and periodicals released by interested organizations as part of their work of informing their constituencies.

The organizations which were kind enough to permit this writer access to some or all files (both dealing with the current civil rights movement and with antecedent developments in all cases) were: the Congress of Racial Equality (CORE), United States National Student Association, Southern Regional Council, and Southeastern Region, American Friends Service Committee. Some files, minutes, releases, etc. of some other organizations were also consulted, in particular those of the National Association for the Advancement of Colored People (NAACP), the Student Non-Violent Coordinating Committee, the Southern Christian Leadership Conference, the Southern Conference Educational Fund, the Highlander Folk School, the American Civil Liberties Union, the Department of Civil Rights, AFL-CIO; and the Department of Racial and Cultural Relations, National Council of Churches. Interviews were conducted with officials of all of the above-named organizations.

The following individuals were particularly helpful in making various documents and files available, and in contributing valuable comments and suggestions: Miss Constance Curry, Southern Student Human Relations Project, USNSA; Miss Rachelle Horowitz and Mr. Tom Kahn, Young Peoples Socialist League; Mr. Richard Ramsay, American Friends Service Committee; and Mr. Robert Walters, USNSA.

In addition to primary and secondary data such as those listed above, personal observation of sit-in activity and conferences dealing with the Movement contributed to this dissertation in three different ways: (1) data collection; (2) the germination of relevant ideas and hypotheses; (3) the establishment of the writer as a friendly participant-observer, hence aiding in access to sources of data within the Movement.

Several important limitations of available data, and impediments to the collection of information, deserve mention in this discussion of source material. In the course of field investigation it was found almost impossible to gain significant access to white opinion, white community leaders, and insight into the white power structure of the community. Thus such questions as: At which point were white businessmen willing to give in, and why did they actually give in? (as distinct from vocalizations)—remain open to speculation only, and have no airtight answers. The chief reason for this is that the social scientist (not only Yankee, but also Southern investigators, from conversations with a number of the latter) who shows interest in the Negro protest movement is automatically assumed by the white power structure (business leaders, police, local government) to be part of that movement, and hence is perceived as an enemy. Information obtained tends to be almost exclusively of the "publicity-release" type, that is, lacking any real content except for the student of propaganda. In some cases an extended stay in the community while attempting to contact Negro student leaders is itself excluded and the investigator is forced to make a "hit-and-run" kind of survey of the area. Local officials sometimes assume he is an organizer for the integrationist group and may even threaten arrest while the investigator is attempting to conduct interviews.

On the other hand, the same assumption is followed by Negro participants and sympathizers of the Movement, and, far from being suspicious of the white investigator, Negro informants tend to be open and free with all but the "insider" kind of information.

There is, however, an important limitation to this, one which also bears on the accuracy of press reports. As Myrdal has pointed out, "Since power and prestige are scarce commodities in the Negro community, the struggle for leadership often becomes ruthless."[1] There is, within the Negro community, a scarcity of both prestigeful positions, and of trained individuals to fill leadership positions requiring technical and organizational skills. When the sit-ins broke out, a large number of prestigeful leadership positions was created, many of which required some organizational and technical skill. In a number of cases Negroes filling these positions tended to be jealous of potential competitors, and tended to inflate their own importance, particularly when their skills were not adequate to the task. Since the press is often dependent upon these leaders (who also tend to be the most vocal), accounts are often distorted to inflate the role of this or that person of the organization which is his "creation," and by an underplaying of other persons or organizations which may not have such a vocal spokesman. A precise picture of what happened in any locality would therefore require an observer to stay (and participate) for months, beginning with the outbreak of the movement. Failing this, any description of a local movement can be accurate only within certain broad approximations.

Added to this is the traditional difficulty of selective perception. Participants in an ongoing movement which concerns their very lives in some instances, which absorbs every moment of spare-time activity (and often much more than that), and which requires of them talents never exercised before (such as organizing, public speaking, keeping financial accounts, legal knowledge, etc.), simply do not keep records of what has occurred. A diary is almost unknown. Minutes of meetings are almost nonexistent on the local level. The danger of "informers" adds to a reluctance to keep careful records of plans, as does the constant danger of police harassment, vigilante action, and the like. Participants, especially when some months have passed, simply do not remember exactly what happened. In one case, only four months after the event, three participants could not remember the date of an important conference which had taken place on their own campus, and ranged in their recall all the way from Thanksgiving Day to Christmas (the actual weekend was that of December 9-11). A general lack of information on ordinary legal details complicates recall of the outcomes of trials, hearings, and the like. Informants in some cases were unable to distinguish between grand jury inquests and trials; between bail and fines; between being out on bail, and being out on parole or probation.

In terms of organization, the main difficulty as to reliability is that any organization which depends for its financial support on dues or contributions from large numbers of constituents must justify its existence in terms of action and results. Hence such organizations overplay, in many cases, their own importance and underplay the roles of their "competitors" within the overall movement. Organizations which have no such "axe to grind" because of independent financing tend to be far more reliable in their data, and more objective in their evaluation. In some cases national organizations deliberately distort their roles, withhold information, or misinform. In other cases they are entirely candid and take the investigator into their complete confidence—particularly when such a confidence damages the competitor.

There are, therefore, no purely objective sources. The observer must take what he can find, compare it to other sources when available, make a judgment as to its accuracy relative to the other facts available, and be prepared to have his findings criticized later by other observers who have found further sources. Thus in many instances the facts presented herein are the best available under the circumstances, and not necessarily *the* one and only truth.

One additional technical factor in analyzing actions for social change should be kept in mind. In the past, social action has often been recorded by letter and telegram, by memorandum and diary. Apart from the limitations mentioned earlier, this is the era of the telephone. One important source of information is therefore entirely eliminated. Much of the business of the Sit-In Movement, especially area-wide and North-South communication, was conducted day-to-day by telephone, and this business appears to be lost to the recorder forever.

It has been suggested that among the research gaps in the area of intergroup relations are: (1) the need to rectify the parochialism of studying white gentile attitudes only; (2) the need to examine what really happens during social change in an integrating situation; (3) the need to examine the workings of minority groups and their organizations; and (4) the need to study the differences between attitudes and behavior.[2] This dissertation is directed towards (2) and (3), rather than towards the area of attitudes and opinions; it is specifically concerned with Negro group behavior on the macrocosmic and microcosmic scale, with what actually happens during integration as a process of social change within the community, and with the organization and functioning of a minority group (or parts of it) as it functions to perform social change.

The sit-ins have been an intensely fascinating experience for the participants, and indeed for anyone who has had any connection with them. The writer was fortunate both as an American and as a student in the field of sociology that the sit-ins happened, and that he was privileged to meet and talk with so many of the very courageous individuals who, through this Movement, helped bring the "American Ideal" a little closer to reality.

TWO

The Social Movement Concept

Social movements (to be defined below) have become an important subject for sociological investigation not merely because they involve large numbers of people, but rather, even more importantly, because they constitute, in a way, small societies, and hence can be studied for the purpose of arriving at a better understanding of such aspects of society as leadership, bureaucracy, group relations, etc. Further, they supply an unending amount of data which seem in many ways ideally suited to a study of the field of social change and social conflict. Finally, in providing the sociologist with important clues about the rate, direction, and consequences of change, the study of movements "can also illuminate for the social planner the possibilities and problems of instituting social change by blueprint."[3] Hence the ordering of the data of social change within the framework of the concepts of social movement theory can provide the student of society with far deeper insights into the workings of society than the mere collection of historical or journalistic data by themselves.

Before attempting to apply social movement theory to the history of Negro protest activity in the United States, it may be useful to discuss briefly some of the schools of thought within this field of theory, and to outline some of the methods of studying social movements in an effort to determine the utility of these concepts and methods when dealing with Negro affairs.

The term "social movement" by itself covers such a range of social action to secure some sort of change, or to prevent change, that it borders on the meaningless. It is only when one discusses the various types of movement and the various methods of analyzing them that order can be brought into a term encompassing such phenomena as panty raids and Peyote Cults, women's suffrage and Naziism. Let us first attempt to obtain some agreement on definition. Theories stemming from a variety of traditions including political science, anthropology and sociology do agree on some minimal definitions. Theodore Abel, discussing Naziism, suggested that a movement is

". . . pluralistic behavior functioning as an organized mass effort directed toward a change of established folkways or institutions. . ."[4]

The anthropologist Anthony Wallace called it ". . . a deliberate, organized, conscious effort by members of a society to construct a more satisfying culture."[5] Turner and Killian included resistance to change, calling a social movement "a collectivity acting with some continuity to promote a change or resist a change in the society or group of which it is a part."[6] King followed this general idea, calling a social movement

"a group venture extending beyond a local community or a single event and involving a systematic effort to inaugurate changes in thought, behavior, and social relationships."[7]

These definitions, however, raise the question of just how much change is to take place within the context of a group of people trying to change the established culture in some organized manner. In particular it has been pointed out that the American Negro protest has been directed in the main not towards changing the basic values of American society, but only towards gaining access to that society, wanting "in" on that society. Even though the American Negro may not want to change much of society, the fact that Negro protest groups want to change at least one society-wide pattern seems to suffice for the definition, for, as King points out, "Few movements have ever sought to change an entire society . . ."[8] In fact, to have any success, a movement must have "some degree of consistency with the society's general culture," as, indeed, most Negro integrationist movements do have. Anthropologists have pointed out that some segments of a culture change more rapidly than others, depending on the extent of deep-rooted feelings involved; the successful movement is often one which has picked as a target for change an area of life in which change is expected, encouraged, and one in which current patterns are not regarded as immutable and inviolate.[9] In fact, one way of classifying movements is to distinguish between those advocating more extensive use of current remedies (this would include most integrationist groups) and those repudiating claims to respectability within the established order.[10]

But this distinction (that is, between the categories of reform versus revolution) is only one of several ways of classifying social movements in the literature of mass action. Blumer has suggested a division, for example, as between what he calls general, specific (planned and structured), and expressive (seeking an outlet in expressive behavior) movements;[11] Turner and Killian distinguish movements from collectivities which are "quasi-movements," such as historical trends, on the one hand, or mere followings and cults on the other;[12] they further suggest that it may be useful to divide movements into those which are primarily value-oriented, power-oriented, or participation-oriented; or, for that matter, into categories according to how they act—legitimately versus illegally.[13]

The literature of anthropology has suggested even more intricate frameworks into which movements (primarily of preliterate societies) may be divided, depending for the most part on their orientations, and responding for the most part to situations of culture contact, culture change, acculturation, or the antagonistic response to acculturation.[14]

This writer, however, would like to suggest that methods of classifying movements, such as mentioned above, remain subsidiary to what it is about movements that the investigator wishes to study. For the interest-field about movements is bound to create typologies reflecting those interest fields. One would not expect the student of individual motivation in organizational participation to classify movements primarily from a historical viewpoint, nor would one expect a student of the relationship between leaders and followers to utilize a typology involving varying reactions to culture contact. Hence it is perhaps understandable, given the goal-orientation of American Negro protest, and the primarily historical orientation of most writers on this subject, that most protest activity has been dealt with in terms of the categories "accommodation" versus "militancy," or some variation upon this theme.[15]

The literature of social movements in general has traditionally fallen into three classes: modern political and/or religious movements as viewed by sociologists and psychologists,[16] movements in preliterate or colonial areas of the world as viewed by anthropologists,[17] and studies of certain historical developments over a span of time as seen by some historians.[18] Few writers have attempted to deal with Negro movements from the angle of social movement theory as such.[19] An overall history of Negro social movements in this country from that viewpoint is still lacking. In the main, work has been framed in terms of single civil rights organizations, or the lives of significant leaders, or at best dealing with a comparison of world-wide movements, with a few words being given to the American Negro.[20] Almost no efforts have been made to compare Negro movements with one another in order to determine how and why changes in format, demands, and results have taken place.

Students of social change and social movements differ widely in their emphasis upon what angle of movement should be studied. Heberle has listed a number of matters properly the subject for study: the ideology of the movement, the attitudes and motivations of its participants, its social foundation in terms of sources of support, its structure (including the differentiation of roles, the distribution of power, the organizational structure), its strategy and tactics, and its functions (both intended and latent) within the total society.[21]

One of the more common means of ordering the data on social movements in terms of a description of process is that of the "life-cycle"; this term has been applied both to a single movement and to various cyclical explanations of series of movements.[22] As Turner and Killian point out:

"The life-cycle consists of an idealized series of stages from the origin to the success or other final form of the movement. . . . It places emphasis on process, which is particularly important in the study of phenomena whose most important characteristic is change . . . (it) is a way of organizing our knowledge about movements so as to permit prediction of forthcoming events. (It) offers a framework within which the many aspects of a movement may be seen working together—leadership, ideology, tactics, membership, etc., rather than studied separately."[23]

The analyst of social change, by utilizing the framework of a life-cycle methodology, is able to circumvent the inherent difficulties of attempting an explanation of such factors as motivations for joining a movement (the difficulty of assessing a person's real motives on the basis of his answers to questionnaires and interview schedules, etc.); he is able to focus directly upon a movement, rather than seeking grandiose explanations in long-term historical theories; and at the same time he has a sociologically useful set of concepts by which to order the data of social change for the purpose of testing important generalizations in the field of collective action, and not merely collecting data for their own sake. For these reasons, the life-cycle approach will be the one utilized in this study.

The life-cycle, or "natural history" approach to social movements often encompasses a series of three to four "stages," into which the history of the movement can conveniently be broken down—a preliminary stage of unrest, a stage of collective excitement and informal organization, a stage of formalized organization, and an institutionalized, hierarchic stage.[24] Implied at one or more of these stages is a series of sociological observations involving such concepts as value conflict and anomie; relative deprivation; group identification; charisma; bureaucracy; cultural innovations, selection and integration; psychological determinants of acceptance of ideology; the role played by idiosyncratic and accidental factors in history; latent functions and meaning; and many others. It is therefore possible to derive a series of propositions and hypotheses from the literature of life-cycle theory of social movements, and test them within the limits of the data available for the Southern Negro Student Movement during 1960.

Most presently available work dealing with American Negro protest movements, as has been mentioned, falls short in one respect; it has not dealt with Negro protest in terms of movement theory, but rather in terms of the division between gradualism and radicalism alone; on the other extreme, data available to this writer would probably not support the grand theory-level generalizations framed in terms of "cycles" of Negro protest movements in America. The latter would more properly be the domain of the historian. Here we must be content with attempting to begin to fill the theoretical gap between ongoing Negro social movements, and social movement theory.

The propositions or hypotheses, derived from the literature, which will serve to order the data on the overall sit-in movement, and which will either be strengthened or weakened within life-cycle theory, follow.

> Proposition 1: *Some necessary, if not sufficient, conditions are conducive to the rise of protest movements. Among these conditions are relative deprivation, group identification, and the appearance of a social context in which action becomes feasible.*

Considerable space has been devoted, in the literature of social movements, to discussions of circumstances conducive to the rise of movements. The themes of relative deprivation, group identification, and a social, historical, or cultural situation making protest actionable, recur, even though these particular wordings are not uniformly used. Let us deal with each one.

In modern industrial, or "mass," society, it has been argued, particularly in societies undergoing rapid change from rural to urban culture, the individual is often confronted with situations in which the old responses no longer

11

apply. Older group ties tend to break down, and cultural conflict (between old and new ways) may take place. In some cases the adjustment of individuals may be so poor that severe personal maladjustment takes place.[25] In many cases anomie ("normlessness"), value conflicts, or cultural confusion occur. Individual discontent, anxiety about the future, frustration, tension, and continuing bewilderment may lead to "large number of people . . . seeking answers they do not have, reassurances that the answers they do have are right, or ways of implementing the answers . . ."[26] This kind of situation creates "an atmosphere conducive to even the most bizarre proposals, many of which thrive and grow. Providing answers and offering durable ideals are part of the 'promise' of many movements."[27] A variety of individual responses, as well as social ones, may take place, as such varying writers as Fromm and Merton have pointed out in their discussions of value conflict and anomie.[28] The above, whether it takes place within the context of urban dislocation or within circumstances of antagonistic acculturation in underdeveloped areas, is what can be called psychological deprivation, in the sense that the individual is deprived of his original "base-line" hold upon a Weltanschauung which had given him a degree of personal security.[29]

In addition to psychological deprivation, there is the physical deprivation of actual material goods such as food, clothing, shelter, educational opportunity, employment, and the like. There may come a time when this kind of deprivation is so acute that a "threshold of suffering" is reached, at which point "something has to happen."[30] This type of movement has been the subject of considerable anthropological study. More commonly, however, the deprivation itself is not as acute as the perception of it within the social context. This gap between existing circumstances (actual or imagined) and circumstances as the group thinks they ought to be, or its patterns of expectation or definition of the situation, is dependent upon the standards of comparison set up by the group undergoing the suffering or deprivation. Hence the concept "*relative* deprivation," as discussed by Stouffer and his associates.[31]

If in fact relative deprivation, either on the psychological and/or material level is a necessary contributing factor in the rise of social movements, then in the case of the American Negro in 1960 the data should support the assertion that there both exists a gap in the circumstances of Negro as compared to white, and that the Negro is somehow more aware of the gap (perceives it more consciously even if the gap is narrowing) than in earlier years.

But deprivation, real and/or perceived, by no means suffices to create movements. The second aspect of it seems to be that it must be channeled into an actionable form. The individual must somehow be made aware that he belongs to a group, and he must be made to see himself as part of a larger whole. In part this is a problem of communication; "If the individual already harbors vague notions about the cause of his ills, he now (in the era of mass media communication—MO) has the opportunity of selecting the expert or leader who is closest to his own position and who crystallises everything . . ."[32] Thus modern communications media at once expose the individual to the confusion of society, and also make it possible for him to have access to plans of action for the alleviation of his troubles. Communication, then, is indispensable to the development of an awareness on the part of many individuals that they do belong to a "negatively privileged group." Conflict behavior, as Coser points out, depends in part on "whether or not the unequal distribution of rights is considered legitimate"[33]; the changing picture of technology in the developing nations often seems to contribute to changes of definitions of self and group.

But the individual must not only become aware of the deprivations which exist for himself and his group; further, the character of the total group's self-identification must become such that it will react against the continuation of a situation in which it is in a subordinate status. ". . . The character of its group identification determine how it (the group—MO) is going to react to the actions of the majority group."[34] In part at least this depends upon the reactions of the superordinate group to early manifestations of dissatisfaction with the status quo, thus bringing into the picture of any developing social movement all earlier social action which is open to perception by members of the minority. The protest movement appears to be one kind of reaction of a group with high morale, or group identification. The conditions for the creation of this kind of group identification are hence of the greatest significance to the rise of a movement. The willingness of the group to engage in combat indicates a degree of security inside the group, and a willingness to risk social action with possible or probable sanctions seems to require that degree of loyalty to the group "which gives the individual a sense of rightness and strength."[35] The technique of achieving this kind of morale, and maintaining it, are important concomitants of success, it would appear.

Both the sense of relative deprivation, and the development of this into group identification, as Rose defines it, appear to be conditioned by the total context, and in turn condition it. The social, cultural and political climate must appear to members of the developing movement as one in which action is feasible and apt to be crowned with success. Communications techniques, particularly the propaganda of the potential movement's early leaders, may help to create the kind of group identification which will make success more believable, but in turn the believability of the ideology will be conditioned by the actions and reactions of the dominant group. "The flourishing social movement is the result of a congenial marriage between elements within the movement and external social conditions . . . an enterprising movement is rarely the original source of a social trend but rather capitalizes on an existing (though sometimes latent) one."[36] Hence the familiar observation that prior concessions (because they make success more believable) and improvements tend to create a climate favorable to further action for more improvements. Those aspects of the total society which, in distinction to an earlier epoch, appear to the members of a movement to have changed and given new promise for the alleviation of suffering, seem to be highly significant in the rise of a social movement.

In an examination of the rise of the Sit-In Movement, then, these three factors ought to be found to be present and operative if this proposition is supported by the data. The background data on the rise of the movement will be organized and examined to try to answer the question as to the presence and operativeness of these factors.

Proposition 2: *The form of response, including ideological, of a movement to the culture which it wishes to change; and the reaction of the culture to the movement, will vary with the relative sizes and perceived strengths of the subordinate and superordinate groups.*

It can be readily seen that a society's reaction to the ideas and challenge of a social movement will be in large part conditioned by the factors which have been discussed under Proposition 1, for example, ongoing technological trends; conversely, the precise form (including ideological) of a movement will be conditioned by similar factors. One would not expect the native population of sections of Melanesia to develop full-fledged political parties; the Cargo Cult is more appropriate as a form. As society changes, the Cargo Cult also alters its form and becomes a "proto-national" formation, and later a political party.[37] In a like manner the protest forms appropriate to the Negro as a slave no longer make sense for the Negro as an urbanized factory worker. Not merely the form of the movement, but even the thought processes of a subordinate group, change with changing cultural factors.[38]

Here, however, this writer would like to make only the proposition that as part of the relationship of a movement to the culture which surrounds it, the relative sizes of populations, and the relative positions of power of the contending groups, are significant. This proposition should be verifiable by examining the comparative data of the movement under study as the relationship of it to its surrounding culture varies.

The Sit-In Movement has as its overt ideology the philosophy of nonviolence, and the data will show that the Movement in fact practices the technique of nonviolence (to be discussed in more detail later). This particular form of response is part of the data of the Movement. It and the reactions to it in the American South, should presumably be somehow related to the societal context in which the civil rights movement and the sit-ins developed; and more particularly its success or failure (which is related to the reaction of the opposing group) should have something to do with the relative sizes of the opposing groups. The following situational variants would tend to modify the responses of both groups when one of them is using nonviolent techniques:[39]

(1) Relative numerical sizes of the opposing groups. If the subordinate group is larger, fear within the dominant group tends to be increased, and change will be more difficult, no matter what technique is used by the subordinate group. All techniques will be perceived and reacted to as violent by the dominant group.

If the subordinate group is smaller than the dominant group, change will be more easily accomplished, especially if the fear of the dominant group is further dispelled by the use of nonviolent techniques.

(2) Extent of a common culture between the opposing groups, including such factors as language, religion, class structure. The more differences in various culture items there are, the more the dominant group will perceive the subordinate group as foreign, strange, uncivilized or subhuman, and the more difficult will it be for the subordinate and dominant groups to communicate with each other. Under such circumstances the technique of nonviolence may be perceived as cowardly, and suffering may be seen as deserved, merited, or exemplifying an incomprehensible masochism. If the defending group in addition places a premium on violence, and has had a monopoly of violence-inflicting mechanisms, the nonviolence of the subordinate group will not only be seen as cowardly, but as usurpation of

the ruler's functions: "So they want to starve, do they? *We'll* show them what starvation is . . ."

(3) Extent of differences of opinion on tactics and strategy within the subordinate nonviolent group. The more divisions within the subordinate group about the feasibility of the nonviolent technique, the less solid will the morale, or group identification be, hence the following which leaders attract will be smaller. Nonviolence as a technique must be culturally acceptable to the subordinate group if it is to become the dominant technique of the movement.

(4) The extent to which the total social context affords an opportunity to the nonviolent subordinate group to make itself visible and communicate its message to the society. In modern societies it appears to be possible to inflict suffering upon individuals and groups to such a degree that resistance collapses. If the society is totalitarian, or "closed," this suffering can to a large degree be kept from the general public by the insulating wall of governmental institutions. If governments take steps to prevent the symbolization of suffering by individual, noted members of the subordinate group, suffering will be undergone by an amorphous mass, and hence will tend to be less visible or comprehensible to the public, should an effective public to which the movement can appeal even exist. If, in addition, the inflicter of suffering is protected by group sanctions which represent the official ideology of the society, he will tend to feel less personal responsibility for his deeds (i.e. the Nazis). Thus the context of society must be open, and an opportunity afforded to the subordinate group to make its movements visible, if the nonviolent movement is not to be destroyed. A violent movement may in some cases replace the ineffective nonviolent one.

(5) The position of the nonviolent group as an attacker or defender. Normally the nonviolent group is in the position of attack, that is, is attempting to change some existing pattern of society. Hence the defender of the status quo has to formulate a method of resistance, which is his choice. He may choose to try to suppress the nonviolent movement violently, or himself use a nonviolent technique, or work out a compromise. However, if the nonviolent movement is defending its position against further encroachments, the nonviolent resister is dependent upon the techniques of the attacker. If the attacker is violent, organized, and a believer in the inherent inferiority of the group being attacked, then the nonviolent group will be destroyed as soon as the attacking group is numerically strong enough. The thesis here is that the attacker always has his choice, and the

defender has his choice only when the attacker has chosen nonviolence. Of course, the word "choice" applies only in academic discussion, since the techniques used in any real situation will depend upon the social context, including all of the factors mentioned above under that broad heading.

In this paper, the role of (1) above will be examined in some detail, and the role of (3) in terms of local movements will also be examined. The other factors, while important, are generally outside the scope of our discussion, since they require access to comparative data of social movements in many locales to a degree not available to this writer.

Proposition 3: *The beginnings of a social movement are characterized by the importance of accidental or idiosyncratic factors; the importance of face-to-face relationships; and a lack of structure, specific ideology, or overall strategy.*

Proposition 4: *a) As a social movement develops, a hierarchy begins to emerge; functions become specialized.*

b) An internal conflict takes shape over strategy: shall the course of strategy be more or less aggressive and militant?

c) Problems of internal cohesion and morale emerge, and with them, techniques of coping with internal problems are developed.

d) The form of reaction to the movement emerges full-scale, the dominant and subordinate groups test each other in the field of social conflict and gauge each other's strengths and weaknesses; and the contending forces modify and revise their strategies and tactics accordingly.

Proposition 5: *Following the modification and revision of strategy and tactics, the movement settles into a more stable, or institutionalized stage, characterized by a lessening of enthusiasm, a more highly developed hierarchy with organizational skills often replacing propaganda skills.*

If success is met, the question of where the movement goes next arises. If success is not met, the question of new tactics arises. These questions tend to be settled by the relationship of power groups within the movement, rather than by the response of the mass of adherents.

Latent consequences, often unanticipated, of the movement arise during this stage, or become apparent, and begin to modify subsequent developments.

The above propositions, derived from the literature of social movements devoted to cyclical or life-cycle approaches, are more or less self-explanatory, and will be more thoroughly treated when the developments of the sit-ins are treated.

In the chapter which follows, the data of the sit-ins will be developed in order to attempt an evaluation of the propositions listed above.

THREE

The Southern Negro Student Movement

This section of the paper will be divided into the following sub-topics, and will be devoted to testing the propositions discussed in the previous section in the light of the data of the Sit-In Movement.

A. Deprivation of the Negro   (proposition 1)
B. Actionable Social Context   (proposition 1)
C. Development of Group Identification   (proposition 1)
D. History of the Movement,
    Framed in Life-Cycle Terms   (propositions 3-5)
E. The Movement's Responses, and the
    Reactions to them, including Ideology
    and Results of the Movement   (proposition 2)

A. The Deprivation of the Negro

The differential status of the American Negro population, relative to the white population, particularly in the Southern states, has been aptly documented and does not, I feel, require renewed analysis here. Since the work of Myrdal during World War II, much progress has been made to close this gap, but,

". . . the Nation still faces substantial and urgent problems in civil rights . . . In some 100 counties in eight Southern states there is reason to believe that Negro citizens are prevented—by outright discrimination or by fear of physical violence or economic reprisal—from exercising the right to vote.

". . . there are many counties in the South where a substantial Negro population not only has no voice in government, but suffers extensive deprivation—legal, economic, educational, and social.

". . . Unemployment in the recent recession, hitting Negroes more than twice as hard as others, underlined the fact that they are by and large confined to the least skilled, worst paid, most insecure occupations . . .

". . . Much of the housing market remains closed in 1961 to millions of Americans because of their race, their religion, or their ancestry; and partly in consequence millions are confined to substandard housing in slums . . ."[40]

Data compiled by the U. S. Bureau of Census, Department of Commerce, amply support the above statement for a variety of indices of standards of living including income, unemployment, years of education, job distribution, and the like, for the period immediately preceding the Movement under study.[41]

However, deprivation is not the same as relative deprivation. As has been suggested above, it is only when the subordinate group sees itself as being deprived (which implies a standard of comparison, a group *relative* to which the deprivation exists, or is perceived) that the type of situation arises in which a solution becomes desired. As other students have pointed out,

". . . the sit-ins and other forms of Negro protest led by middle and upper class Negroes are best interpreted by reference group theory and the concept of relative deprivation."[42]

Reference group is the group to which the deprived group refers as a standard of comparison, the group relative to which it sees itself. Some data do exist as to which reference groups seem to be appropriate to participants in the sit-ins: Northern white students, Negro leadership groups such as clergymen, professionals, and the like, so that the students who participate in the Movement "appear to be committed to the society and its middle class leaders."[43]

The fact of deprivation and the existence of a disprivileged group relative to another group, plus the existence of reference groups, does not, of course, demonstrate relative deprivation, that is, a large-scale sense of *awareness* on the part of members of the disprivileged group that, compared to the dominant or other groups, they are, indeed, disprivileged. This would require an opinion survey of the group being studied. However, numerous observers have noted statements of this kind, albeit not formalized in the form of a methodologically sound survey. These statements generally are formulated in terms of a refusal to accept present conditions, or the slow rate of progress, any longer. As Howard Zinn, Professor of History and Social Science at Spelman College, Atlanta, has suggested,

"Modern science . . . radio . . . television . . . air travel . . . national newspapers and magazines . . . Air Force or Marine Corps units in the area . . . All of these influences have acted on Albany Negroes and created expectations far beyond the crawling progress and kindly tolerance which Albany white leaders thought . . . sufficient."[44]

And again, in the words of Rev. Martin Luther King, Jr., "We have come to the day when a piece of freedom is not enough . . . a piece of liberty no longer suffices . . ."[45]

B. Actionable Social Context

What seems to be of greater significance is not so much that a subordinate group has a reference group relative to which it can feel a sense of deprivation, but rather what societal factors account for the development of a consciousness of relative deprivation, and what societal factors account for this or that group, rather than others, being the reference group in question. These factors appear to be involved with the general field of social change, as one observer has suggested:

". . . the movement has some of its deepest roots in the fabric of social change and reorganization . . . the effective cause of the spread of the 1960 sit-ins was a profound impatience over *the rate of change*, and that the largest factor in that was disillusionment over the progress of school desegregation."[46] (emphasis mine—MO)

The suggestion here is that consciousness of relative deprivation in the instance of the Sit-In Movement equates the deprivation with a rate of improvement of conditions not sufficient to satisfy members of the subordinate group.

This is somewhat akin to Crane Brinton's suggestion, in connection with the causes of revolution, that in fact the makers of revolution may be improving their lot, but that the new prosperity "was certainly most unevenly shared . . . The men who made the French Revolution were getting higher real income—so much that they wanted a great deal more. And above all . . . they wanted much that cannot be measured by the economist."[47] It is true that Brinton also suggests the importance of negations of improvements,

21

such as the nullification or repeal of important reforms by the Old Regime, but he emphasizes, in line with this proposition, the creation of even half-hearted reforms as in turn generating higher hopes, particularly for those social groups not receiving the full benefits of even the half-hearted changes. What conditions of change in the society contributed to this dissatisfaction? The author cited above, as well as others, has suggested that urbanization with its many components is the phenomenon responsible.

Among the components of urbanization particularly tending to heighten a sense of consciousness of relative deprivation and group identification might be (1) the development of a Negro community with a diversified occupational structure to service it; hence the development of a "Black Bourgeoisie;"[48] (2) the absorption of many Negroes into occupations that are unionized; hence the development of union-influenced ideology;[49] (3) the gradual extension of Negro voter-registration in urban areas; hence local improvements in such things as police protection, educational facilities, health and welfare facilities;[50] and the easier diffusion of propaganda and ideology leading to heightened group identification that goes with living in closer proximity to others of the same group.

The urbanization of the Southern Negro takes two forms: the shrinking of the so-called "Black Belt," and the concentration of Negroes in urban areas, both Southern and non-Southern. The "Black Belt," while shrinking steadily, still exists as a potent political and social force. It is here that Negroes constitute heavy proportions of rural population, and it is here, too, that the greatest gap between Negro population and Negroes registered to vote is found. Louisiana, in the presidential year of 1956, had four counties in which Negro percentage of the population ranged from 61% to 73% in which not one Negro was registered to vote; Mississippi had seven counties ranging from 60% to 72% Negro in which not a single Negro was registered. Most of the counties in which Negroes have high percentages of the population and low percentages of registered voters are:

". . . in a rough area extending from southside Virginia to East Texas—the old plantation country, or Black Belt. Here is to be found still the highest rate of Negroes . . . This historic agricultural region has lost much of its economic importance, but not its political dominance. The old Black Belt, which, through inequitable legislative apportionment dominates the politics of several states and heavily influences the politics of others, is the area of highest concentration of Negro population, and of discrimination."[51]

Conversely, Negro voter registration tends to be greater in the urban areas. In 1956, in Virginia, over half the state's Negro registrants lived in thirty-two cities, although less than half the Negro population was in those cities. In Florida, two counties (Jacksonville and Miami) contain about one-fourth of the state's Negro population, one-third of its Negro voters. More than one-third of Georgia's Negro voters live in the eight counties with the largest county population in the state. In Alabama about half the total Negro vote, even though small, is from cities. In Mississippi, about one-third of all Negro voters live in the three counties which contain the cities of Jackson, Meridian, Biloxi and Gulfport.[52]

TABLE ONE

Percentage of Negroes living in Urban Areas,
1900 to 1950, for Southern Areas[53]

	Total U.S.	South Atlantic	East-South Central	West-South Central
1900	22.7	18.7	15.5	16.7
1930	43.7	33.1	28.6	32.6
1950	62.4	48.0	42.7	53.1

TABLE TWO

Voter Registration by Negroes, by State,
for the Southern States, 1947-1958[54]

	1947	1952	1956	1958
Alabama	6,000	22,224	53,366	70,000
Arkansas	47,000	61,413	69,677	64,023
Florida	49,000	120,900	148,703	144,810
Georgia	125,000	144,835	163,389	161,958
Louisiana	10,000	120,000	161,410	131,068
Miss.	5,000	20,000	20,000	20,000
North Car.	75,000	100,000	135,000	150,000
South Car.	50,000	80,000	99,890	57,978
Tennessee	80,000	85,000	90,000	185,000
Texas	100,000	181,000	214,000	226,818
Virginia	48,000	69,326	82,603	92,172
Totals	595,000	1,008,614	1,238,038	1,303,827

It is not easy to state categorically that there is a definite, provable relationship between the phenomena of disprivilege, or deprivation on the one hand, the trend of urbanization on the other, and the development of a consciousness of relative deprivation and group identification.

However, the urbanization trend did not take place alone. Along with it a series of movements to better the conditions, both legal and social, of the American Negro arose; and a series of advances in the legal status of the Negro gradually accompanied the development of group identification among the newly urbanized Negroes. It would be idle to suggest that one or another aspect (urbanization or group identification or socio-political advances) is primarily responsible for developments in the other two areas; they are interrelated and seemingly develop together over the years, even though this or that aspect takes the lead in this or that specific circumstance, or short-run period. A correlation does exist, even though a causation cannot be proven. Thus these seemingly related phenomena all form necessary, if not sufficient, conditions for the rise of a protest movement, which is the primary concern of this paper.

The legal developments which gradually accompanied the trend towards urbanization, and the trend towards political awakening, form part of the actionable context because they aid in continuing the other trends, and particularly seem to play a relevant role in developing a sense of relative deprivation among those Negroes who are able to take advantage of the reform, yet find themselves still disadvantaged because of the slow rate of reform, as they see it, and/or because these reforms do not hit areas of life considered important by them.

On July 26, 1949, President Harry Truman signed an executive order putting equality of treatment of the races in the armed services into effect "as rapidly as possible . . ."[55] During and six years after the Korean War desegregation in the armed forces was virtually completed on the federal level; Negro servicemen were thus able to see for the first time sharp differences in treatment on and off posts, hence to develop a perception of deprivation with their own group as the reference group.

This was accompanied, in the field of education, by a long series of cases which gradually repudiated the "separate but equal" theory of school segregation.[56] In the *Gaines* case in 1938 the U.S. Supreme Court held that Missouri did not meet requirements by sending Gaines to a non-segregated school in another state, and obligated Missouri to admit Gaines to its own hitherto segregated law school. In 1948 this was extended to say that equal training must be provided within the state without undue delay, or else the student must be admitted to the white law school (*Sipuel* v. *University of Oklahoma*). In 1950, in *Sweatt* v. *Painter* (Texas), and in *McLaurin* v. *Oklahoma State Regents*, the Court held that a segregated law school within the state could not really provide equal opportunity. Then, in cases that had been before it since the fall of 1952, the Court handed down, on May 17, 1954, its famous decision in a consolidated opinion under the title of *Brown* v. *Board of Education* (Kansas). The decision stated that "separate educational facilities are inherently unequal," hence plaintiffs had been denied equal protection of the law as guaranteed by the 14th amendment to the U.S. Constitution. A full year later, on May 31, 1955, the Court directed District Courts to require school authorities to "make a prompt and reasonable start" towards full compliance with the May 17, 1954, ruling, and recognized local difficulties in complying with the phrase "with all deliberate speed." Nevertheless,

"In public education there still are three states—Alabama, Mississippi, and South Carolina—where not one public school or college conforms with the constitutional requirements enumerated by the Supreme Court seven years ago. In May, 1961, 2,062 of the 2,837 biracial school districts in the 17 Southern and border States remained totally segregated."[57]

This picture on the one hand enabled some Negroes to attend better schools than heretofore, obtain better education, and hence qualify them for potential leadership positions within their own group, and on the other portrayed in vivid tones the inconsistency between declarations of American democracy, and actual day-to-day practices, a type of perception that must distinctly be placed in the category of relative deprivation.

At the same time, there was wide-spread reaction to the Supreme Court's decisions by segregationists, hence aiding the development of group identification by the Negroes in that they were confronted with a series of vocal, well-organized anti-integration groups aimed against what Negroes generally perceived as their interests. Less than two months after the May 17 decision, the first White Citizens Council was organized at Indianola, Mississippi. On April 7, 1956, the Citizens Councils of America were formed at a secret meeting in New Orleans, with delegates from eleven states. By 1957 there were 550 local Councils, with over one-quarter million claimed members, and 50,000 more members of similar groups.[58] In the year 1954

25

also, the Klan saw a revival, and within three years there were at least four Klans competing in the South. Since the 1954 decision at least twenty groups have appeared, including the KKK, the National Association for the Advancement of White People, the Citizens Councils, and local groups, many of which have leading and respected citizens as members.[59]

C. Development of Group Identification

The development of group identification and morale cannot be viewed independently of such historical trends as those enumerated above. But the prime index of this development is the body of data coming out of the Negro protest movements antecedent to the sit-ins, for these movements are the response of the subordinate group to the culture which it wishes to change or amend. In their ideologies, furthermore, we can see the image that participants in these movements have of themselves, and wish the society at large to have of them. Hence a brief survey of these antecedent developments, with emphasis upon those aspects which seem to carry over to current developments, must be undertaken.

The development of group identification, morale, or cohesion can be seen not only through a historical survey of antecedent developments organizationally. On the one hand, the development of group identification is in response to certain historical trends; on the other, the formation of organizations serves to continue, modify and develop the already existing trends, and create a further sense of group identification. Thus such a survey is not only an index to the development of group identification, but also a clue as to the direction and form of further group identification.

Our account begins in the spring of 1941, when A. Philip Randolph, a socialist and President of the Brotherhood of Sleeping Car Porters, seized upon the opportunity of a European war, the slogans of anti-facism, and the dissatisfaction of Negro labor at continued discrimination, to call for a mass march on Washington, D.C., with the objective of securing full integration in the labor market through federal action. The National Association for the Advancement of Colored People had called mass meetings and pickets in some twenty-three states to protest discrimination in defense hiring, and joined Randolph's call, which became known as the March on Washington Movement (MOWM). However, NAACP's national leadership remained only formally involved, and was not enthusiastic. In March, Randolph's union paper, *Black Worker*, issued the formal call (the date was to be July 1).

On June 13, 1941, Mrs. Eleanor Roosevelt asked Randolph to call off the march. On the 15th President Roosevelt issued a memorandum to the Office of Production Management urging it to eliminate discrimination in defense hiring. On the 18th the President conferred with some Negro leaders and asked that the march be cancelled. On June 24th, Mayor LaGuardia told MOWM leaders that President Roosevelt would issue an Executive Order concerning discrimination. They demanded that it cover government employment, and this was done. Executive Order 8802, prohibiting discrimination in defense employment or in government service because of race, creed, color or national origin was issued the next day. Randolph then cancelled the date of the march, and the organization finally petered out without ever going to Washington. Estimates of potential participation ranged widely, up to 100,000 being claimed by some. Integration of the armed forces, another of Randolph's demands, was not included in the Executive Order.[60]

MOWM was the first American Negro protest action officially endorsing the principle of nonviolent direct action. Said Randolph,

"The MOWM has proclaimed its dedication to and advocacy of non-violent good will direct action as a method of . . . meeting . . . discrimination . . . Before any form of direct action is engaged in, all the resources of negotiation are exhausted . . . Every individual who participates in such a project is pledged to non-violent action, to the extent of not even using violent language against the management or the employees . . . Contrary to many hysterical and intemperate attacks upon Non-Violent Good Will Direct Action by some of the Negro intelligentsia and petty bourgeoisie . . . this form of social protest and revolt was used . . . before and after the Civil War."[61]

MOWM continued its organization for some time; during a Madison Square Garden rally on June 16, 1942, Harlem was successfully blacked out in response to MOWM's call. Later that summer several local marches under MOWM leadership took place to protest the execution of Odell Walker in Virginia July 2 of that year. In September, 1942, Randolph called for a one-week campaign involving civil disobedience against discrimination in public accommodations. Randolph then switched his energies to the National Council for a Permanent FEPC.[62]

In that same year (1942), in Chicago, the Congress of Racial Equality, embodying many of the principles enunciated by Randolph for MOWM, was founded. CORE will be discussed in more detail later.

In April, 1949, during debate prior to the enactment of a new Selective Service Law, Randolph announced the formation of the League for Non-Violent Civil Disobedience Against Military Segregation, and told the Senate Armed Service Committee that if segregation were not eliminated he would lead a civil disobedience campaign urging Negroes and sympathetic whites not to register for the draft. Walter White, then executive secretary of the NAACP, and other Negro leaders, disavowed the idea.[63] The act was passed with no desegregation proposals, but both major political parties, meeting in convention in July, adopted anti-discriminatory platforms. President Truman's Executive Order of July 26, 1948, paving the way for armed services integration, accompanied these moves, although the presence of Henry A. Wallace's Progressive Party on the scene may also have helped.

The Korean War and the McCarthy era which accompanied it may account in part for the lack of any outstanding civil rights activities during the years from 1949 to 1954; action proceeded, however, on the legal front and culminated in the well-known Supreme Court decisions of 1954 and 1955 in the field of education. The counter attack by segregationist groups has been mentioned.

On December 1, 1955, Mrs. Rosa Parks, a Negro seamstress and former secretary of the local NAACP branch, boarded a bus in downtown Montgomery, Alabama. Tired, she sat down in the first seat behind the section reserved for whites. She and three other Negro passengers were ordered by the driver to move back in order to accommodate boarding white passengers. (This is not the general Southern custom. Normally whites fill from front to rear, Negroes from rear to front, but Negroes are not generally asked to give up seats to whites once the Negro section is filled.) Mrs. Parks refused, and was arrested. From December 5, 1955, until November 14, 1956, sparked by this arrest, the Negro community of Montgomery stayed off the buses. They returned to the buses only after a U.S. Supreme Court decision on November 13, 1956, affirming a District Court decision declaring Alabama's state and local bus segregation laws unconstitutional.

The Montgomery Bus Boycott, as it was to become known, created as its formal structure a group, the Montgomery Improvement Association, which formed the pattern for similar Negro groups in other communities in the years to come; and it catapulted onto the stage of American history a young Baptist minister, the Rev. Martin Luther King, Jr., who soon became the symbol of Negro non-violent protest.[64]

About a week after the boycott started, a white woman, Miss Juliette Morgan, wrote a letter to the *Montgomery Advertiser*, comparing the protest with the Gandhian movement in India. This observation struck King, who began consciously to develop non-violent resistance as the technique of the Boycott. In the mass meetings that he addressed, rotating from church to church, he stressed the role of Christian love, and insisted that Negroes meet "the forces of hate" with the power of love. According to King's account,

> "In a real sense, Montgomery's Negroes showed themselves willing to grapple with a new approach to the crisis in race relations. It is probably true that most of them did not believe in nonviolence as a philosophy of life, but because of their confidence in their leaders and because nonviolence was presented to them as a simple expression of Christianity in action, they were willing to use it as a technique. Admittedly, nonviolence in the truest sense is not a strategy that one uses simply because it is expedient at the moment; nonviolence is ultimately a way of life that men live by because of the sheer morality of its claim. But even granting this, the willingness to use nonviolence as a technique is a step forward . . ."[65]

While at Crozer Theological Seminary some years earlier, King had been exposed to pacifist ideas in a talk by A. J. Muste, probably America's leading radical pacifist. Then he heard a sermon by Dr. Mordecai Johnson, just returned from India, on Gandhi. He then began a study of Gandhi's writings. In 1954 he took the position as pastor of the Dexter Avenue Baptist Church in Montgomery.

Because of the wide reading Rev. King's book received among leaders of the sit-in movement, and because King himself spoke widely, and to large audiences, on the same theme in the years following the Boycott, it might be of interest to summarize briefly the main principles of nonviolence as he saw them:

(1) Nonviolence is not for cowards. It is not "passive," but rather an active resistance to evil, without physical aggression.

(2) Nonviolence does not seek to defeat or humiliate an opponent, but rather to win his friendship and understanding.

(3) Nonviolence is directed not against persons who happen to be doing evil, but rather against the forces of evil themselves.

(4) Nonviolent resistance is a willingness to accept suffering without retaliation on the theory that unearned suffering is redemptive and can convert the opponent.

(5) Nonviolence avoids not only physical violence, but also the violence of the spirit, that is, of thought and feeling against the opponent.

(6) Nonviolence is based on the conviction that you will ultimately win because the universe (God, the future, world opinion, etc.) is on your side, regardless of your personal immediate future.[66]

The basic demands of the Montgomery Bus Boycott were quite simple—to raise standards up to those in the rest of the South, for the most part. They were: (1) courteous treatment by bus operators; (2) passengers to be seated on a first-come, first-served basis, Negroes back to front, regardless of any "line"; (3) Negro drivers on predominantly Negro routes. The first two demands were conceded, after the Supreme Court decision, more or less, that is, bus riders are no longer segregated by law, but only self-segregated. The bus company, several years after the end of the boycott, had not hired any Negro drivers.

A series of converging phenomena linked to the general phenomena discussed in this paper as being necessary (although not always sufficient) to the rise of a protest movement seem to have been present in Montgomery, and seem to account adequately, if not with certainty, for the "catching on" of the Boycott. Rev. King suggested the hand of God, but He had helpers. When Mrs. Parks was first jailed, her bond was signed by Mr. E. D. Nixon, an active NAACP member and a member of Randolph's Brotherhood of Sleeping Car Porters; it was Nixon who turned out the mimeographed flyer which called for an initial one-day boycott on December 5, 1955. The white press then gave the movement a tremendous push by publicizing this leaflet, thus bringing it to the attention of many Negroes who would otherwise not have seen it. The dynamic personality of King, who was able to combine the idea of a mass boycott with Christian ideology, and at the same time create a tactical weapon (nonviolence) sufficiently militant to attract the support of Negroes, yet respectable enough not to alienate white supporters elsewhere, was certainly a crucial factor. Yet without an idiosyncratic factor of the kind created by Mrs. Parks there would have been no movement at that time. But there would have been neither incident nor an atmosphere in which such an incident would catch on, without the development of a social context—including circumstances of relative deprivation and group identification—in which action could be perceived as feasible by the leaders-to-be of the MIA-to-be, and in which this feasibility could be made believable by these leaders to their followers.

After a local success for mass action such as in Montgomery, and in Tallahassee, Florida, where a Bus Boycott was also tried (although with less success);[67] and after Rev. King catapulted onto the national stage, it seemed only a matter of time before the March on Washington idea would be revived by organizations and individuals inside organizations enthused by the example of Montgomery. King quickly became a symbol of an alternative tactic to Northern Negro and liberal forces who were weary of the NAACP's lackluster lobbying and court battles, and for Southern Negroes increasingly aware of the slowness of the pace. Pacifist groups such as the Fellowship of Reconciliation were quick to make use of King's action in order to rally new supporters and revive the flagging faith of old ones, somewhat battered by the apparent indestructibility of the status quo; the Hungarian Revolution had created a "ferment" on the small American left, sufficient to restore some energy to the democratic (anti-Stalinist) section of it, and the civil rights movement quickly became the focus of enthusiastic attention for younger people associated with liberal and independent left groups, and even for students not previously organizationally-minded. At last something was happening! At last a crack in the Establishment! At least so the American left viewed the situation.

Late in the fall of 1956 a group of Northern Negroes, aided by whites close to a variety of pacifist groups, and primarily organized by A. Philip Randolph, scheduled a mass "prayer Pilgrimage" to Lincoln Memorial in the nation's capital. The date set was May 17, 1957, the anniversary of the Supreme Court's school integration decision. There was no organizational sponsorship, but King was present, and the NAACP was represented on the platform by Roy Wilkins. This initial revival of the MOWM idea was not a success; with 400,000 Negroes in Washington alone, total attendance was only about 20,000 (police said 15,000, the NAACP said 27,000). One observer suggested some of the difficulties: there was little labor support; the white press scarcely mentioned it; there were rumors of Communist infiltration; the whole thing seemed to be a compromise between those leaders who wanted no mass moves, and those who wanted a really big turn-out—so there was no really serious effort to get people out; the leadership was not typical of the "new leadership" such as King; the whole thing was too prayerful: "It will take more than prayer to move white politicians preparing again to bury the civil rights issue."[68]

The lessons of the Prayer Pilgrimage were, however, not lost on the forces grouped around Randolph and King, particularly on their strategist, Mr. Bayard Rustin, a Negro pacifist and ex-Communist employed by the War Resisters League. Rustin, who was to remain active for several more years as an unofficial tactical adviser to King, shifted the focus of MOWM-type activity to the youth arena, and kept organizational work outside the official channels of the NAACP. His first try massed some 8,000 students, mainly from the North, in a march down Constitution Avenue to Lincoln Memorial. A delegation sent to the White House reported back: the White House had nothing to say. The date was October 25, 1958.[69]

His next try—and the last prior to the outbreak of the sit-ins less than a year later—was set for April 18, 1959, and included the presentation of several hundred thousand petitions. The petition, calling for full and speedy integration of schools, was signed at the top by figures such as Harry Belafonte, Rev. King, George Meany, Randolph, Walter Reuther, Norman Thomas, and Roy Wilkins. Rustin acted as coordinator of the March. For leg-work he had at his service the now actively reorganized Young Peoples Socialist League, youth section of Thomas' Socialist Party. Rustin's office was located at 321 W. 125th Street in Harlem, an address which was to become the Northern center for the Randolph-King forces in the early months of the sit-ins.

Some 25,000 young people turned out for the March and rally which followed. This time a deputy assistant to President Eisenhower, Mr. Gerald D. Morgan, had a statement:

> "The President has asked me to give you his best wishes and to tell you of his regret that he had planned to be away from Washington . . . The President is just as anxious as you are to see an America where discrimination does not exist . . . The President is proud of this progress that has been made during his administration . . . In your march you are performing a valuable educational function . . . and I congratulate you for it."

Possibly Mr. Morgan was referring to the passage, on September 9, 1957, of the first civil rights bill since 1875, and the establishment with it of a Commission on Civil Rights, a body empowered only to investigate, study, appraise, and make findings and recommendations. The Commission had no enforcement powers other than to issue subpoenas and seek Court enforcement of the subpoenas. It received its first voting complaint (the franchise being one area of its jurisdiction) on August 14, 1958, and held its first hearing (on voting) in Montgomery, Alabama, December 8, 1958. On September 9, 1959, it printed its *Report* for the initial period of its activity, and transcripts of the various hearings were also published. A second report, following further activity, followed in 1961. In 1960, again under the Eisenhower Administration, a second Civil Rights Act was passed. It strengthened the power of the Federal Government in the field of denials of the right to vote, obstruction of Federal court orders, and violence to schools and churches.

The publicity attendant upon the Marches (even though it was restricted to a limited sector of the population), and the information disseminated by the Commission on Civil Rights (again, limited to persons interested in the first place in most cases) both helped to educate a certain section of younger people, particularly Negro students, and probably enhanced to some degree their sense of group identification. Yet the specific technique which could involve persons on an individual basis in the civil rights struggle, as it was beginning to be known, was not available, or if it was available, it was relatively unknown.

The Congress of Racial Equality (CORE) experimented, and obtained success, with sit-ins at restaurants in Chicago as early as 1942. CORE's membership at this time, however, was small, and consisted largely of intellectual whites with pacifist and conscientious objector backgrounds. Very slowly CORE, over the years since World War II, began to expand. In the years 1949-53, CORE's St. Louis chapter negotiated, picketed, and sat-in until they succeeded in getting downtown dime stores to integrate eating facilities. In 1949, also, CORE's Washington, D.C. group staged one of the first "stand-ins" at a movie theater. In New Jersey, at Palisades Park, a two-year stand-in campaign marked by numerous incidents of violence was also successfully concluded in this period. In State College, Pennsylvania, CORE secured integrated barbershop facilities. In 1959 CORE staged sit-ins in Miami, Florida, without success.

And, in 1947, twenty-three persons associated with CORE and the Fellowship of Reconciliation, carried out a Freedom Ride in the Upper South to test an early Court decision on interstate travel.[70] The idea of the sit-in, based on nonviolent direct action techniques, spread slowly, even though nonviolence itself was becoming better known because of the activities of Rev. King. On August 19, 1958, the NAACP Youth Council in Oklahoma City began the first formal sit-in by predominantly Negro students. Within two weeks all but one of five stores selected for action changed their serving policies. Ages of the participants ranged from six to seventeen, with fifteen-year-old Barbara Ann Posey acting as spokesman. Miss Posey, who subsequently became the NAACP's chief claim to be the originator of the sit-in idea, related later that when she was fourteen she joined the Youth Council, and that the Council adviser had told the youngster the story of Rev. King and the Montgomery Bus Boycott. She had also attended an NAACP youth rally in New York City, the most significant part of her trip being her exposure to the integrated public facilities in New York, certainly an aspect of relative deprivation.[71]

On Sunday, August 24, 1958, twenty pairs of Negro youths attended twenty white churches; they were refused admittance at only three, making Oklahoma City the first city to have a "pray-in," though the term had not yet been coined. On September 22, 1958, a Citizens Committee on Human Relations was formed in the city, foreshadowing similar developments during the main wave of sit-ins later; some 114 prominent citizens, mostly white, signed a statement supporting the effort. By February 10, 1960, thirty-three stores had opened their facilities to Negroes; by the end of the first wave of sit-ins in 1960, sixty-one restaurants and other facilities in the city had desegregated.

On August 29, 1958, the NAACP Youth Council in Wichita, Kansas, staged a sit-in at the Dockum Drug Store. The idea had come through official NAACP channels from Oklahoma City. After four days of sitting, the manager of the store called the NAACP branch president and told him the policy of the store would be changed to serve everyone equally. The news spread and sit-ins took place in Enid, Tulsa and Stillwater, Oklahoma, and in Kansas City, Kansas, with varying success. In the latter city a single Negro minister had effected a policy change at a drug store chain three years earlier; now, in November, 1958, picketing of five downtown stores commenced. The campaign hit its high point during the Christmas rush, when it was accompanied by requests that Negroes cancel their charge accounts at the stores. Protracted negotiations followed without result. Then, when Negroes scheduled a downtown protest parade for Saturday, February 28, 1959, four of the five stores in question gave in. The parade was cancelled. The 1958 sit-ins resulted in no major wave of activity elsewhere. Several reasons can be suggested for this: (1) They took place around the border of the South, and Southern Negro students did not really perceive these events as having anything to do with themselves. In other words, the younger members of the Oklahoma and Kansas Youth Councils were not a group with whom the

Southern college students would compare themselves. (2) There was no general press or radio coverage; communication, diffusion of information, contagion was cut down. There were no face-to-face relationships between students in different locales, hence no communication on the personal level to inspire further action. On the other hand, organizations such as the NAACP apparently did not have the campus followings that would have responded to a call to spread the sit-ins from the national level.

One further activity just prior to the outbreak of the sit-ins can be mentioned. On New Year's Day, 1959, and again a year later, mass Negro "pilgrimages" from many communities in Virginia centered in the Mosque in Richmond to protest (in 1959) the state's massive resistance program against school integration and (in 1960) to protest the closing of public schools in Prince Edward County. Sympathizers claimed audiences of 2,000 and 3,000 for the two years. Rev. Wyatt Tee Walker, later to become prominent as the leader of the Petersburg sit-ins, and still later as a leading official of the Southern Christian Leadership Conference, was coordinator of the 1959 pilgrimage, and public relations director of the 1960 one.

Also on New Year's Day, 1960, a rally took place at the airport in Greenville, South Carolina. Some 600 Negroes gathered in snow and sleet to protest segregated facilities, a pilgrimage growing out of an incident the previous spring, when Jackie Robinson, invited to address a local NAACP meeting, was ejected from the waiting room. The local CORE president coordinated the rally. A delegation read a message to the whites seated in the white waiting room: "We will no longer make a pretense of being satisfied with the crumbs of citizenship while others enjoy the whole loaf only by the right of a white-skinned birth."[72] A prayer service followed. The above statement is a clear expression of the concept of relative deprivation: the subordinate group compares itself to the white group, in this case its reference group, and finds itself deprived relative to it.

Perhaps a word or two more on the use of the term "reference group" might be in order here. The bulk of the statements ascribed to members of the subordinate group to indicate their sense of relative deprivation used so far merely imply that the members of the subordinate group compare themselves to members of the dominant group, and find themselves to be disprivileged, or deprived relative to the others. But what must be added here is that short of a sense of psychological identification such a feeling of relative deprivation would not exist, in all probability. A psychological identification seems to exist, indeed, for members of all kinds of subordinate groups with their oppressors.[73] The difficulty arises when trying to evaluate the reasons for the transitions from simply a sense of psychological identity, to the kind of psychological identity which creates a sense of dissatisfaction sufficient to cause an individual to do something about it. This type of evaluation has been attempted by writers elsewhere, but does not fall within the scope of this paper.[74]

The data developed up to this point indicate, within the framework of social movement theory, some of the necessary if not sufficient prerequisites for the outbreak of a movement. Deprivation and the growing awareness of it relative to the progress envisioned, and relative to the privileges enjoyed by the dominant group have been suggested, although a full development of this theme has not been attempted; the data of deprivation on the one hand are readily available in other sources, and the data of a psychological sort necessary to demonstrate the indices of relative deprivation are not within the main focus of this inquiry. Resources necessary to this kind of research were not available to this writer at the time of the outbreak of the Movement. It might be suggested here that this particular lacuna could be profitably filled by students of movements in the future.

The social context, particularly the growth of a political superstructure which on the one hand afforded to Negroes the appearance of federal interests and protection, and on the other created certain instruments for the further development of skills of operating a movement (such as education) while tending to intensify a demand for more and more reforms, has also been indicated, chiefly in terms of urbanization and legal reforms.

In addition, the organizational background to the current student movement has been outlined on the one hand as a response to the social context and as a result of a certain level of group identification, and on the other hand as a factor tending to continue and modify a further sense of group identification, or morale. These necessary strands now converge in the form of the initiating incident of the Sit-In Movement of 1960.

D. History of the Movement

1. *Beginnings*

Lacking the kind of circumstances discussed above, there can be many beginnings which fail to find roots, and simply die; many of these remain unrecorded, so that there is no real way of knowing what the ratio of movements to simple events which do not expand into movements is. Either kind of initiating event, whether it fizzles or expands into an actual movement, is, or seems to be, an accident or coincidence; most initiating incidents are not deliberately planned to develop into movements, though some are. The sit-ins were an example of an uncalculated action of the former type; the Freedom Riders were an example of a planned move, but themselves formed only as an aftermath of the sit-ins and as a result of the institutionalized structure growing out of the sit-in.

Greensboro, North Carolina, seat of Guilford County in the heart of the state's Piedmont industrial region, is the location of Greensboro College (white, coed, Methodist), Women's College of the University of North Carolina (tokenly integrated but almost entirely white, state-supported), Guilford College (white, coed, Quaker), Bennett College (Negro, Methodist, women), and North Carolina Agricultural and Technical College (Negro, men, state-supported). Twenty-five percent of the city's 123,000 population is Negro, in an area of the state historically opposed to the political domination of the plantation counties of Eastern North Carolina.

Among the students at A&T in the fall of 1959 there were four who were in the habit of getting together in the campus rooms of two of them—the two others roomed off campus—for "bull sessions." The youngest of the four had gone to high school in Wilmington, North Carolina, where during his senior year a sit-in had been planned, but had never jelled. The four would come together for supper and talk. After a while, they assigned each other books—Frederick Douglass, Langston Hughes, Gandhi. They watched a television documentary on Gandhi that fall. In the latter part of January, 1960, one of the boys read Robert E. Davis' *The American Negro's Dilemma*,[75] the opening paragraph of the foreword to which reads:

"It is the considered view of this writer that the problem of the Negro in the United States is basically the result of his own actions, or rather inactions. Whatever the original cause of the present dilemma, it is the Negro's apathy which is largely responsible for its continued existence . . . Until the Negro realizes that he must do something on his own to alleviate his burdens, he will constantly be plagued by double standards of justice, cynicism, and other nefarious treatment . . ."[76]

According to a study by J. Allen Williams (see note 76), one of the four boys remembered an idea he once had several months earlier. He had been in a store downtown, and had thought how nice it would be to sit down and have a drink. He suggested that they go downtown and remain seated until they were served. At this point the four had almost no notion of what they might be getting into, and were quite unprepared for opposition, should any arise. All were, or at some point had been, members of the NAACP Youth Council, but were not in consultation with the NAACP at this point; however, some months earlier they had corresponded with NAACP's national office and had asked for pointers on how to deal with this kind of situation. There had been no reply, so they determined to go on their own.[77]

At 4:30 p.m. on February 1, 1960, the four went into the F. W. Woolworth store in downtown Greensboro and sat down to wait for service. There was no service, and there were no incidents. After the first day, they came back with other students, and the "sit-ins" rapidly grew in size. Girls from Bennett College joined in after the first two days. The boys went to the local head of the NAACP branch, who promised legal assistance; they also organized a group on campus, the Student Executive Committee for Justice. About three days later, the local NAACP president, realizing that he had potential dynamite on his hands, and recognizing that he himself had no experience in this type of activity, called the national office of CORE. A field secretary, Gordon Carey, came to Greensboro at once and talked with the students involved in the action, briefing them on the principles and tactics of the nonviolent action technique. By this time, that is, after about a week, the Greensboro action had been picked up by the press and radio, and Negro students in Durham and Winston-Salem were already engaged in similar activities.[78]

At this point, and from then on, it can be observed that in microcosm the Greensboro movement followed in its stages the general pattern of social movements, moving rapidly from a situation lacking any organizational form and dependent entirely on the face-to-face relationship of only four individuals to one in which a structured local organization with an ideology and a strategy, supported by several hundred students, linked itself to at least two nation-wide civil rights groups. The organization made contact with representatives of the local merchants, and the conflict between those representing the status quo (segregated facilities) and those desiring to change it, became concrete and structured in the form of negotiations.

After the first week of sit-ins, a truce was negotiated at the students' initiative. This was extended one time on February 20. Negotiation between the student committee and store managers dragged on until the beginning of April, when sit-ins were resumed. The meaning of this development will be discussed in the next main section. In late April, 1960, some forty-five student demonstrators were arrested by local police and the student committee shifted to picketing rather than sitting-in. The mayor then appointed a bi-racial commission,[79] a development also important in terms of the dynamics of intergroup conflict to be discussed below; this commission recommended that stores have both a white and integrated section. Students agreed, but managers of stores concerned did not. Finally, after school had closed for the summer, all Greensboro stores affected by sit-ins agreed to reopen on an entirely integrated basis July 25; thus Greensboro became the fourteenth city to integrate as a result of the sit-ins.

After the Student Executive Committee for Justice had achieved lunch counter integration, it succumbed to an organizational crisis also typical of developments elsewhere. The apparatus and leadership of the group were no longer able to present to its followers any cogent, dynamic reason for continuing existence. The Committee changed its name to the Intercollegiate Council for Racial Equality, but was unable to muster students to further actions. The NAACP assumed a strong role in the group, which alienated some students, particularly from the white colleges, who did not wish to be handicapped by this (in the white community) unpopular label. By the end of the year 1960 only a small core of students was on hand to answer the call of the all-Southern Student Nonviolent Coordinating Committee (SNCC) to begin picketing movie theaters. None of the initial four was still at A&T. They had all gone to other schools or had left school altogether in response to the larger demands of "the movement."

It is this writer's impression, based on contacts with leaders of sit-ins in several communities, that there is a high rate of drop-outs among such leaders from their initial protest college. Some of this seems to be due to scholastic failure as a result of too much concentration of time on the Movement; some is due to expulsion or suspension; some is due to offers of jobs by groups such as CORE and NAACP (one of the Greensboro students worked for the NAACP for a time). What seems to happen in both the last-named category, and to some other students, however, goes further. Student leaders are exposed to a large number of new acculturative factors including such things as trips to New York City. Unaccustomed status and prestige ("fame") comes to them. The Movement, particularly once one is swept into it beyond the home town situation, is an exciting and stimulating new world. It is difficult indeed to settle back into the routine of study after the glamour of being a famed leader. Much the same thing has been pointed out for trade union leaders faced with the necessity of returning to the workbench.

Within the first week the sit-in idea, carried by press and radio reports primarily, reached Durham and Winston-Salem. Within two weeks the demonstrations leaped state lines to Virginia and South Carolina—on the 10th, Raleigh, the state capital; on the 11th, High Point and Hampton, Virginia, on the 12th, Concord, North Carolina, and Norfolk and Portsmouth, Virginia; and Rock Hill, South Carolina; on the 13th, to Nashville, Tennessee, and Tallahassee, Florida. The demonstrations spread quickly along a wide crescent, with Durham at one end, Greensboro in the center, and Rock Hill at the other end, then leaped to the Virginia shore to the urban and industrial complex there; then scattered farther out to the more traditional centers of Negro urban life (and often Negro urban protest) like Nashville, Tallahassee, Baltimore, Orangeburg and Montgomery. As the movement caught on, often for idiosyncratic reasons to all appearances, colleges nearby would also pick it up, almost as a matter of competition—they could not permit themselves to be shown up if a nearby college sat-in, so they also sat-in, hence continuing an image of a quickly spreading, dynamic, energetic, and spontaneous movement.

In terms of these idiosyncratic factors, one student of the movement has pointed out that eleven of the first fifteen sit-in communities are in the Piedmont region within a 100-mile radius of Greensboro. He suggests the presence of a basketball circuit, with Greensboro A&T playing five games in two weeks and students at each of the five opponent schools being involved shortly thereafter as a factor. In interviews, however, this writer has not been able to substantiate the basketball theory. Other idiosyncratic factors include letters from students at one college to friends and relatives at other institutions; dating patterns, etc. The most common source of information is attributed by students to the radio and newspapers. The fact remains that the sit-ins caught on in the manner of a grass fire, moving from the center outward, in general.[80]

The graph on page 41 shows the number of initial demonstrations, week by week. This information is based largely on the author's newspaper files, and on accounts published by the Southern Regional Council, particularly its *The Student Protest Movement*, Winter, 1960. The table on pages 42 and 43 shows the dates of the first occurrence of demonstrations in a locality.

GRAPH ONE
Number of Initial Demonstrations
Week by Week, February-May 1960

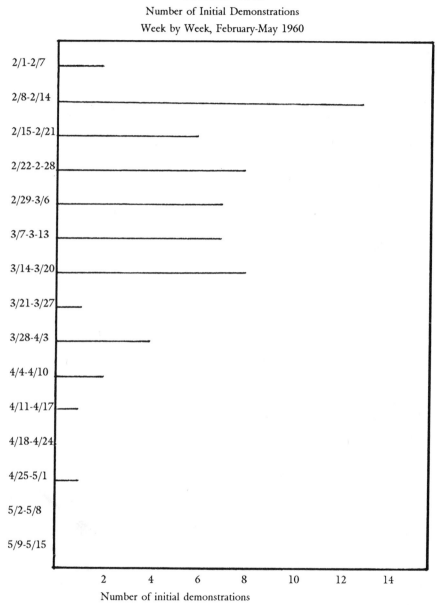

Number of initial demonstrations

TABLE THREE
First occurrence of sit-ins in a locality

DATE	CITY
Feb. 1, 1960	Greensboro, N.C.
Feb. 5	Chevy Chase, Md. (not a sit-in)
Feb. 8	Durham, N.C.; Winston-Salem, N.C.
Feb. 9	Charlotte, N.C.
Feb. 10	Raleigh, N.C.
Feb. 11	High Point, N.C.; Hampton, Va
Feb. 12	Concord, Norfolk, Portsmouth, Va.; Rock Hill, S.C.
Feb. 13	Nashville, Tenn.; Tallahassee, Fla.
Feb. 14	Sumter, S.C.
Feb. 16	Salisbury, N.C.
Feb. 17	Chapel Hill, N.C.
Feb. 18	Charleston, S.C.; Shelby, N.C.
Feb. 19	Chattanooga, Tenn.
Feb. 20	Richmond, Va.
Feb. 22	Baltimore, Md.; Frankfort, Ky.
Feb. 25	Montgomery, Ala.; Orangeburg, S.C.; Henderson, N.C.
Feb. 27	Lexington, Ky.; Petersburg, Va.; Tuskegee, Ala.
Feb. 29	Tampa, Fla.

Others initiated during February: Newport News, Suffolk, Whaleyville, Va.

March 2	St. Petersburg, Daytona Beach, Fla.; Columbia, S.C.
March 3	Atlanta, Ga.
March 4	Miami, Fla.; Houston, Tex.
March 7	Knoxville, Tenn
March 8	New Orleans, La.
March 10	Little Rock, Ark.
March 11	Austin, Galveston, Tex.
March 12	Jacksonville, Fla.
March 13	San Antonio, Tex.
March 15	St. Augustine, Fla.; Statesville, N.C.; Corpus Christi, Tex.
March 16	Savannah, Ga.
March 17	New Bern, N.C.
March 19	Memphis, Tenn.; Wilmington, N.C.; Arlington, Va.
March 26	Lynchburg, Va.
March 28	Baton Rouge, La.
March 29	Marshall, Tex.
March 31	Birmingham, Ala.

Others initiated during March: Annapolis, Md.; Bluefield, W.Va.; Columbus, Ga.;Douglasville, Ga.;Deland, Fla.; Denmark, S.C.; Elizabeth City, N.C.; Fayetteville, N.C.; Florence, S.C.; Huntsville, Ala.; Lenoir, N.C.; Monroe, N.C.; Orlando, Fla.; Rutherford, N.C.; Sarasota, Fla.;Shreveport, La.; Xenia, Ohio;Charleston, W. Va; Greenville, S.C.; Oklahoma City, Okla.

TABLE THREE, cont

April 2	Danville, Va.
April 4	Darlington, S.C.
April 9	Augusta, Ga.
April 17	Biloxi, Miss.
April 28	Dallas, Tex.

Others initiated during April: Jackson, Miss. (boycott, no sit-ins); Pensacola, Fla.

Initiated During May: Columbia, Mo.; Starkville, Miss.
Initiated During June: Kansas City, Kansas and Missouri
Initiated during July: Killeen, Tex.; Rockville, Md.; Spartanburg, S.C.; Fredericksburg, Va.
Initiated during August: Hopewell, Va.; Jefferson City, Mo. (concluded that month; initial date not known); Murphysboro, Ill.; Myrtle Beach, S.C.; Glen Echo, Md. (not known precisely).
Initiated during September: Huntington, W. Va.; Jackson, Tenn.; St. Louis, Mo.
Initiated During December: Covington, Ky.

(Note: From February through April, "others initiated" indicates communities concerning which precise dates are not known, or those in which the sit-ins were not sustained, or concerning which there is inadequate information upon which to base any real discussion.)

During the first sixty days of the demonstrations they spread to nearly eighty communities as far removed as Xenia, Ohio (where state laws for equal accommodations were being violated) and Sarasota, Florida. In the North, civil rights, labor, student and liberal political organizations discussed below moved to assist the demonstrators. Delegates to a fourteen-state Midwest Democratic Party conference adopted a proposal which supported equal rights at lunch counters in part.[81] Campuses which had seen no political demonstrations since the 1930s or late 1940s saw picketing in support of the Southern students. White church groups issued proclamations favoring the nonviolent actions, including many in the South (details will be given later). Within these first sixty days, some facilities in some six upper and middle Southern communities were opened on an integrated basis.[82] Also within these first two months (the high-water mark of sit-in activities in terms of initiating incidents, with nearly half of all communities which were to have sit-ins having them in this period for the first time) nearly 1,000 Negroes and white sympathizers were arrested (388 in Orangeburg, South Carolina alone); hundreds of students suffered one form or another of harassment and intimidation, ranging from tear gas, police dogs, burning cigars on clothing,

43

and beatings, to suspension and expulsion from school. Specific incidents will be related while reporting on particular communities. The civil liberties, academic freedom and related legal issues, since they are not the chief focus of this paper, will be discussed only briefly below.

These first sixty days of the sit-ins can be characterized as the beginning of the sit-in movement as such. No overall structure has been developed, the ideological side of the movement was still in its extremely tentative stage, and the response to the movement by the national civil rights organizations had not yet been clarified. Nor had any consistent pattern of response or reaction to the movement by opponents within Southern communities made itself felt as yet. There had been arrests and violence in some places. In others, truces had been arranged. But by and large the movement remained localized, as did the reaction to it. No overall strategies had emerged as yet, and much of what happened depended on local circumstances, often on personal factors such as those suggested earlier.

2. The Developing Movement

This situation, however, did not last long. Even within the first two months of the sit-ins, national organizations began to intervene in the situation with lawyers, organizers, and advice. At the same time, local sit-in groups began the process of organizing themselves to cope with a series of technical problems, and thus local hierarchies emerged. The "Workshop" came forth to supply to the rank-and-file not only training in the mechanics of direct action, but also to function as a cohesive, morale-building mechanism which could serve to infuse an ideology into the Negro student participants.

The developing stage of the movement, beginning in late March and early April, took several forms which paralleled each other. From press and radio reports, a "public image" of the sit-in was developing. This publicity was partly developed and utilized by civil rights groups such as the NAACP, CORE, the Southern Christian Leadership Conference, and others in their publications to aid the movement financially, organizationally, and legally. It is worth speculating that, by aiding it, they could attempt to create a movement which would be publicly identified with their particular set of initials, hence helping the growth of the organization in question. For this purpose a nationally-linked student movement which could be influenced, as opposed to a helter-skelter of localized protest groups independent of "outside" support or influence, was optimally desirable, and a number of national groups began to work toward this goal.

At the same time, the students actually involved in the struggle in the South began to sense the need for some more overall coordinated structure in order to provide legal and financial help, and coordination, to what was rapidly becoming a vast network of protest groups hardly in touch with each other, but working toward the same end by similar means in most cases. The Southern Christian Leadership Conference (SCLC), itself a federation of local civil rights groups on the adult level, secured the endorsement of CORE, AFSC, and the Fellowship of Reconciliation, and scheduled a conference, thus putting itself into the organizational lead, and securing for its particular ideological slant a definite advantage. The conference, held April 15-17 at Shaw University in Raleigh, North Carolina, marked the beginning of an overall sit-in organization, and hence the end of the early, informal stage of the movement. The Raleigh Citizens Association, a Negro group, was also co-sponsor.

More than 200 delegates, representing fifty-two colleges and high schools, from thirty-seven different communities in thirteen states and Washington, D.C., were present. Representatives of colleges in eleven border and Northern states also participated but did not vote. This move was apparently dictated not only by an acute sense of public relations (by attempting to offset opponent's charges of "outside meddling in our affairs"), but by a genuine feeling on the part of the Southerners that this was to remain their movement, indigenous, Southern, and predominantly Negro, not controlled by any organization, adult, Northern, or otherwise.[83] This feeling has remained with the movement consistently.

Drama attended the opening of the Conference on Friday, April 15. First, Dr. Grady Davis, head of the Raleigh Citizens Association, pastor of the Oberlin Baptist Church and an assistant professor of Philosophy and Religion at Shaw, announced his candidacy for the state house of representatives in the May Democratic primary. Then, a white visitor to the conference was struck by a passer-by during a picket demonstration in front of the Woolworth store. His wound required seven stitches. The attack came moments after the same assailant had hit another visitor, a West African student at Shaw. Local regulations limiting picketing were passed as a result. The new ordinance, however, forbade interference with pickets.

This "Leadership Conference in Nonviolent Resistance," as it was officially called, was addressed by a series of persons who were to become well-known

45

in the Movement, or who were already well-known. These included Rev. King, Jr.; Rev. James Lawson, coordinator of the conference; and Miss Ella Baker, SCLC executive secretary. Delegates went on record then, as later, agreeing unanimously to go to jail and refuse bail if arrested, a policy never really followed through by many participants. Lawson, in a keynote speech, was quoted as calling *Crisis*, official organ of the NAACP, the magazine of the "black bourgeois club," and, in a later closed session the NAACP was subjected to some criticism for its ideological and organizational conservatism. Miss Baker, asked by a *New York Times* reporter if this were true, remarked, "I wouldn't be a bit surprised," but reiterated that for the record the only differences between her organization and the NAACP were differences of emphasis. This note of attempting to cover up disagreements with an appearance of unity for the benefit of the public was a theme to be repeated again and again later in the year. This appears to be a factor in maintaining strong in-group identification.

In its closing hours the conference established a coordinating committee officially called the Student Nonviolent Coordinating Committee (SNCC); within a few weeks it set up staff in Atlanta in the offices of SCLC (later it moved across the street to its own smaller quarters), and became as much as anything ever would be the Southwide apparatus and image of the total movement. Lawson and Miss Baker were both closely associated with these early steps toward the establishment of a permanent apparatus for the Sit-In Movement, and were as responsible as anybody for the continuing independence of SNCC of adult organizations, including SCLC. Much of the later suspicion of students within SNCC toward adult groups and their "interference" was bolstered publicly in remarks made by Lawson at Raleigh, and both Lawson and Miss Baker subsequently, especially after the latter had left SCLC's employment. While this suspicion toward adult groups was by no means limited to the NAACP, that organization received the brunt of suspicions, since it combined apparent efforts at interference with a generally conservative reputation on the national level (see the remark about the "black bourgeois club" earlier), though this was not true in many localities.

On April 17 the Conference adopted the following statement of purpose, written by Rev. Lawson, and significant because it verbalizes the ideology of the movement at least in theory:

"We affirm the philosophical or religious ideal of nonviolence as the foundation of our purpose, the presupposition of our faith, and the manner of our action. Nonviolence as it grows from Judaic-Christian traditions seeks a social order of justice permeated by love. Integration of human endeavor represents the crucial first step towards such a society.

"Through nonviolence, courage displaces fear; love transforms hate. Acceptance dissipates prejudice; hope ends despair. Peace dominates war; faith reconciles doubt. Mutual regard cancels enmity. Justice for all overthrows injustice. The redemptive community supersedes systems of gross social immorality.

"Love is the central motif of nonviolence. Love is the force by which God binds man to himself and man to man. Such love goes to the extreme; it remains loving and forgiving even in the midst of hostility. It matches the capacity of evil to inflict suffering with an even more enduring capacity to absorb evil, all the while persisting in love.

"By appealing to the conscience and standing on the moral nature of human existence, nonviolence nurtures the atmosphere in which reconciliation and justice become actual possibilities."

Almost needless to say, such an ideological commitment does not at all indicate the degree of agreement of each and every participant in the sit-in movement. Many participants probably never saw the statement; many others probably did not understand it, much less agree with its full implications of pacifism and Gandhiism as it is understood by American pacifists. Many, understandably, saw no inconsistency between voting for this statement and at the same time belonging to Reserve Officers Training Corps units—segregated. At this point very few saw that there might be a connection between nonviolence as espoused by a general movement, and nonviolence as practiced by individuals in everyday life.

This developing stage of the Southern movement, characterized in the first place by the April Conference, was paralleled in the North, where a series of more or less localized support actions had taken place, usually in the form of picketing of Northern outlets of chain stores which were the targets of sit-ins in the South. Thus the sit-ins began to have a wider effect on students, and particularly on student government leaders. The United States National Student Association (USNSA) was almost immediately affected by demonstrations or support actions in its member schools. In the educational field a need to understand, and assist the movement began to be voiced, and two conferences in Washington took place which indicated these needs in a more formal way.

One of these was the White House Conference, a regular gathering which celebrated its golden anniversary in 1960, when nearly 7,000 people came together. The 1,400 full delegates were divided into five "theme assemblies" and eighteen forums, and subdivided into 210 workgroups. The conference was intended to deal with matters affecting "opportunities for children and youth to realize their full potential for a creative life in freedom and dignity."

Conference resolutions ranged from one on mass media (intended to decrease emphasis on horror, crime and violence) to education (in support of a federal scholarship program).

One of the accredited organizations at the Conference was the Young Adult Council, youth section of the National Social Welfare Assembly, which, in turn, comprises twenty-six national student and youth groups, one of which is USNSA. On March 29, in the midst of the Conference, YAC quietly gathered together its delegates into a caucus determined to get the Conference to support the sit-ins. They drafted a petition, which was circulated generally, and in addition agreed to introduce into each workshop a resolution incorporating the major ideas of the petition. To back all this up dramatically, they laid plans to set up a picket line in the heart of downtown Washington. The activities of the "secret" caucus were carefully leaked to the press, and were fully covered by the *New York Times*, among others. Within two days the caucus had succeeded in getting six workshops to pass resolutions in general support of the sit-ins, and the caucus then selected spokesmen for Forum 18, "The Young With Social Handicaps," which went on to pass a resolution of the same kind. Some of the delegates then picketed Kress' store in Washington. The final resolution, however, omitted part of the proposal, to take President Eisenhower to task for his lack of leadership in implementing the U.S. Supreme Court decision on school integration.

The passage of this resolution demonstrated the extreme diffusion of results stemming from the organized actions of a very few individuals who had some overlapping responsibility with the sit-ins. Specifically, not more than a dozen delegates to the Conference, all from YAC, who in turn represented constituent groups with a direct stake in civil rights, were able, due to the popularity of the issue, to move a body of 1,400 delegates who, without the presence of the caucus, would probably not have moved despite the popularity of the issue. The leaders of the caucus of sixty or so included Curtis Gans, national affairs vice-president of USNSA, who had just returned to national headquarters in Philadelphia from the South; Don Hoffman, president of USNSA; Herb Wright, Youth Secretary, NAACP; Charles Van Tassel, of Students for a Democratic Society; and Evelyn Rich, a regional representative of CORE. The caucus had been formed by them as individuals, not in the name of YAC, and it had been done on the spur of the moment in response to a lack of direct concern with the issue of integration by the Conference as a whole.

While the direct effect of the Conference on the Movement as a whole was negligible, the success of the YAC caucus served to put on record in favor of the sit-ins a broad and highly respectable body of educational opinion.

The national affairs vice-president of USNSA, Curtis Gans, a former student at the University of North Carolina, following the broader pro-integrationist policies of his organization, had gone to the South in mid-February to make a determination for USNSA on the credentials of the movement so that the organization could support it and give assistance. Upon his return to national headquarters in Philadelphia USNSA did issue a statement supporting the movement and corresponded frequently with its approximately 350 member student government organizations requesting a variety of actions. Some sixty college student government bodies, for example, responded to USNSA's call to send telegrams to Nashville upon the arrest of students there during a sit-in. On another occasion, over $1,000 was raised from student governments inside of three days during a walkout of students in Montgomery, Alabama, protesting the expulsion of student leaders there, for use in legal fees, etc. USNSA received continuous reports from its contact people and representatives on the scene of sit-in activity.

The officers, upon hearing Gans' report, determined to hold a conference in order to "present participants with a coherent picture of the . . . Southern movement . . .," to involve student leaders elsewhere in support activity, to create national publicity, to ascertain efficient means of obtaining and giving support, and to channel human relations program interest into campus-level action.[84] One hundred and eighty-four official delegates—student body presidents or their official representatives—attended the Conference, which was held in Washington, April 22-23. Presentations included panels on the history of the movement, supporting actions of students elsewhere, discussion groups, and sessions for dealing with the recommendations.

The Conference was not a success, in the opinion of USNSA observers themselves.[85] Handicapped by insufficient planning and inadequate preparation, the Conference immediately bogged down. Southern participants were too involved locally to be able to give thought to planning of a national scope; Northern students, desperately seeking identification with the

Southern movement, wanted more thoughtful leadership and insight than Southerners were able to give at the moment. Furthermore, Northern students were less able to see the deeper social blocks facing their Southern colleagues, and hence were more superficially concerned with the mechanics of campus problems; the Southerners were more deeply involved with their whole society, its inhibitions as well as its difficulties, but were not able to vocalize these concepts.

The usual, and expected, resolutions favoring the sit-ins, the philosophy of nonviolent action, and the like were passed. They condemned reprisals upon student protest leaders. They "recognized" that the movement was based on the ideology of nonviolence and was not a movement "merely using nonviolence as a technique," though this was clearly not true in a general sense. They went on record in support of a variety of specific plans such as petitions, nationwide one-day demonstrations, letter-writing campaigns, fund-raising activity, and the like.

The question of just how representative such conferences and such resolutions within the framework of USNSA are has often been raised, and continues to be raised after each national conference every year. Delegates and observers to such conferences are chosen in a variety of ways, the most common being delegation by student government groups of their own members, and/or personal appointment by student government leaders of individuals not members of student government but interested in the issue at hand. Thus the question of representativeness reduces itself in part to the question of how representative student governments are of student bodies. This appears to vary widely from campus to campus, as does participation in the elections for student governments, which seems to be at least a moderately sound index of representativeness. Ultimately, and frequently, however, conference participants select themselves out of the student government and student body on the basis that they are sufficiently interested in the issue to go to a conference. Thus it can be said with a fair amount of accuracy that USNSA conferences are representative of those students from affiliated campuses who are interested enough in the issue (pro or con) to attend.

The USNSA's Southern Project will be discussed later; in the North the Conference aided in stimulating other, smaller conferences which helped to focus Northern students' attention upon the issue of civil rights. Several examples will be illustrative: On May 6-7, the New England Region of USNSA sponsored a Conference on Civil Rights at Wesleyan University in

Middletown, Connecticut. On May 7, a conference took place at St. Mary College, Xavier, Kansas, with five colleges in the vicinity of Atchison, Kansas, participating. During that spring also, Students for a Democratic Society held a fairly large conference along similar lines at Ann Arbor; later in the year, on October 8, students from twenty-four Midwestern colleges met at Antioch College, Yellow Springs, Ohio, to form a coordinating body for civil rights action; on October 21-22, Philadelphia area colleges did the same at the University of Pennsylvania, forming a Philadelphia Student Civil Rights Coordinating Committee. A number of other conferences and symposia also featured civil rights and the sit-ins. "Challenge," a discussion group at Yale University, was host to students from many Eastern colleges early in the spring of 1960; the guests heard A. Philip Randolph speak, and funds for the sit-in movement were collected at an evening musical benefit which followed the close of the official program, and which ran into the early morning hours.

Thus the movement in the South, and its supporters in the North, began to develop an overall structure, with a hierarchy and a coherent ideology. The beginnings of conflict, in the form of argument as to the extent of outside and/or adult control or influence over the Southern movement, came into evidence.

A second pattern during the developing stage of the movement emerged on the local scene in terms of the white community's reaction to the sit-ins—particularly in the border states. The initial wave of sit-ins abated after the first sixty to ninety days following February, 1960. Many communities involved in these first sit-ins were now in "cooling-off" periods, during which students held off demonstrations pending the outcome of one form or another of negotiations. In many cases these were simply delaying actions on the part of the white power structure, which was as yet unconvinced that the movement could last beyond a week or so of relatively uncoordinated and disorganized sitting-in. In other words, the cooling-off periods, when they were simply delaying actions, were the result of a misunderstanding as to the real strength of the student movement, which had not yet been really tested.

When it became apparent to student organizations in such communities, that results would not be forthcoming without more direct pressure, more sit-ins and picketing resulted. These in turn gave rise to renewed demands for "real" negotiations on the part of both students, and segments of the white community interested in minimizing community conflict. As one participant-observer has suggested, the white middle class businessman will surrender to whatever party takes the initiative in disrupting business: in the case of public schools it was the segregationists, and rather than have further disruption, school integration was delayed. In the case of the sit-ins, those who disrupted business were Negro, hence businessmen, once convinced of the seriousness of the situation, gave in to them. The sit-in movement placed ". . . the fear of community disturbance on the side of civil rights" for a change, and therefore businessmen ". . . decided they risked greater losses by not desegregating than by desegregating. This is *the one decisive reason* for the speedy success of the movement" where it did succeed.[86]

By the end of May, 1960, many Upper South and border communities realized that the students were not going to be put off by delaying tactics. Businessmen began to seek an avenue for realistic negotiation which would give them a graceful out vis-a-vis the segregationist groups. Local government leaders responded to this by creating, within four months of the initial sit-in in Greensboro, local race relations committees in some thirty cities in eight border and Upper South states to work out local problems. Most were sparked by local, or nearby sit-ins. Only one Deep Southern city, Savannah, Georgia, had such a committee in this period. A few others in the Deep South set them up later. On a statewide level Oklahoma, Kentucky and Florida had previously set up race relations commissions; some thirty-three cities throughout the U.S., most of them Northern, had such commissions with staff and professional help. Governor LeRoy Collins of Florida set up such a group, the Commission on Race Relations, which had a number of advisory bodies, on March 20, 1960. He was the only Southern governor openly to state that he was opposed to discrimination against Negroes at some sections of stores when they were being served at other sections.[87]

Six weeks after his statement setting up the Florida Commission, twelve communities in Florida had local interracial committees functioning; eight of them had been in action before. By the close of the year there were fourteen. Texas and North Carolina also had extensive community organizations, although not all local committees were by any means uniformly successful in negotiating local settlements or ends to the sit-ins and the discriminatory practices which gave rise to them. Other Southern states continued generally without such committees. Among North Carolina cities stimulated by local sit-ins to organize local biracial committees were Greensboro, Winston-Salem, High Point, Raleigh, Durham, Charlotte and Salisbury. In Texas, a negotiating committee was set up in strifetorn Marshall, but it failed. On the other hand, in Corpus Christi there were no demonstrations at all, and within a short time, in response to action elsewhere, several stores were integrated through the efforts of some of the store managers. In San Antonio, following a mass rally of Negroes, local ministers brought negotiations into the picture. Stores were integrated. In Galveston, after sit-ins, an all-white mediating committee of businessmen and ministers succeeded in getting Negro leaders and store managers to agree on some conditions, and stores were integrated.

By October 25, twenty-nine cities had government-appointed committees, and seven others had informal committees. Only eight had existed prior to the sit-ins. The committees more frequently successful, according to the Southern Regional Council's survey, were in communities small in size, where committees were officially appointed, biracial, composed of "respected civic figures," and generally in communities where some other facilities had already been integrated prior to the lunch counter issue, particularly where Negroes voted and held some political power.[88]

In a study by Grigg and Killian, based on questionnaires sent to 389 cities in twelve Southern states, it later developed that only fifty-five of those responding had biracial committees. But of these, only five had existed prior to 1954, nine more had been established in the years 1954-1959, and the remaining thirty-nine in the years 1959-1961, inclusive. The most important factor in the creation of these latter committees was the sit-in movement.[89]

In the case of Governor Collin's Commission, it is interesting to note that in a plea to set up such committees sent to local civic leaders, the prime emphasis is placed on good business. Twelve reasons are given by the Florida Commission to suggest a change in the race relations "climate." Number one is that Negroes in the South represent three billion dollars worth of purchasing power, and that through selective buying Negroes could exert great economic pressure. Several other reasons emphasize the legal difficulties facing continued segregation, and the diplomatic embarrassment for the U.S. involved in continuing these practices. Another group of reasons suggested that Negroes have changed and will no longer tolerate segregation patterns. Only one reason, number seven, suggested that equality per se was a good thing, and this mainly because twenty-nine religious bodies were on record, hence forming a pressure group in their own right, backing the Judeo-Christian ethic of equality of all men before God. The Florida report, in the best of business tradition, drew a parallel between race relations and labor-management relations, stating that "No large industry would operate today without a well-functioning grievance procedure . . . This is just a simple operating maxim of good management and public relations in general." This was because "a worker with a grievance who has no place to take it tends to build up resentment and increase the probability of irresponsible behavior."[90]

Obviously much of this language was calculated in terms of an appeal to "hard-headed" businessman's rationale, and as a rhetoric had no necessary connection to the actual results. Regardless of Governor Collin's real motives, he appealed, through the Florida Commission, to businessmen in terms of the rhetoric he thought they would "buy." And regardless of whether or not local civic leaders set up local committees in response to the rhetoric, businessmen did. No implication is included here that because the rhetoric was business the motive was business—although when rhetoric also is profitable, it is probable that a profit-motivated rhetoric is also a real motive.

In a few cases—notably some East Texas cities, and Nashville, Tennessee, these committees secured early settlements. But in most of the Upper South states, Negro students remained locked in battle at the lunch counter, on the picket line, or across the negotiating table. In the Deep South there were virtually no negotiating tables, and the lunch counter and picket line activities were frequently broken up by superior police force, so that the movement in a number of instances was effectively broken up as a going concern. Merchants in some cases wished to wait the students out, hoping that when they went home for the summer the whole thing would die down.

But in this they were generally disappointed. The developing student movement, in the course of organizing and turning to adult groups for help (while rejecting adult control), brought adults from local Negro communities directly into contact with direct action techniques. In many cases, Negro citizen groups and NAACP chapters called boycotts on the chain stores which were the student targets. In some cases Negro groups on the adult level took over the picketing in the absence of the college students; high school students from the local area came into the picture to replace their slightly older colleagues. In cities such as Greensboro and Charlotte, North Carolina, merchants found their hopes that the movement would die in the summer months frustrated. By June 6, 1960, nine communities had come to terms with the Movement, and had integrated lunch counters; by August, twenty-seven Southern cities and counties had capitulated. These were: Miami, Chapel Hill, Charlotte, Concord, Durham, Elizabeth City, Greensboro, High Point, Salisbury, Winston-Salem, Frankfort, Knoxville, Nashville, Austin, Corpus Christi, Dallas, Galveston, San Antonio,

Alexandria, Arlington County, Fairfax County (Va.), Falls Church, Fredericksburg, Hampton, Norfolk, Portsmouth, and Williamsburg. Some stores had also been integrated in Richmond, Petersburg, and Houston. "Non-Southern" cities of Xenia, Ohio, Las Vegas, Baltimore, Kansas City, Missouri, and Oklahoma City, had also desegregated some eating facilities. Almost every one of these communities had had some kind of local demonstrations.

Thus the first segment of segregated facilities fell to the Movement. But now the students were faced with the much more difficult problem of how to handle the harder cores of resistance in the Deep South states—and at the same time they had to answer the question of what to do with their local organizations now that victory was won.

The answer to these questions, as it developed, marked a long-range strategic shift for the student movement, the latter phases of which are no longer within the subject matter of this paper. This answer can be summed up in the term Political Action, in which the students' share was primarily in the field of voter registration in the Deep South states—a share they are still carrying on, and which is by no means near fruition.

The early impetus toward this shift of strategy, which still belongs to the developing stage of the Movement, came from outside, from the North. 1960 was a Presidential election year, and even before the sit-ins broke out a number of interested persons, led by Bayard Rustin, had envisioned mass action in the South, in various localities, to put pressure on convention delegates of both major parties, and at the convention to press for a clear stand on civil rights in both platforms. At a meeting in honor of his seventieth birthday, A. Philip Randolph said he intended to call for marches on the conventions. Although the NAACP indicated it was in favor of the project, particularly the appeals on local levels to put pressure on convention delegates, not much action was forthcoming. Randolph was tied up with the formation of his American Negro Labor Council, the SCLC was facing financial difficulties given the outbreak of the sit-ins, and the need for funds to support them, and the NAACP's national office efforts were likewise being deflected. In early March Rustin opened a New York City office of SCLC to drum up support for Rev. King, after he had been arrested on an income tax evasion charge in Alabama. This too diverted resources.

Despite these difficulties, on June 9 King and Randolph issued a call for a "March on the Convention Movement for Freedom Now!" to present a list of questions to all the candidates, and in general put pressure on the conventions. Headquarters for the Marches was 312 W. 125th Street, Harlem, also the office of SCLC's Northern outlet, the Committee to Defend Martin Luther King and the Struggle for Freedom in the South, headed by Rustin. A Chicago office was opened to coordinate the March on the Republican Convention, and a Los Angeles office followed.

Then, on June 25, the *Courier* chain of Negro newspapers (Pittsburgh, Philadelphia, New York, etc.) published a story datelined Buffalo, where Representative Adam Clayton Powell (D., N.Y.) had addressed delegates to the National Sunday School Congress June 19. Powell stated that Rev. King had been "under undue influences" ever since Bayard Rustin went into Montgomery, Alabama, to help in the bus boycott. He said Randolph was the "captive of socialist interests." It came out against the Marches, though Powell did not explicitly oppose them. A few days earlier a column in the New York *Journal-American* said that Communists had plans to capture and infiltrate the Marches, and quoted Roy Wilkins of the NAACP as saying that he feared left-wingers in the picket lines.

This faced Randolph, King and Rustin with a serious crisis. Representative Powell, important in Democratic Party circles, was smearing all three, and was forcing the NAACP to shy away from the Marches. The NAACP, never strong on mass action, could undercut the Marches by failing to mobilize its supporters in the convention cities. On the same day that Powell's charges hit the newsstands, he came out praising Senator Lyndon Johnson of Texas as "the most able man in Congress," but said he still preferred Senator Stuart Symington of Missouri. The next day, June 28, Rustin resigned as King's Special Assistant, and as Director of the New York office of SCLC. In his resignation, he charged that Representative Powell "seeks to weaken, if not destroy, the March on the Conventions for his own obvious political reasons."[91]

Plans for the Marches, however, continued and both did in fact take place, in Los Angeles and Chicago, respectively, on July 10 with some 5,000 participating in the former city, and on July 25 in the latter city. Picketing of both conventions took place. In Los Angeles as many as 500 per day joined the lines until July 13, when activity ceased. In addition, a number of statements were submitted, and individuals appeared, before the Platform Committees of both parties, to advocate clear-cut civil rights planks. The Student Nonviolent Coordinating Committee sent four spokesmen to both Los Angeles and Chicago. They asked for planks advocating implementation of the 1954 Supreme Court School Decision; federal action for equal job opportunities; the unhampered exercise of the franchise; and legal protection of the sit-ins.

On May 31, the Leadership Conference on Civil Rights, which includes the American Civil Liberties Union, American Jewish Congress, American Veterans Committee, and similar bodies, set forth a seven-point civil rights program and said it would send representatives to call on all the candidates to ask them to specify where they stood.[92] Roy Wilkins, of NAACP, was chairman of the Conference.

Meanwhile, on June 24, Senator John F. Kennedy (D., Mass.), praised the sit-in campaign as a sign that "The American spirit is coming alive again." A few days later, during the preliminaries of the convention in Los Angeles, however, Representative Powell told reporters he would stick to Senator Symington for a while, perhaps switching to Senator Johnson later. Powell did not actively campaign for Kennedy until October.

The Congress of Racial Equality also appeared before the Democratic Platform Committee with a brief statement, as did Robert Armstrong, a member of Tallahassee, Fla., CORE and a student at Florida State University (all-white).

As a result of these various pressures, added no doubt to the pressures applied on delegates before they arrived at the convention sites, both major parties passed civil rights planks bolder than any since Reconstruction. The sit-ins were mentioned indirectly in the following manner in "The Rights of Man," the Democratic Platform:

"The peaceful demonstrations for first-class citizenship which have recently taken place in many parts of this country are a signal to all of us to make good at long last the guarantees of our Constitution . . ."

The Republican Party's declaration was similar. In Chicago Governor Rockefeller of New York addressed the NAACP-sponsored rally on the eve of the opening of the Convention, and the date of the Chicago March on the Convention, July 25.

The Civil Rights issue, needless to say, played an important role in the campaign. Exactly how critical it was will probably never be determined. It is possible that it was decisive in the election of President Kennedy. On October 19, fifty-one sit-in demonstrators, including Rev. Martin Luther King, Jr., were arrested in Atlanta, Georgia, in the course of a sit-in at Rich's department store. King at this time was under a suspended sentence of twelve months, imposed for driving without a Georgia license some time before (he had moved to Georgia from Alabama during 1960). DeKalb County Judge Oscar Mitchell set aside the twelve-month sentence, imposed a four-month sentence, and Dr. King found himself in Georgia State Prison. Bail was denied.

Senator Kennedy then made a special plea to Mayor Hartsfield of Atlanta, who used his good offices to obtain the release of twenty-two sit-in demonstrators from the city jail, and thirty-nine more from the Fulton County jail, leaving only King incarcerated. Kennedy was said to have personally telephoned sympathy to Mrs. King. As a result, King's father, Rev. Martin King Sr., publicly said he would vote for Kennedy. A member of Kennedy's family whose identity has never been revealed,[93] interceded with Judge Mitchell, who, on October 26, released King on $2,000 bail. Mitchell claimed he was releasing King on the merits of the case only, and not due to the pressures put upon him. The Republican presidential candidate, Mr. Nixon, was silent on the issue.

In both Texas and South Carolina President Kennedy swung the states by less than the number of Negro voters—according to the *New York Times* (November 27, 1960), Kennedy carried Texas by about 45,000 voters. He got about 100,000 Negro votes there. In South Carolina the President carried the state by approximately 10,000 only. About 40,000 Negroes were estimated by the *Times* to have voted for him there. In North Carolina, where some 70,000 Negroes voted for him, Kennedy carried the state by 58,000. Narrow margins in many other states, including Northern states, were also exceeded by the number of Negroes voting for him. But in the South Negroes who had voted Republican, and districts that had gone to Adlai Stevenson by small margins, shifted to Mr. Kennedy in large numbers. Said the *Times*,

"The most important single campaign move was undoubtedly Senator Kennedy's telephone call of sympathy to the wife of the Rev. Dr. Martin Luther King, Jr., when the Southern integration leader was briefly in a Georgia prison on a traffic charge. Mr. Nixon made no comment on the King episode.

"In the last week of the campaign, various committees and groups favoring Senator Kennedy printed and distributed 2,000,000 copies of a four-page pamphlet headed "'No Comment' Nixon Versus a Candidate With a Heart, Senator Kennedy." It simply gave some quotes on the affair from Dr. and Mrs. King and others.

"In Chicago alone, 250,000 copies of the pamphlet were handed out . . . in a state that (Kennedy) carried by 8,000 votes."

Kennedy's victory in the South appeared particularly important for civil rights because of the growth of the Republican Party there; traditionally segregationist Democratic areas in a number of instances went Republican. In Atlanta the nature of the campaign by the Republicans was generally to try to out-segregationist the Democratic segregationists. In Alabama, too, usually Democratic votes went to unpledged electors, and six out of the state's eleven electors did not vote for Kennedy. In Mississippi he lost the state to an independent ticket. The Republican Party carried the Southern states of Virginia, Kentucky, Tennessee, Florida and Oklahoma. The Democratic Party carried West Virginia, North Carolina, South Carolina, Georgia, Louisiana, Texas, Arkansas, Missouri and five out of eleven electors in Alabama.

The two candidates were separated in the popular vote by about a single percentage point; 400,000 votes out of a total of sixty-two million votes cast made the difference for the victor. Senator Kennedy's phone call—a situation impossible without the sit-ins as a backdrop—conceivably may have made him President.

One further note to the election of 1960 must be added. At the first formal conference of the Student Nonviolent Coordinating Committee, held in Atlanta October 14-16, delegates decided on Election Day demonstrations with the themes of calling attention to the lack of voting rights of Negroes in some areas, and demanding action to implement the platforms of the victorious candidates. Northern delegates were aware in advance of this forthcoming decision and, with the assistance of a mailing through the good offices of USNSA organized demonstrations at polling places and campaign headquarters in a number of cities. The demonstrations came off, generally unreported in the public press, in about a dozen Northern cities, sparked by local college students. Between two and three thousand students were involved.[94]

3. The Institutionalized Stage

The sit-in movement as such, following its initial successes in attaining lunch counter integration in the Upper South, reached what can be called a semi-institutionalized stage with SNCC's second conference in Atlanta, Ga., in October, 1960. For the purpose of this paper, the final months of 1960, and the first part of 1961 mark the concluding stage of what can be called the sit-in movement proper. But, in the same period, something else began to emerge—the Southern Negro Student Movement. The Sit-In Movement, confronted with success on the one hand, and virtually immobilized by local opposition in the Deep Southern states on the other, went into a transitionary stage in which it experimented with a series of devices such as stand-ins, kneel-ins, and the like, before finally committing itself to a voter registration campaign. At that point it can no longer be called the sit-in movement, even though the organizational framework of the student movement remained SNCC.

Its semi-institutionalized stage, following the resumption of school in the fall of 1960, was marked by the emergence of SNCC as the apparatus and the public image of the Negro student movement in the South. SNCC more and more came to direct local protest groups, or at least seriously coordinate them, and give local groups a semblance of tactical direction, strategic guidance, and ideological training and leadership. Its decision-making processes, its control, and its conflicts are therefore of importance to an understanding of this stage of the movement.

The second conference of SNCC (the initial one being at Raleigh, April 17), from which the Election Day demonstrations emanated, took place in Atlanta, October 14-16. The first business of the Conference was to send telegrams to both presidential candidates protesting an attempt on the life of an organizer for the Southern Christian Leadership Conference, holding its annual meeting in New Orleans a few days before. Then, on the evening of October 14, Miss Ella Baker, adviser to SNCC (no longer officially with SCLC) and Rev. King, Jr., gave keynote speeches. Miss Baker continued on the theme she had developed earlier, warning against a leadership-centered movement, and against being taken over by "other interests." There were rumors, later substantiated, that she had had a falling-out with Rev. King. King himself added little new, and his talk was basically a more sophisticated version of the philosophy outlined in his book, *Stride Toward Freedom*.

Ninety-five voting delegates were present, plus SNCC staff which voted, plus thirteen alternates. Of the ninety-five, perhaps a dozen were white. In addition there were ninety-eight registered observers, of whom twelve, representing eleven different groups or publications, were members of the Socialist Party-Social Democratic Federation or its youth affiliate, the Young People's Socialist League, or both. State by state the delegation broke down as follows:

SNCC CONFERENCE, OCTOBER, 14-16, 1960

Alabama	8 delegates	(5 campuses)
Arkansas	4	(2 ")
Florida	6	(3 campuses, 1 high school)
Georgia	13	(7 ")
Kentucky	1	
Louisiana	5	(4 campuses, 1 high school)
Mississippi	1	
Maryland	5	(3 ")
North Carolina	13	(6 " 1 " ")
South Carolina	6	(4 ")
Oklahoma	2	(1 " 1 " ")
Tennessee	12	(7 " or areas)
Texas	6	(3 ")
Virginia	8	(2 " 1 " ")
D.C.	5	(2 ")

A listing of the groups or publications sending observers is of significance in terms of the range of support for the movement, both locally, and in the Northern states. Groups are listed by type:

Religious

Anti-Defamation League (Atlanta)
B'nai B'rith Hillel Foundation (Atlanta)
National Student Christian Federation
United Christian Youth Movement (New York)
American Friends Service Committee (Regional)
Congregational Christian Church (minister)
National Student YWCA
Southern Regional YWCA

Unions

United Federation of Teachers, AFL-CIO (New York)
An *unofficial* representative of George Meany, President, AFL-CIO

Civil Rights Groups

SNCC (advisers)
Southern Regional Council
Massachusetts Commission Against Discrimination, Atlanta Branch
NAACP, South Side Chicago Branch NAACP, South Side Chicago NAACP Youth Council
Freedom Walk Committee of Ithaca, N.Y.
Cornell Committee Against Segregation
Southern Conference Educational Fund
Regional Council of Negro Leadership (Mississippi)
CORE
NAACP
Highlander Folk School

<u>SNCC CONFERENCE, OCTOBER, 14-16, 1960 (cont.)</u>

Civil Rights Groups, cont.

Fellowship of Reconciliation
Minneapolis Students for Integration
Oberlin College Chapter NAACP
Amherst College Students for Racial Equality
Ann Arbor Direct Action Committee
Antioch College Chapter NAACP
Nashville Student Leadership Council
Baton Rouge NAACP Youth Council
Philadelphia Coordinating Committee for Civil Rights
Indiana University NAACP
Atlanta Committee on Appeal
Etc.

Publications

New America
The Worker
The National Guardian

Student Groups or Students not representing groups

USNSA
Students for a Democratic Society
Shimer College Student Council
Oberlin College YMCA
Oberlin Student Council
University of Chicago (grad. student)
Central State College (student)
Antioch College Peace Group
Harvard (grad. student)
Swarthmore Student Council
Swarthmore *Albatross*
University of Michigan (student)
Colorado State College "LSA and HRA"
Antioch NSA Committee
Pomona College (student)
Mt. Holyoke College (student)
Va. Union University (student)
Morgan State College Civic Interest Group
Fisk University (student)
Clark College (student)
Spelman College (student)
Va. State College (student)

Misc. World University Service (Atlanta)

Precise classification is open to argument, since some of the civil rights groups should perhaps be classified under student groups, or vice-versa.

On the second day of the Conference the basic issue of local autonomy versus centralized control by state area or Atlanta came to the floor. A compromise was worked out so that local "protest areas" composed of local groups within one or contiguous communities would be the basic unit of voting. SNCC's original compromise that state areas be voted as units was defeated. Workshops then took place on a variety of topics. Dr. Lewis Wade Jones, social scientist from Tuskegee, and Rev. James Lawson, expelled from Vanderbilt Theological Seminary, spoke at an afternoon session. Lawson strongly advocated going to jail rather than paying bail. He attacked the Negro elite for raising money for bail: they should have attacked "the system." "We lost the finest hours of our movement when we left the jails for bail . . . perhaps we can never again recover," he added. During that evening workshops took place in the areas of "political activity," "public facilities," "employment," "education," "relationship with national and non-Southern groups," and "jail vs. bail."

It was in the political activities workshop that one of the resource persons stated the case for election day projects; actual proposals would have to originate in workshops, and SNCC's idea for such a project would not come to a vote on the floor unless it was raised and adopted by a workshop. The resource person to raise the issue was Michael Harrington, correspondent (and later editor) of *New America*, and an alternate national committeeman of the Socialist Party-SDF.

Students from outside the South arranged a separate caucus later in the evening but gave it up to join the workshop on Relationship with National and Non-Southern Groups. Two viewpoints were being debated here: Should SNCC be only a coordinating committee or should it "call the shots"; it was merely another version of the morning's argument on the Conference floor. Northern support groups, then in the process of picketing local outlets of chain stores being demonstrated against in the South, wanted guidance from some central spokesman. But the local movements were not in a position to delegate such rights to SNCC in Atlanta. One reason for this was that local groups affiliated to NAACP found themselves with divided loyalties: not only were they part of SNCC, but they were attached to a local NAACP chapter, and to a National NAACP Youth Section as well, all of which might at any point have some conflicting interests.

Late on Sunday, with only thirty-five voting delegates remaining (the rest were attending a rally nearby), the election day proposals passed. The proposal was supposed to be "secret," and the press was officially excluded from the session, although loudspeakers carried the proceedings clearly outdoors.

Lack of leadership training among the leaders of the Movement was obvious at this conference. A parliamentary shambles was avoided on the first day only when the national affairs vice-president of USNSA, a Negro (Timothy Jenkins), took the chairmanship of the session from the previously delegated chairman. Many of the delegates seemed to have little inkling of political organization; any well-organized caucus could easily have rammed anything through, but there were no such groups.

However, there were individuals, like Jenkins, Rev. Lawson, and others, who had a fairly solid grasp of what was going on. Lawson, in addition, had around him a small group of out-and-out believers in the philosophy of nonviolence who were quite coherent. Further, the significant number of socialists among the observers added even more numbers to the group in Atlanta which, while not forming a formal caucus, were vocal and had ideas about strategy. The socialists in particular were interested in the electoral action issue, and informally broached the subject throughout the weekend. The socialists, considering the civil rights movement the first real breakthrough for social change in the U.S. in a decade, had been active in Northern support all along, and had become respected and open allies of such persons as Rustin there; now they had come to Atlanta, relatively more experienced, certainly with a more far-reaching view than the average Negro participant, and certainly vocal in a quiet way. Hence, without in any way "taking over" or "using" the Conference, the socialists exerted some influence.

In this semi-institutionalized stage, then, groups with experience, able to voice an ideology coherently, were able to give a measure of direction to the overall structure of the sit-in movement, which otherwise existed in a vacuum. In other words, the very lack of organized interest groups within the movement gave leadership to persons who, without themselves forming a caucus, or even being a specific interest group in a formal sense, had some organizational experience and talent, no matter how limited. In some cases these individuals had contact with one or more of the traditional civil rights groups, and thus brought the influence of these groups to bear on the direction of SNCC. Given the role played by the various civil rights organizations not only in terms of organizational, financial, and legal support to the Negro students in the South, but also in terms of their influence upon the direction the student movement would take, it might be well at this point to describe briefly each of them. These descriptions will emphasize the functional relationship of each group to the student movement, and particularly to the developing sit-in movement during its first year, 1960.

Let us describe first, however, the structure of SNCC as it was set up at the Raleigh and Atlanta conferences. SNCC is a committee which maintains a staff and office in Atlanta, Georgia, and which is supported financially by interested adult groups and by private donations raised at rallies, meetings, and the like. There are some twenty-five members of the committee, seventeen of whom are delegates from the various Southern and border states and the District of Columbia. Three student groups, USNSA, the National Student Christian Federation, and the National College and Youth Branch of NAACP are also represented by voting delegates. About nine adult groups at one time or another have acted as observers at SNCC meetings: AFSC, American Civil Liberties Union, CORE, the Fellowship of Reconciliation, NAACP, SCLC, the Southern Conference Educational Fund, the National Student YMCA, and the Southern Regional Council. The Committee meets every two months or so to coordinate, in a loose way, its constituent parts. Local protest groups remain autonomous, sometimes organizing statewide groups to maintain contact more directly with SNCC. During the period under discussion the only salaried official of SNCC was the administrative secretary, who was largely responsible for the publication of SNCC's official newsletter, *Student Voice*. His salary was $3,000 annually. Since shifting to voter-registration in its emphasis in a later period, the SNCC staff has been expanded considerably, but this did not happen until the Freedom Rider period, and is thus outside the scope of this paper.

The following organizations will be discussed in the next few pages: NAACP, CORE, SCLC, ACLU, SCEF, Southern Regional Council, AFSC, FOR, USNSA, and the Highlander Folk School. The role played by official religious bodies in the sit-in movement will also be summarized.

The National Association for the Advancement of Colored People (NAACP) was one of the three groups which formed a kind of adult organizational shield over SNCC and the sit-ins during their first year, and still today forms the main legal weapon of the civil rights movement. The well-known legal cases which it had undertaken formed a critical part of the social context which made further group identification possible, and which made other kinds of social action appear feasible.

Structurally, the NAACP really consists of three sections: the national organization, with headquarters in New York run by Roy Wilkins; its Legal Defense arm, a separate legal entity, formerly directed by Thurgood Marshall, now a federal judge; and the local branches, which carry out actions on local levels consistent with national policy but often independent of the national office. The NAACP, with its national emphasis on the contesting of legal issues, and on lobbying, is widely considered the organizational spokesman for the Negro elite, the group termed by Dr. E. Franklin Frazier as "The Black Bourgeoisie."[95] The bulk of its national and local leadership come from the ranks of this sector of the Negro community. It has the largest membership of any Negro civil rights group, and the vast bulk of its members are wage-earners. Its primary role has been that of resorting to the legal channels of social change, particularly the courts, in order to obtain for Negroes a share in American society, rather than attempting to change that society as a whole.

In the past the NAACP has been cautious about entering the field of direct action; MOWM and the sit-ins are examples of this caution. On its national level the NAACP has been extremely careful not to risk its hard-won gains by gambles in untried fields. MOWM and the sit-ins both had to show that they were more than adventures of the fly-by-night sort before NAACP extended more than token support. Thus is has often been perceived as a go-slow, or conservatizing influence in terms of innovations in the field of social action.

Locally, NAACP branches differ widely, not only in numbers and type of activity, but even in extent of democratic representation of the local membership. Branches range in size from a handful to more than 10,000 in a few cases. In some branches there is an active social life, with most members participating in the decision-making process. In others, few members attend meetings, and activity is limited to a small minority. In some cases local groups are little more than social cliques; in others the branch forms an important part of local civil rights activity, and plays a large role in Negro community affairs. Generalizations, as with so many other nationwide American institutions, are therefore difficult.

In relation to the sit-ins the national leadership of NAACP has played different roles at different times. Its spokesmen have opposed some facets of the Movement, such as the idea of going to jail rather than accepting bail.

At the same time, local branches have on many occasions supported local sit-ins not only financially and with legal aid, but in some areas have actually been the movement and have done the sitting-in. The exact number of organizers, attorneys and other staff persons supplied by, or supported by, the NAACP for the sit-in movement is not known, nor is the amount of money spent nationally and locally on behalf of the movement known.

The NAACP has, in addition, hired a number of participants in the sit-in movement for its national and local staffs, sponsored a number of conferences, especially on local levels, for its youth and campus members concerned with the sit-ins, and has had present as speakers at its national conventions and local rallies a large number of sit-in participants. It has, like all other civil rights groups, benefited in terms of growth in membership from the sit-in movement.

Probably due to an early underestimate on the part of the national leadership, in particular those heading the youth and campus programs, of the potential of the sit-ins, a number of unfortunate statements have come from NAACP spokesmen. The most damaging of these was probably the remark made by Thurgood Marshall at a meeting in Nashville during April, 1960, when he said, "Once you have been arrested, you've made your point . . . If someone offers to get you out, man, get out . . ." The early caution of the NAACP at the national level vis-a-vis the sit-ins, plus this statement, plus the natural suspicion which the students had of all "adult interference" probably account for the fact that the NAACP, of all the groups in this field, has been most criticized and resented by the students. Other groups have been resented as well, but not so severely, probably because of a friendlier initial response to the tactic of direct action on the part of the national staffs involved.

The *Congress of Racial Equality* (CORE) forms the second part of the organizational shield of the sit-in movement, and today still symbolizes on the adult level that sector of the civil rights movement which is primarily committed to the weapon of nonviolent direct action as a lever to attain full citizenship for American Negroes. Its early pioneering work in this field suited CORE ideally for the task of orienting and training local sit-in organizations in the techniques of nonviolence, while NAACP moved into the legal arena of support for the movement. As a result of these activities, CORE has expanded its membership and its annual budget ten-fold since February, 1960. CORE's utilization of workshops as a training technique will be explored in more detail in a later section of this paper.

When the president of the NAACP branch in Greensboro, N.C., heard of the sit-ins by the students at the A&T College, he called in CORE, whose reputation in the field of direct action was known to him. Subsequently CORE sent a series of field secretaries into the South to assist in the organization of sit-ins, aid those already in progress, and in some cases affiliate local groups to itself. In some cases, as with NAACP, these efforts by adult outsiders antagonized local student groups. In a number of other cases local leaders became, after leaving the area due to expulsion from school or the like, members of CORE's staff. CORE, while cooperating on a formal level with NAACP, tends to ally itself more with SCLC on the local level, sharing with the latter group an ideology which places primary emphasis on nonviolent direct action. Local antagonism between CORE and NAACP over the relative priorities to be given to the tactics of direct action versus court cases has been observed in a number of localities.

It was CORE which, under its new director James Farmer (who had been throughout the early months of the sit-ins NAACP's program director; he has also been one of the founders of CORE) initiated the "Freedom Rides." Farmer, a Negro, had played an active role in adult support of the sit-ins, and had also maintained close personal contact with SNCC and its personnel. He was arrested May 24, 1961, in Jackson, Mississippi, and served forty days of a sixty-seven-day sentence, including some time at the State Penitentiary at Parchman, Mississippi.

The *Southern Christian Leadership Conference* (SCLC) forms the third part of the organizational shield of the movement. It supplied, on the adult level, an ideological symbol to the student movement through its President, Rev. Martin Luther King, Jr.; further, due to its roots in many Southern Negro communities, it was able to give logistical and training support to the sit-ins based on a common commitment to a similar ideology, that of nonviolent resistance.

SCLC was originally set up as the Southern Leadership Conference in 1957. It became a federation of local community groups, such as the Montgomery Improvement Association, and now has as its main purpose a resource and coordinating function similar to that of SNCC on the youth level. From October, 1959 until August, 1960, Miss Ella Baker was SCLC's executive director. At that time, in part due to a personal disagreement with Rev. King, she left the post, and it was taken over by Rev. Wyatt Tee Walker, formerly leader of the protest activities in Petersburg, Virginia. Only one of its officers is not a minister; about thirteen of its twenty-one-member Executive Board in 1960 were also ministers.

One of SCLC's most important functions has been to serve as a channeling body for the training of Negro leaders suggested by its affiliates. It has utilized the Highlander Folk School for this purpose to some degree. Attempts have been made by forces antagonistic to integration to interfere with this, not only by harassing the School, but also by outright violence to SCLC personnel. At its annual conference in Shreveport, Louisiana, on October 11, 1960, the police of Shreveport detained four prominent SCLC figures for over an hour in the station; their car, meanwhile, had the letters KKK scratched into it. Then, one day following the close of the conference, Rev. Larry Blake, SCLC field secretary, was fired on from a passing auto in Shreveport. The bullet missed him, lodging in the front seat of the car an inch from his shoulder.

SCLC's Northern supporters, particularly around persons such as Randolph and Rustin, have been important in organizing support activities for the sit-ins, as well as defense funds for some of the legal cases arising out of the Southern activities, especially the income-tax evasion case involving Rev. King himself.

NAACP, CORE, and SCLC, being large membership organizations functionally closely related to the student movement, formed the chief adult support for SNCC. But a number of other organizations which are either not mass membership groups with the type of resources that would constitute them as part of the "umbrella" of the movement, or are not directly or chiefly concerned with Negro rights also played important, though differing roles. Many were important in the development, structure, and success of the movement, either in terms of support of a financial or personnel kind, or in terms of aiding in the formation of public moral support for the students' efforts, a factor which eased the acceptance of the movement in U.S. society at large, or both.

The *American Civil Liberties Union* (ACLU) had no affiliates in any Southern state except Florida, Kentucky, and Louisiana, and its only city affiliate outside these three states, in the South, was one in Houston, Tex. ACLU did assist in the defense of some sit-in leaders in a number of areas other than those mentioned, and helped when civil liberties issues arose in the course of Northern support picketing. But aside from this, the context of Southern justice is such that ACLU did not have much chance to be effective.

Extra-legal harassment of white integrationists and Negro leaders is a commonplace in many areas of the South, and to this there is often no appeal because such vigilante action is often taken with the support or collaboration of local police. Nor can appeal be taken to state authorities, particularly in the tier of Deep South states, for they are often involved in the extra-legal activities themselves. Civil liberties groups often do not exist; if they existed they would be subjected to the same kinds of extra-legal action, which has varied from outright terrorism (assassination attempts, arson, bombings, etc.) to milder forms of harassment such as phone calls during the night, malicious mischief upon automobiles belonging to integrationists, harassment through arrest for minor offenses, traffic violations, etc.

In many parts of the South the white integrationist in particular may find himself virtually an exile once he becomes known, and he is often forced to move as a result of evictions and the like. His appearance on integrationist picket lines increases, normally, the probability of violence, and in cases of violence chances are it will be directed at him first. There are some islands of safety in the South, some exceptions to this—areas in which the integrationist may operate in a community of liberals, such as that of Atlanta or Chapel Hill; but it remains true that concepts of constitutional guarantees of civil liberties, where known, are often not practiced in the Southern states, particularly in the Deep South.[96]

The *Southern Conference Educational Fund*, with headquarters in New Orleans, is another of the group which lends support to the sit-in movement by publicizing it, raising funds, etc. It is largely associated with the names of Carl and Anne Braden, the former of whom recently finished serving a term for contempt of the U.S. Congress after utilizing the First Amendment to the U.S. Constitution and refusing to answer questions relating to his political activities and associations. SCEF, which stemmed from the Southern Conference for Human Welfare, has been widely alleged in the South to be a Communist front organization. The Bradens were involved in a Kentucky sedition case originating in a bombing in Louisville, but all the defendants were ultimately acquitted. SCEF's publication, *The Southern Patriot*, probably has had more thorough coverage of Southern civil rights news than any other publication with the exception of the *CORE-lator*.

The *Southern Regional Council*, in Atlanta, and its predecessor, the Commission on Interracial Cooperation, have been in existence since 1919. Its chief function is that of a research and publishing-of-research agency with the essential aim of educating the South for integration. Its large volume of files can be matched only by the Southern Educational Reporting Service, which fulfills a similar function, but which limits itself largely to the field of education.

The *American Friends Service Committee* (AFSC), Southeastern Regional Office in High Point, N.C., leaped into the sit-in fray early in 1960, and became an important auxiliary group supporting the movement financially, in terms of organizational training, and in terms of publicizing the aims of the movement among its constituents and friends. The Regional Office and the College Committee of the Region, through its then secretary, Max Heirich, drafted the following statement, which was widely released and quoted in the press:

> "It is our conviction that these demonstrations stem from an unmet need in our society . . . we believe there should be no barriers to equality of opportunity . . . As an organization devoted to nonviolence as a way of life, we commend the approach taken by most of those who have participated in the lunch counter protest demonstrations . . . We urge proprietor, manager, and customer alike to accord equal treatment to all, regardless of race, creed or color . . ."

Prior to the outbreak of the sit-ins, AFSC had been involved in a program for employment equality, in collaboration with the Durham Committee on Negro Affairs, a Negro civic group.[97] Its experience there in acting as an agency to bring employers and the Negro community leaders together was soon transferred to the new events. The College Committee particularly became important because of its prior experience in running workshops and conferences, and in playing a leading role in integration efforts at Duke University (admission policies) and in Chapel Hill (theaters and restaurants). A series of projects, broadly in connection with civil rights and the sit-ins, followed in 1960. A summer work camp was set up in connection with the Montgomery Improvement Association to assist it in a voter registration campaign; members of the college committee (particularly Paul Wehr of the University of North Carolina and Charles Jones of Johnson C. Smith University in Charlotte) participated in local actions; staff and committee members helped the mayor of High Point set up a human relations committee to negotiate a settlement there; a workshop in nonviolence for high school students was organized and sponsored on April 2, in Chapel Hill; the Regional Office co-sponsored the Raleigh Conference; the then

71

college secretary spoke at the USNSA conference in Washington, D.C.; and other integrated workshops were held.

During the planning of the Montgomery voter registration project, the college secretary of AFSC Region at the time, Max Heirich, was arrested, photographed, and questioned by police in Montgomery, and his wife awakened and questioned at the motel where the couple was staying. It was subsequently considered impossible by AFSC to hold an integrated project under what were termed "police state" conditions and thereupon the project was cancelled.

In September, 1960, a new college secretary, Richard Ramsay, was instated. He continued AFSC's participation in the SNCC as observer, and personally participated in attempts to integrate theaters in Greensboro. He also organized the first integrated overnight work camp in Charlotte during the spring, 1961.

A smaller organization, the religious pacifist *Fellowship of Reconciliation* (FoR), also played a role in the sit-ins, but on a more limited scale. A team of FoR personnel was instrumental in the sit-ins in New Bern, North Carolina. Also, FoR, during the summer of 1960, hired as its youth secretary Charles Jones, mentioned previously as the leader of sit-ins in Charlotte, but was forced to release him when friction developed between him and CORE. FoR publications are utilized in a number of areas, particularly in Nashville, Tennessee, where Rev. James Lawson, a pacifist, uses FoR material in training sessions and workshops.

While the labor movement in the South has divided feelings on the question of segregation and race relations, a number of important labor bodies in the South did take stands for the sit-ins, and hence contributed to the climate of public opinion favorable to the student efforts in some areas. On March 18, 1960, the North Carolina AFL-CIO, meeting in convention in Raleigh, adopted a resolution without dissenting vote which said, in part,

". . . this Third Annual Convention of the N.C. AFL-CIO expresses its approval of the efforts of these Negro student groups and expresses our disapproval of the unwarranted police actions now being carried out . . ."

The West Virginia Labor Federation also took a strong stand against discrimination, including in restaurants and other places of public accommodation. The Texas AFL-CIO also supported the nonviolent policies of the sit-ins, as did the District of Columbia Central Labor body. National policy, it went without saying, vocally supported the Movement. In addition,

George Meany, through AFL-CIO Executive Council, put up some $5,000 to assist SNCC in holding its October conference, and then later voted another $4,000 for Fayette County, Tennessee. An administrative assistant from Meany's office attended the conference, almost the only labor representative there. In addition, Edward P. Morgan, news commentator sponsored by the AFL-CIO gave prominent coverage to the sit-in events, and on at least one occasion interviewed sit-in participants.

On April 18, 1960, in a speech at Ithaca, former president Harry S. Truman charged that Communists were engineering the student sit-downs just as sit-downs in the auto factories in 1937 had been "engineered entirely" by Reds. Two days later, in refutation of this, and while Meany and AFL-CIO vice-president Walter Reuther were signing pledge cards to refuse to patronize stores segregating Negro customers, Reuther called Truman's charges, both in regard to the 1937 auto sit-ins, and the 1960 student sit-ins, "nonsense." Truman then claimed he had been misquoted, but reporters stated they had checked with a tape recording of the offending press conference, and had found the remarks correct as originally quoted. It was the only such charge made by a nationally prominent and respected figure during the course of the year.

One of the most important auxiliary groups in the sit-ins was the *U.S. National Student Association* (USNSA), with national headquarters in Philadelphia. USNSA's general support activities have already been discussed above in connection with the conference it held in Washington, D.C., on the sit-ins. In April it also set up a Legal Defense and Scholarship Fund to channel money collected from member schools and other sources. Some $3,000 was raised for this fund, apart from funds raised by individual schools and handled directly by them.

USNSA set up, in Atlanta, in December, 1959, a Southern Student Human Relations Project, supported by a $60,000 grant from the Marshall Field Foundation. It was to last two years. The Project was to educate and stimulate action to solve problems in the area of human relations. The Project grew out of several prior Human Relations Seminars and Conferences from 1958 on. A number of participants in these conferences actually did later become leaders of the sit-ins in their localities, probably more because participants were selected on the basis of leadership already evidenced, than because the seminars provoked them to this specific type of action.

The Third Seminar, held August 1-21, 1960 at the University of Minnesota in conjunction with USNSA's Congress directly thereafter, gathered together sixteen participants, all from the South. Several of the participants again either were, or became, leaders in local protest action. At least half of the sixteen were so involved later.

The Southern project, the involvement of USNSA with the sit-ins, and the on-the-spot reportage to USNSA's member schools by the project's director, Miss Constance Curry, landed USNSA into almost immediate trouble with its Southern affiliates. A significant number of Southern schools disaffiliated due to USNSA's sympathy with the sit-ins, and joined instead a rival group set up shortly after the U.S. Supreme Court's decision on school integration, the all-white Southern University Student Government Association (SUSGA). Subsequently, almost no white schools in the Deep South remained affiliated to USNSA. At regional meetings in the Deep South, a small group of Negro schools are often the only USNSA members participating, and hence the issue of civil rights almost automatically becomes the central topic of discussion, thus alienating the all-white schools even further from USNSA.

The director of the Southern Project at this time, a white woman, on a number of occasions risked her life by appearing at the scene of demonstrations which involved violence, and has on a series of other occasions been constantly harassed. In Atlanta she had been evicted from an apartment, has been plagued by telephone calls during the night after her telephone number appeared in a segregationist newspaper, and has had her automobile damaged by vandals. She is a native Southerner.

The case of the *Highlander Folk School* illustrates the difficulties facing integrationists and integrated auxiliary groups in the South when government bodies are determined to move against them. The School was organized in 1934 primarily as a leadership and training school in adult education, with emphasis on the labor movement. It remains today the only leadership training institute for civil rights in the South that is run on a continuing basis. Partly because of its labor orientation in its early years and partly because it admitted anyone who chose to come, including Communists, it also achieved a communist-front reputation similar to that of SCEF, even in Northern liberal circles.

In 1959 the Tennessee state legislature investigated the School and recommended that its charter be revoked. On July 30, 1959, the School was raided by police and members of the staff were jailed. After a jury trial in which defense counsel took a long series of exceptions based on the introduction of allegedly prejudicial material, the School and its director, Myles Horton, were found guilty on several counts. Appeals were denied and the school was forced to close, reopening some months later in Knoxville.

Highlander is important in the context of the sit-in movement because it has played a small but significant role in the training and development of student leadership. It held a college workshop in April, 1960, on the subject of "The New Generation Fights for Equality," and had eighty-two students present, both white and Negro. A workshop in May on "The Place of the White Southerner in the Current Struggle for Justice" brought sixty-four white and Negro adults together. Its Citizenship School Training Program was for a long time the only long-term program to train Negroes in the South for voting and registration. SCLC funnels persons from its constituent bodies to this school, and other organizations not scared off by the "red" label also cooperate with Highlander.

The issue of radicalism, raised in the discussion of Highlander and SCEF, highlighted by the disproportionate number of socialists present at SNCC's October Conference in Atlanta, emphasized by the organizational pasts of a few individuals such as Bayard Rustin and the Rev. James Lawson, and constantly raised by the Southern opponents of the integrationist organizations in order to smear them with the "red" label, deserves some discussion and cannot simply be dismissed as segregationist "red-baiting."

The influence of white left-wingers in the field of civil rights can be attributed to two factors primarily: one is the positive impetus of the leftists themselves in entering the field, and the other involves the negative factor of a vacuum in the area of training and experience.

When it comes to groups like Highlander and SCEF, we are dealing with a radical milieu which originated in the 1930s or even before; the sit-in movement and radical influences upon it involve a new generation of younger leftists, those who were developed in the McCarthy and immediate post-McCarthy era, but who were trained and/or influenced by the radicals of the 30s. Both the older and the newer generation of radicals have a common outlook in terms of civil rights: they view the so-called "Negro Struggle" as one of several crucial areas within American society which function as a lever for social change, and as such, if combined with the other areas (the labor movement, the peace movement, etc.), it could become a significant factor in going beyond its present goals to a more fundamental alteration of the American social structure.

Hence the radical, be he of the 1930s generation or of the newer, younger generation, operates within the framework of civil rights with a two-fold goal in mind: (1) to attempt to move the integrationist groups beyond their present goals of obtaining a rightful share *in* American society to one of changing the society as such. Functionally this fact of radical strategy usually involves attempts to involve civil rights groups in a more direct, face-to-face conflict with the status quo in the form of mass marches, boycotts, and direct action rather than the less obvious, less mass-scale nature of court action and lobbying. The tactical point of this is an educational one: to demonstrate to large numbers of Negroes (particularly those who have some connection with labor, such as trade unionists) the limitations of the status quo (and of their demands upon it) in terms of meeting and answering their everyday problems of jobs, education, housing, status, etc. Subsidiary to this, but increasingly important in recent years, has been an attempt to refocus civil rights activity into the political arena on the theory that once Negroes in the South begin voting in significant numbers the Dixiecrat-Republican coalition can be sufficiently weakened so that more social welfare legislation will be possible, and a friendlier atmosphere for more radical ideas will be created by the removal of the present legislative roadblocks.

(2) The radical also attempts to demonstrate, particularly in the campaign for voter registration, that the Negro has important common interests with organized labor, and with the peace movement; this attempt is also undertaken by radicals working in both of the other arenas for each of the others. The goal of this is to fuse these three presently separate movements (presently also hostile to each other in some degree) into one movement which represents interests all different from, or hostile to (in varying degrees at different times) what is termed "the ruling circles," "the Power Elite," "the Capitalist Class," or "the military-industrial complex."

This somewhat abbreviated presentation of the radical's rationale for participation in the civil rights field, and for his particular strategic endeavors in that field, indicates why the positive impetus for radical activity exists—apart from, and by no means negating other important reasons, such as the basically humanistic outlook of many individuals in radical circles which puts them almost automatically on the side of any "underdog" cause. This factor, in fact, may precede the actual radicalization of the individual involved in this or that cause; he becomes a radical only after he has failed to attain his goals within the context of the single movement, and often only because of the presence as invaluable allies of radicals in the cause to which he is committed. Thus the recruitment factor forms a third facet of the radical's activity, being more or less incidental depending largely upon the extent of the individual radical's commitment to the organization with which he may be affiliated.

Now, not all radicals are equally adept at moving sufficiently fast, but not too fast, in each of these areas of tactic. Many radicals, being impatient with the slowness of change, will move too fast, being tactically personally crude or rude. It is here that antagonism develops between the individuals who place the interests of the specific movement first, and those radicals who seek to revolutionize the movement before time and circumstance are appropriate. This is, or was, particularly true of radicals associated with the Communist Party and its milieu in the 1930s, when the C.P. dealt in an extremely heavy fashion with various movements, particularly the Negro movement, when the interests of the movement conflicted with the immediate need of the Soviet Union's foreign policy.[98]

The negative factor of radical influence is one that is attributable to the lack of organizational and agitational skills in any movement which is composed of persons lacking in formal education, organizational experience, and intellectual tradition, in other words any movement of the lower income groups. Radicals, being positively committed to such movements, tend to move into this vacuum and assume a disproportionate share in doing the kinds of jobs that others lack the know-how to do. This was true of the early years of the C.I.O. until the labor movement gradually developed these skills within its own ranks; it is now true of those sectors of the civil rights movement which are relatively new, or young. The older and adult groups have also developed their own skilled personnel but the radical influence of the 1930s generation still hangs on in a few cases. Given the students' lack of experience and organizational know-how, it is to be expected that young, Northern radicals will obtain some foothold in the movement. What is surprising is that this foothold has not been greater. The failure of radicals to be even more influential than they are in civil rights youth circles is probably due to two factors: One is the natural suspicion of the Negro students of *all* outside influence, a suspicion which served to minimize the radical foothold, as well as the adult foothold in organizations like SNCC; plus the additional public-relations consciousness of the Negroes which would in any case make them leery of outside "agitators," particularly so in the case of known radicals. The other factor has to do with the historical development of the American Left in this period, which resulted in the elimination from effective participation in civil rights of those segments of the Left which would tend to be "pushy." The Communist Party itself was still in the throes of post-Hungarian internal dissention, and in addition was still receiving a large amount of attention from Congress and the Justice Department, hence was effectively eliminated from *open* participation; in addition, the current "line" of the "People's Anti-Monopoly Coalition" minimizes actions in the name of the Party, and maximizes the tactic of being as much like a liberal as possible.

The Trotskyists have, in places, attempted to "use" local support actions in the North for recruiting purposes, but have found it difficult to become part of an overall movement which has, even in its Northern support, put forward the image of nonviolence, a concept repugnant to Trotskyism. Hence others have usually managed to take leadership out of the hands of the Trotskyist youth. Therefore the only radical youth which was left, centering in the Young Peoples Socialist League and the Students for a Democratic Society, two groups which can be broadly described as social-democratic (in the sense that the word is used in Europe, meaning one who generally advocates some radical transformation of the economy in the direction of socialization and central planning by means of traditional Western parliamentary action) in outlook, took on the chief burden of radicalizing the sit-in movement. Their conception was, however, that since the Negro movement was not "their" movement, they would play down their own particular viewpoints and pretty much go along as loyal allies. While not noted historically for an affinity to nonviolence, they were prepared to go along with that, too, partly because it kept the Trotskyites out, partly because it might serve, in the future, as a bridge between the Negro organizations and the peace movements in which they were equally interested, and partly because they had not been asked their opinions in the first place.

Both the YPSL and SDS played not insignificant roles in the first year of sit-ins, and continue today to promote the broad goals suggested above, SDS primarily in the field of education as sponsor of civil rights conferences both North and South, and YPSL as the functional inheritor of many liberal-left groups on a campus level, that is, as a group which was best able to recruit on campuses from among those few Northern students for whom civil rights formed only one interest among others such as peace, capital punishment, Cuba, ROTC, the House Committee on Un-American Activities, etc. YPSL was also able to secure, for the first time in decades, chapters in white colleges in the South, directly as the result of sit-in leadership and action. YPSL members representing other groups, primarily student in nature, participated in the October SNCC Conference in Atlanta, and helped draft and promote that section of the program dealing with Election Day demonstrations. Some twelve of the ninety-eight observers to the Conference were members of YPSL or its parent affiliate, the Socialist Party (usually identified with the name of Norman Thomas). Of the 100 regular delegates, perhaps three or four were YPSL members, but this number would be considerably increased were such a conference to be held now, given the growth of YPSL in some Southern cities meanwhile.

Despite these radical influences, evidence seems to indicate that the charges of "red agitation" levelled by some segregationists are not based on the above data. It is not known just how familiar segregationist circles are with this kind of data. It seems rather to be the case that the "red" label is applied indiscriminately to the integrationist cause without any attempt to differentiate the regular civil rights groups from actual radicals, or radicals from one another, or in fact to make any charges that could be substantiated by examining the facts. In cases where specific individuals are named, as in the controversy over the confirmation of Mr. Thurgood Marshall as a federal judge, the allegations stemmed from activities in the 1930s and not from current alleged radical activity; and in any case the allegations were inaccurate to one degree or another, or so out of proportion as to seem ludicrous.

Hence the rationale used by opponents of the sit-ins that they are leftist-inspired appears to be a function of the need on the part of the segregationists to associate phenomena of change which are not readily comprehended with a type of "devil" theory akin psychologically to the German "stab-in-the-back" theory of the losing of World War I, or the theory that American setbacks in the world today are the result of a conspiracy in the White House. On a small scale a number of persons have observed the inability of Southern whites to accept the fact that other Southern whites are for the sit-ins, and actually march on their picket lines. The elaborate structure of rationale which some Southern whites have constructed in the effort to explain discrimination to themselves is so threatened by "the white picket" (on the rare occasions when there is one) that he is forced to dismiss the phenomenon as a "light-skinned Negro," or an "outside agitator," or, if a woman, a prostitute. In the same manner, it is so inconceivable, so threatening to some white Southerners to realize that Southern Negroes are now involved in a movement to attain equality, a movement indigenous to the South and directed by Southerners, that they cannot recognize the real nature of the movement. They must rationalize so that they can deal with it within the framework of their existing patterns of thought. This can be done by labelling it an outside conspiracy, and the rationale is strengthened in terms of prevailing American values which see much of the world's unrest as the result of "international communism" by attaching the Communist label to this conspiracy.

Thus by an ironic convergence of history, in an era when American radicalism is organizationally weaker than it has ever been except in the days of McCarthyism, the issue of radicalism has been thrust into the Southern student movement.

An important part of the superstructural "umbrella" of the sit-in movement was the general public image of this movement as indicated in the public press, radio and television for the Upper South and throughout the United States and other parts of the world. Without attempting a content analysis of this image as seen through the mass media, it can be said that in general the mass media saw the sit-in movement in a favorable light, that it had a good "public image." The correspondence of the movement to the stated American value system, the respectable appearance of the students, their advocacy of a nonviolent policy, and the moderation of their demands undoubtedly played a role in the creation of this public image.

But aside from the students' own influence upon this public image (and only in part due to it) was the support of a large number of religious bodies within the white community for the movement. That is, the churches, even in parts of the South, particularly the Upper South, took positions favoring the movement, not only because of the movement's own image up to that point, but also because many church groups were seeking opportunities for social action and involvement; the student movement, with its religiously-centered value structure, and with its respectable and moderate appearance, met this need and presented this opportunity. From then on many church bodies assisted the movement and in turn furthered the image of the movement as they wished to see it, thus gaining even more support among Southern "moderate" elements. Not only local religious groups, but also their national parent bodies, voiced support of the students.

The following is, then, a partial listing of national church bodies which have adopted positions generally in favor of the sit-in movement and/or its nonviolent tactics.

(1)   The Board of Managers of the United Church Women meeting in Minneapolis April 26-28, 1960, supported the principle of service without

discrimination at lunch counters and the principle of nonviolent protest as a means of securing social justice.

(2)   The General Board of the National Council of Churches on June 2, 1960, adopted a statement released through its Department of Racial and Cultural Relations, Division of Christian Life and Work which recognized the nonviolent demonstrations as just, protested unequal enforcement of law, and reaffirmed its commitment to work for a nonsegregated church.

(3)   The Episcopal Society for Cultural and Racial Unity, at its first annual meeting in Williamsburg, Virginia, January 8-11, 1961, supported one of its members, Rev. Theodore Gibson, in his refusal to turn over lists to a legislative committee in Florida; attacked continuing segregation in public schools; and recommended use of sit-ins and kneel-ins to its members to secure integration. The Board of Directors of the Society, meeting the previous September 23-24, approved of "kneel-ins." On July 10, the Executive Director had sent telegrams to both presidential candidates urging endorsement by them of the student sit-in movement; a few days later plans for kneel-ins began to be discussed by the Society.

(4)   One of the earliest church groups to act, the Central Committee of the National Student Christian Federation on March 6, 1960, sent a letter to Christian students and student chapters which gave the background to the sit-ins and supported justifiable use of civil disobedience against wrong laws.

(5)   The National Council, Protestant Episcopal Church, distributed a background paper from its Division of Racial Minorities and Division of Christian Citizenship arguing strongly that Christian teaching supports the right of civil disobedience under some circumstances, that it could affirm the dignity of the law, and stating that the demonstrations were the outgrowth of Christian teaching.

(6)   On April 28, 1960, the Board of Home Missions of the Congregational and Christian Churches adopted a statement supporting the students in their demonstrations against discrimination, and promised financial aid in cases of dismissals of students because of their activities.

(7)   The Board of Christian Education, the Rev. Eugene Carson Blake, chief executive officer, and the whole General Assembly of the United Presbyterian Church at various times in April and May supported the sit-ins, kneel-ins, and called for a nonsegregated church in a nonsegregated society.

(8)   The National Board of the YWCA on April 11, 1960, went on record in support of the objectives of the nonviolent demonstrations.

(9)   The American Friends Service Committee's national office on April 1 supported the idea of no barriers to equality of opportunity, whether at lunch counters or schools, housing or employment.

(10)   The Council for Christian Action, United Church of Christ, on June 15 commended the student demonstrators and supported their demands, urging all Christians to join in this support.

(11)   The Executive Committee of the liberal Religious Youth, meeting April 15-17 in Boston, voiced support of the movement, and the convention, meeting September 5 at Geneva Park, Ontario, Canada, unanimously regarded nonviolent action as a moral and valid means toward the aim of brotherhood and peace. It is affiliated with CORE.

There were, of course, protests against these actions by various groups, including church groups and ministers. For example, the Bishop of the Protestant Episcopal Diocese of Alabama, Rt. Rev. Charles C.J. Carpenter, asked the National Council of the Church to repudiate its expression of sympathy for the sit-ins.

In addition to the above formal expressions of sympathy, a series of church publications supported and/or gave publicity to the movement. *The Presbyterian Outlook*, March 21, 1960, covered developments sympathetically. *The Interracial Revue*, May, 1960, a publication of the Catholic Interracial Council, covered the origins of the sit-ins. *Social Action*, January, 1961, published by the Council for Christian Social Action of the United Church of Christ (the merged group of the Congretational Christian Church and the Evangelical and Reformed Church) devoted the entire issue to the sit-in movement. The National Federation of Catholic College Students devoted two issues of its series on Social Action, those of series I, nos. 1 and 7, to discrimination and student protest activity. The *New World*, newspaper of the Catholic Archdiocese of Chicago, covered the seventh annual midwest College Student Conference on Human Relations, sponsored by the Catholic Interracial Council of Chicago, and gave news of resolutions passed there in favor of the sit-ins. *Concern*, semi-monthly publication of the National Conference of Methodist Youth, put out a special issue on the sit-ins dated March 18, 1960. The *Social Action Newsletter*, Department of Social Welfare, United Christian Missionary Society, June, 1960, gave a summary of sit-in activity and covered church support of the movement. (This is a body of the Disciples of Christ.) *Campus Encounter*, October, 1960, published by the United Campus Christian Fellowship (Disciples Student Fellowship, Student Fellowship Council, United Student Fellowship and

Westminster Student Fellowship) reported the sit-ins and support for them. *Christianity and Crisis*, May 29, 1961, the editors of which include Reinhold Niebuhr and John C. Bennett, devoted its whole issue to Race in America. The above is obviously only a partial account, but it gives an idea of the kind of coverage the sit-ins received in the journals of the churches.

Also, a number of local church bodies took action, in the South, in support of integrated facilities. The list below represents mainly *white* church groups, with the possible exception of the first:

(1) The Arkansas Council of Churches, in November, 1960, heard, without opposition, a report from its Christian Life and Work Committee which sympathized with the student protests.

(2) The twenty-one-member Executive Council of the Baptist Student Union at (white) North Carolina State College in Raleigh, representing about 450 students, came out in March, 1960, for the sit-ins, and resolved to boycott Raleigh stores being picketed by Negro students from Shaw and St. Augustine's in that city.

(3) The Charlotte Meeting, Society of Friends, urged, in a letter to the local newspapers, understanding and sympathy for the movement for integration in general.

(4) The Unitarian Fellowship for Social Justice, organized in North Carolina in 1959, actively participated in the sit-ins in Charlotte (as individuals); the minister of the Charlotte Unitarian Church marched with white supporters of the Negro students on one occasion, and the participation of the white Unitarians appears to have been a crucial factor in the settlement here.

(5) In Chapel Hill the local Ministerial Association issued a statement on March 20, 1960, signed by thirty Protestant, Catholic and Jewish clergymen, pledging support for any business which gave equal service, and commending the student leaders for the nature of their protests.

(6) In Nashville, the Minsters' Association, composed of Christian ministers, circulated a statement to the Mayor urging open facilities. The Wesley Foundation, which includes Methodist students and faculty at Vanderbilt, Scarritt and Peabody in the same city, gave complete coverage to the local sit-ins and to the Lawson dismissal, all sympathetic to the movement.

A list of ministerial associations which participated in negotiations in various communities to some degree or another is not available, but there were many. We have attempted here to cite only the more obvious as examples. Other specific instances will be found in the summaries of what happened in each community.

The above section has summarized the institutionalized stage of the movement. It has been shown that in the case of the sit-ins this stage cannot really be said to be final in any sense, thus the use of the term "semi-institutionalized." The crisis besetting the movement after it achieved success in some parts in the South, while it seemed to fail in other parts, was only beginning to be resolved in the direction of political action (voter registration) at the October, 1960, SNCC conference, when SNCC, due to the internal strength of the vocal advocates of a political turn, came out for Election Day demonstrations. For some months following this, however, the movement continued to vacillate, experimenting with such tactics as cinema stand-ins, pray-ins, skate-ins, and the like, while continuing some mopping up operations in outlying areas of cities already integrated (i.e. shopping centers in the suburbs of Charlotte were picketed and sat-in during April, 1961). But a dwindling number of Negro students were sufficiently enthusiastic about these less immediate and less electrifying events.

It was the Freedom Riders who formed a bridge between the semi-institutionalized stage of the sit-in movement, and the breakthrough of the sit-in movement and SNCC into the political arena. This stage, however, is not within the jurisdiction of this paper. Here it can only be pointed out that some of the latent and perhaps unanticipated (at that time) side-effects of the movement (particularly in terms of the effects of the movement upon the 1960 elections, and of the election issue upon the individual students—educating them in the area of politics—) had a significant effect upon later developments. The original Freedom Rider effort was rapidly expanded by SNCC—the organization originally conceived for sit-ins only—into a wave of freedom rider activity in several states. This gave SNCC organizers and agents access to areas of the South, and Negro communities in the South, which they had never had before, thus creating community-wide bases of power for future action. SNCC, in view of this newly-made-available arena, then expanded into the field of voter registration on a larger scale late in 1961, and by 1962 was sending dozens of teams of integrated students from North and South into Deep Southern rural areas to set up and run voter registration projects. It was this activity which focused the attention of the nation's press upon the reaction to it—the well-known church burnings in September, 1962.

E. The Movement's Responses, and the Reactions to Them

The discussion of Proposition 2 on pages 14-17 above made the point that the subordinate group's position of defender or attacker would limit its choices of tactics, and that as far as effectiveness is concerned the attacker has a choice of weapons. This point, however, does not tell us why it was that the student movement chose to respond to this situation of social action for change by utilizing the techniques of nonviolence. We cannot accept the notion put forward in some quarters that nonviolence is *the* specific historical device developed by Negroes as part of their slave-plus-Christian heritage, or that,

> "A special combination of cultural factors—namely, oppression . . . and a religion which promises that through suffering power will be gained over the oppressors—has channeled one type of adaptive behavior similar to that of the masochist."[99]

But this does not tell us why this type of behavior is utilized at one time and not at another, or by one group sharing these factors and not another. For we know from a study of American Negro history that violence in many forms is a common method of adaptive behavior just as nonviolence is. While Christianity may be a rationale for nonviolence it is not necessarily a reason for it. That is, Christianity may make nonviolence acceptable to large numbers of rank-and-file members of the subordinate group, but it does not exclude other techniques, had they been proposed first.

In the case of the sit-in movement the chief explanation for the utilization of the technique of nonviolence must lie in the area of more or less accidental historical factors. The immediately preceding civil rights direct action campaigns had been, in part due to their sponsorship by ministers, of the nonviolent type; the Greensboro students had chosen to sit-in, a tactic not suited to violence (i.e. they did not choose to conduct an armed raid on the police station, or to assassinate the governor, or burn down the local KKK headquarters); and the national civil rights groups which came to their aid had a background of experience, to one or another degree, in the tactics of nonviolence.

The reaction on the part of the White South to this movement varied within certain broad limits to a considerable degree. Racial discrimination, as one social scientist has pointed out, is "ultimately based on power relationships between a dominant and a subordinate group," and therefore it should follow that ". . . the greater the power advantage to be maintained and the smaller the white resources, the higher the relative degree of mobilization of whites there must be" in order to maintain that power advantage, that dominant relationship.[100] In other words, the will to preserve segregation (even at the lunch counter) is directly related to the social and economic gains derived from segregation. In terms of what can be described as a value conflict between the values of maintaining the Southern status quo and the values as they are often stated outside the South (the "American Dilemma"), the will to preserve segregation is also inversely related to contact with the value system outside the South.[101]

This dominant-subordinate power relationship can be empirically examined in terms of the proportion of the local population that is non-white. "Key conclusively demonstrated that much Southern political behavior is highly correlated with the proportion of the local population that is Negro."[102] Hence the tendency will be that the larger the local proportion of Negroes, the greater will be the income differential between Negroes and whites; likewise, the vote for Senator Strom Thurmond as opposed to the vote for President Truman in 1948 was strongest in counties with the largest proportion of Negroes; and the like.[103] Furthermore, white persons residing in towns with high densities of Negro population tend to be more strongly in favor of racial segregation and less optimistic about the eventual acceptance of desegregation in the South; thus ". . . the proportion of Negroes living in a particular community appears to be of crucial significance in desegregation attitudes."[104]

This point, with all of its theoretical implications as developed by Key and others, holds true, however, only for certain *states* where, statewide, there are large proportions of *rural* Negroes; and for specific communities of rural composition associated with the traditional Black Belt plantation areas of the South. Hence the resistance to integration in this type of environment seems to be related to the perception on the part of current politically dominant groups that Negroes do in fact threaten the political status quo and might upset it if they were to be refranchised.

The point is not, however, valid for urban areas either in the South or elsewhere, where there are in fact large proportions of Negroes in the population, yet where they do vote, have some political power and because of this power are able to attain other desegregation gains.

Yet very little attention has been paid in the literature to this comparison, and therefore the suggestions which follow as a possible hypothesis for this differential must be viewed as being extremely tentative. There are at least three factors which seem to be important in explaining why in urban areas with large proportions of Negroes in the population Negroes do participate in the political process, and in rural areas of similar proportions do not. One is that in the rural area the Negro has, since slavery, been a high proportion of the population; this proportion (say, 30% or more) has not gone up but tended to go down.[105] In urban areas, on the other hand, the proportion of Negroes was initially quite small (a thin, entering wedge) and has tended very gradually to increase over the decades. Hence while in one place the threat has always been present, in the other it has very gradually crept upon the white, so that in effect before he perceived the threat it had already achieved certain political rights.

A second factor involves the political competition which seems to be more inherent in urban than in rural areas. In the latter, a relatively small group of local politicians shared power among themselves, hence never bothered to appeal to the Negro vote. In urban areas, on the other hand, there appears to be more political competition, necessitating an appeal to the Negro voter in order to be politically effective, hence also necessitating the franchise. A third factor which is suggested by this differential between rural and urban rights despite similar proportions of Negroes to the total population involves the notion of "visibility." In the rural community the Negro seems to be perceived in all of his roles at once—as Negro, wage-earner or share-cropper, political threat, social threat, etc., and thus when he attempts to improve his position in any one role, the dominant white culture perceives this attempt as an attempt to improve his total role because, simply, in a small rural town he is more totally visible, and one comes into contact with him in many roles at once. In an urban place, on the other hand, contact between people tends to be that of contact in one role at a time. The individual is not totally visible in all of his roles, since he plays one role at home, another on the job, etc., and most of them are geographically separated and involve contact not with the same whites, but different whites in different roles. The Negro and the white therefore never confront each other in their entirety. When the confrontation between the races is only partial, then, the threat is only partial and exists in only one role at a time, and is not as intensely perceived as when the confrontation is in many roles at one time. The simple size of the urban areas, and the resultant anonymity, seems to be the key variable here. In the rural community the Negro is often a well-known personally to everyone in the town. He is more visible and any deviation from the expected behavior will be immediately noted.

It therefore appears that the dominant-subordinate power relationship of a community has important repercussions in the domain of attitudes of the white population of rural areas, and hence in their receptiveness toward action for social change. Thus,

"... it appears that nonviolent direct action is most effective when the prevailing attitudes of the locality are in sympathy or at least geared toward bringing the laws and policies of their communities in line with those of the federal government. When more than token resistance is offered, however, it appears that ... the principal means through which Negroes gain increasing civil rights seem to be through gaining a significant voting power and winning victories in the federal courts or through the intervention of the federal government ..."[106]

The crisis of the sit-in movement in its semi-institutionalized stage, and its subsequent turn toward voter registration was in part caused by a realization of just this, it would appear.

Thus the reaction of Southern white communities to the student movement varied with the relative sizes and perceived strengths of the dominant and subordinate groups. Information gathered on sixty-nine different communities in fifteen Southern states (Alabama, Arkansas, Florida, Georgia, Kentucky, Louisiana, Maryland, Mississippi, Missouri, North Carolina, Oklahoma, South Carolina, Tennessee, Texas and Virginia) for which data covering either more than a single demonstration or covering an extended period of time are available, seem to support this. In the four pages following, in outline form, a few of the more relevant facts in terms of this statement are presented for these communities:[107]

    State and city
    Total population of community
    Percentage of Negro population in city
    Percentage of Negro population in county
    Name of school or college involved
    Total recorded arrests
    Total convictions to date
    Unusual incidents
    Approximate order of participation in sit-ins
    Success or failure of initial efforts in 1960

Another important aspect of the subordinate-dominant power relationship is not only how the white community will react in terms of resistance, but also (and even prior to anything happening) the Negroes' expectancy of what the whites will do, i.e. their perception of the power structure and its possible consequences. It should follow, empirically, then, that not only will the white reaction to the sit-in movement be more negative in areas of high proportions of Negroes in the population *when the movement does occur*, but that the movement will tend to occur less, in such areas.

Let us, therefore, see first of all, where the sit-in movement took place, and perhaps more importantly where it did not take place. The table on the following page will illustrate the fact that the movement did not reach vast segments of the South, at least in terms of absolute numbers of communities.

CITY	POPULATION	%NEGRO	%NEGRO IN COUNTY
Alabama		30.1	
Birmingham	521,330	38	34.6
Tuskegee	1,750	24	83.5
Montgomery	142,893	33	38.3
Arkansas		21.9	
Little Rock	185,017	23	21.5
Florida		17.9	
Daytona Beach	37,395	30	16.9
Miami and			
Miami Beach	852,705	13	14.9
St. Augustine	14,734	24	27.4
St. Petersburg	181,298	13	8.9
Tampa	274,970	17	14.0
Tallahassee	48,174	33	32.9
Jacksonville	372,569	27	23.4
Georgia		28.6	
Atlanta	768,125	27	34.8
Augusta	123,698	32	31.8
Savannah	149,245	35	34.1
Kentucky		7.2	
Frankfort	18,365	13	8.4
Lexington	111,940	16	15.3
Louisville	606,659	11	12.9
Louisiana		32.1	
Baton Rouge	193,485	33	31.8
New Orleans	845,237	31	37.4
Maryland		17	
Baltimore	1,418,948	35 (no separate county)	
Chevy Chase	2,405	2	?
Glen Echo	not available		
Rockville	26,090	6	3.9
Mississippi		42.3	
Biloxi	44,053	12	16.1
Missouri		9.2	
Kansas City	921,121	11	2.9
North Carolina		25.4	
Chapel Hill	12,573	11	23.7
Charlotte	209,551	27	24.6
Concord	17,799	23	15.9
Durham	84,642	35	32.2
Greensboro	123,334	25	20.9
Henderson	12,740	44	5.4
High Point	66,543	17	20.9
New Bern	15,717	43	34.9

FOUR

SCHOOL	ARRESTS	CONVICTIONS	OTHER	ORDER	SUCCESS/FAILURE
	28	0	3 beaten	55	failure
Tuskegee Inst.			1 fired	29	"
Ala. State	60	45	9 exp.	24	"
			1 fired		
Philander Smith	13	13		39	failure
				32	failure
	20	20		35	success
Fla. N & I				44	failure
Gibbs Jr. Coll.				31	success
				30	success
Fla. A & M Univ	46	11		14	failure
Waters Coll.	114	57		42	failure
Atl. Univ etc	182	0		34	failure
Paine Coll.				58	failure
Sav. State T.C.	41	2 plus		47	failure
			12 exp.		
Ky. State			2 fired	23	failure
				27	success
	300			69+	success
			17 exp.		
Southern U.	16	16	1 dead	53	failure
Xavier, Dillard	10 plus	?		38	failure
Hopkins, Morgan	11	?		22	success
				2	success
	25	?		66	success
				63	success
	20	20		59	failure
	6	0		61	success
U. of N.C.	10	9		17	success
Johnson Smith	3	2		5	success
Barber-Scotia	18	7 plus?	1 beaten	9	success
NCC & Duke	107	7 plus?		3	success
A & T, Bennet	45	?		1	success
Kittrell Jr. Coll.	1	1	1 wht. beaten	26	failure
	3	3		7	success
	29	26		48	success

CITY	POPULATION	%NEGRO	%NEGRO IN COUNTY
Raleigh	93,931	24	26.1
Salisbury	21,297	28	16.8
Shelby	17,698	23	22.4
Statesville	19,844	22	17.8
Wilmington	44,013	38	?
Winston-Salem	128,176	33	24.2
Oklahoma		9.5	
Oklahoma City	429,188	9	10.4
South Carolina		34.9	
Charleston	160,113	31	36.5
Darlington	6,710	50	44.4
Columbia	162,601	27	32.6
Greenville	126,887	20	17.6
Orangeburg	13,852	42	60.1
Rock Hill	29,404	25	28.7
Spartanburg	44,352	32	22.1
Sumter	23,062	35	46.8
Tennessee		16.5	
Chattanooga	205,143	22	19.9
Knoxville	172,734	13	9.1
Memphis	544,505	36	36.4
Nashville	346,729	21	19.2
Texas		12.6	
Austin	187,157	13	12.8
Corpus Christi	177,157	5	4.7
Dallas	932,349	15	14.7
Galveston	67,175	27	21.4
Houston	1,139,678	20	20.1
Killeen	23,377	5	?
Marshall	23,846	40	43.4
San Antonio	641,965	7	6.9
Virginia		20.8	
Arlington (County)	163,401	5.6	
Danville	46,577	6	5.6
Hampton	89,258	21	28 (County figures are for the Newport News—Hamptom urbanized area)
Hopewell	17,895	18	23.8
Lynchburg	59,319	20	21.1
Norfolk	305,872	25	26.2
Petersburg	36,750	48	61.7
Portsmouth	114,773	34	26.2
Richmond	333,438	30	5.2

FOUR (continued)

SCHOOL	ARRESTS	CONVICTIONS	OTHER	ORDER	SUCCESS/FAILURE
Shaw & St. Aug.	43	0	2 beaten	6	success
Livingstone				16	success
			1 beaten	19	failure
	12	12	4 fired	45	failure
	some			50	success
W-S T.C.	23	23		4	success
				56	success
	24	24		18	failure
			3 exp.	57	failure
Allen & Benedict	225	?		33	failure
	35	35	1 beaten	56	failure
SCS, Claflin	396	329	gassed	25	failure
Friendship JC	72	72		11	failure
	4	?		64	failure
Morris	50	?		15	failure
	22	?	riots	20	success
Knoxville Coll.	11+	?		37	success
	98+	48	4 fired	49	failure
Fisk, etc.	163	85	1 expelled	13	success
U. of Texas				40	success
				46	success
				60	success
				41	success
Texas Southern			1 mutilated	36	success
	2	?	2 fired	62	failure
Bishop & Wiley	250	?	1 fired	54	failure
				43	success
Howard U.				51	success
				56	success
Hampton Inst.				8	success
	95	31+		65	failure
	13	13		52	success
Va. State Coll.	7	7		10	success
	83	42		28	success
	27	?	riot,beatg	11	success
Va. Union U.	37	34+		21	success

If one considers the large proportion of population, not only Negro, still living in rural areas (for Negroes, ranging from Missouri's 9% to Mississippi's 68%, with a low of 37% in rural areas in Louisiana for the Deep Southern tier of states), it can be observed that only that proportion of Negroes living in large cities actually had any contact at all with the sit-in movement. This does not mean that centers of population are necessarily over-represented in incidences of sit-ins; the contrary might actually be the case. But it does mean that the vast bulk of sit-ins did occur in the larger centers of population.

TABLE FIVE

Cities in which sixty-nine sit-in movements occured, by population size.[108]

	Less than 10,000	10-100,000	over 100,000	total sit-ins
Alabama	1	0	2	3
Arkansas	0	0	1	1
Florida	0	3	4	7
Georgia	0	0	3	3
Kentucky	0	1	2	3
Louisiana	0	0	2	2
Maryland	2	1	1	4
Mississippi	0	1	0	1
Missouri	0	0	1	1
N. Carolina	0	11	3	14
Oklahoma	0	0	1	1
S. Carolina	1	4	3	8
Tennessee	0	0	4	4
Texas	0	3	5	8
Virginia	0	5	4	9
Totals	4	29	36	69

From this it is apparent that sit-ins during 1960 tended, for those communities about which information over an extended period was available, to be concentrated in the larger centers of population; a majority of demonstrations occurred in cities of over 100,000 population, and only four occurred in cities of under 10,000 population. Of these four, it might be mentioned, two were in Maryland not far from Washington, D.C.; and one was the series of incidents set off by the gerrymandering of Tuskegee,

Alabama, also not a typical situation. Thus the movement tended, as might be expected under this hypothesis, to steer clear of the rural "Black Belt" areas, probably as the result of the perception on the part of the students that in rural black belt areas the opposition would tend to be most severe.

Since, however, some 56.5% of the communities in this study (thirty-nine out of sixty-nine) involved the presence of a college or university as a decisive factor in the demonstrations, it can be further suggested that colleges, rather than urban conditions, may be decisive in the outbreak of the movement, and that, since many colleges are located in cities, the urban phenomenon is an intervening variable. This problem is made even more significant by the realization that of the 104 Negro colleges and universities listed in the U.S. Department of Health, Education and Welfare's *Statistics of Negro Colleges and Universities: 1951-52 and Fall of 1954* (the latest published), at least fifty-four and probably a few more, or at least 53.4% participated in some way in the sit-in movement during 1960.

The question therefore arises as to which factor, the non-Black Belt characteristic, or the college characteristic, is the independent variable? Our hypothesis suggests that the former is the case; hence an examination of the communities *with* colleges in which *no* demonstrations took place should indicate that they are rural, with high proportions of Negro population.

This hypothesis is, in fact, substantiated insofar as the data are available. There are 103 Negro colleges and universities listed by the *HEW* study for the South; at least fifty-four of these definitely participated in the sit-in movement. Concerning an additional twenty-six information is either not available at all, or the possibility of their participation exists because they are in communities in which demonstrations took place. Nine junior colleges were eliminated from consideration, leaving fourteen colleges and universities about which we do know definitely that during 1960 no activity involving them took place.

Firstly, of the fourteen colleges and universities ten were located in the Deep Southern states of Alabama (2), Georgia (2), Louisiana (1), and Mississippi (5). Of these ten, two were located in one community of over 100,000 population in a state (Mississippi) which had no sit-ins at all that year. One was located in a large West Texas city with almost no Negroes in the population—and no segregation in city lunch counters. Only one other college was located in a non-Black Belt county in Texas; the rest were all located in counties in the traditional Black Belt. Six had city populations of under 10,000, and four had populations of between 10,000 and 100,000.

Now let us see whether the nature of support (private versus public) played any significant role in the sit-in movement. Of the 104 colleges listed in the U.S. *HEW* study, thirty-eight, or 36.5% are publicly-supported. Of the total colleges in our study (forty-eight Negro, ten white, or fifty-eight in all), twenty, or 34.5% were state-supported. The specific percentages for the forty-eight Negro colleges are 35.4%, for the ten white schools, 30%. This differential of 1.1% among the Negro school in our study, and the total Negro schools does not appear to be significant.

As to whether or not the presence of a college, or the type of college, affected the success or failure of a sit-in situation in overall terms, this factor does not seem to be significant within our study. Of the sixty-nine communities in this study, thirty-nine (56.5%) had a successful outcome within the first year of the movement. Of these, twenty involved colleges—51.3%, and nineteen did not—48.7%. These two percentages do not differ significantly from the total figures.

Twenty-nine different colleges were involved in the twenty successful communities just noted. Of these, eleven, or 38%, were state-supported, including white schools involved. In eleven communities in which *only* a state-supported institution was involved (including white), five, or 45.4% were successful; of twenty communities in which *only* non-publicly-supported institutions were involved, ten, or 50%, were successful. It seems therefore that this factor is either not significant in terms of the outcome; or that a sufficient number of cases is not available to make a definite statement in this matter.

Even if we look at the five Deep Southern states of Louisiana, Alabama, South Carolina, and Georgia, we find that, where demonstrations were unsuccessful, nineteen Negro schools were involved, of which six, or 31%, were publicly-supported, again no significant deviation from the national total.

This still does not explain precisely why nineteen schools did get involved in the Deep South while ten did not; this represents a nearly one-third non-participation rate, as compared with the fact that elsewhere almost every Negro college or university in every Southern state (including South Carolina) did participate. Thus, while the hypothesis is not completely borne out, it is strongly supported.

Having now discussed population of the community as a possible independent variable in terms of the hypothesis that the reaction of the movement to its community, and vice-versa, will be related to the proportion of the Negro population in the community, that is, the black belt or non-black-belt character of the community, let us examine this reaction in terms of resistance of the white population as measured by the failure of the movement to attain its goals. Our hypothesis should be supported by data indicating that the higher the Negro proportion of population, the less successful the outcome of the movement might be (because of the higher degree of resistance by the white population). In fact this is so.

TABLE SIX

Successful and Unsuccessful Outcomes,
by Percentage of Negro Population in the County, for Sixty-Nine Communities

	0-14%	15-29%	30-49%	50% or more	Totals
Successful	14	19	5	1	39
Unsuccessful	4	10	14	2	30
Totals	18	29	19	3	69

It therefore appears that not only do sit-ins appear to take place in areas with lower percentages of Negro populations, but also that chances of success will decline inversely to Negro proportion of the population.

Apart from incidence of occurrence, let us look at the success-failure problem. 75.4% of the communities in our study were found outside the tier of five Deep Southern states; of these fifty-two communities, thirty-nine (75%), had successful outcomes. In the Deep South, during the first year, there were no successful outcomes.

TABLE SEVEN

Sixty-Nine Communities by State
with Number of Successful Outcomes Noted in Parentheses
by Upper vs. Deep South

UPPER SOUTH		DEEP SOUTH	
Arkansas	1(0)	Alabama	3(0)
Florida	7(4)	Georgia	3(0)
Kentucky	3(2)	Louisiana	2(0)
Maryland	4(3)	Miss.	1(0)
Missouri	1(1)	S.C.	8(0)
N.C.	14(11)		
Oklahoma	1(1)		
Tennessee	4(3)		
Texas	8(6)		
Virginia	9(8)		
Totals	52(39)		17(0)

Briefly summarizing then, the factors contributing to the outbreak of the sit-in movement appear to be (1) a community in which the population is large—preferably over 100,000; and (2) one in which there exists a Negro college or university. Further, (3) the area in which the community is located should not be one in which the total Negro proportion of the population very much exceeds 30%, particularly if a successful outcome is desired within a reasonable period of time. In other words, such a community should not be in the tier of five Deep Southern states, or located in that section of an Upper Southern state commonly associated with Deep South or plantation conditions. Only six cases were successful where Negroes constituted over 30% of the population in our study, out of thirty-nine successful cases in all.

It can also be added here that in almost every case which appears to be "deviant" from this hypothesis (i.e. a sit-in movement breaking out in a Deep Southern black belt community), peculiar idiosyncratic conditions can be found to account for this deviation. In two cases sit-ins were conducted by "raiding parties" from a larger nearby metropolis; one case is that of the Tuskegee Institute, long engaged in a local fight over suffrage; one case involved an extremely strong, long-established and unusual community organization; one case (to be discussed in more detail later) involved the convergence of two Negro colleges in a black belt county seat with some tradition of protest; and one other case was really a protest against a ban on selective buying by some high school students, rather than a sit-in in the normal sense.

———————

In terms of the propositions or hypotheses set out on pages 11 through 18, this section has been an attempt to order the data of the student movement in the South in such a way as to validate, or show invalid, those propositions. Each of the five propositions has been shown to be valid in large measure as the sit-in movement unfolded itself from its social and historical antecedent conditions, went through its various stages, and achieved success or failure relative to its power position in its local community. The next section of this paper will deal with a new set of propositions dealing with the dynamics of social conflict in intergroup and intragroup relations in the testing of which further data will be developed.

The Dynamics of Inter-Group Community Conflict

The sociology of conflict includes an increasingly large body of theoretical literature. It is not the purpose of this paper to develop this body of literature further, and no purpose would be served in summarizing the available work here. This has been done by Coser, Bernard, and others.[109] Here it is proposed only to take some of the more common observations concerning inter- and intra-group conflict, draw up a brief series of propositions or hypotheses which summarize them, and, as with the previous sections on social movement theory, examine a series of cases of communities involved with sit-ins and other demonstrations for integration to see how applicable these propositions are in situations of real-life stress.

As with social movement theory, conflict theory does not stem from any single trend in theory. There are those who have been primarily interested in intra-group conflict from the angle of control, or power;[110] while others have put their emphasis more into the field of community relations, and inter-group conflict, or "group relations."[111] Overlapping both emphases is the field of sociometry and the study of small groups.[112]

Much of the theoretical background in this area comes from the work of the German formal sociologists, in particular that of Georg Simmel, who was interested in patterns of interaction in a variety of forms.[113] In terms of the applicability of this to community-level conflict, Simmel was one of the earlier writers to point to the "correlation between the structure of any social group and the amount of antagonisms permissible among its members."[114] This, it would seem, is a fruitful point of departure if one wishes to study such phenomena as the structure of any local sit-in movement.

It was Lewis Coser who, in his work, *The Functions of Social Conflict*, succeeded in bringing together some of these various emphases, added to work of psychologists including some of the theories of Freud, and derived from this literature a series of propositions which analyze social conflict from a functional standpoint. In Coser's words

> ". . . Social conflict may fulfill a number of determinate functions in groups and other interpersonal relations; it may, for example, contribute to the maintenance of group boundaries and prevent the withdrawal of members from a group . . ."[115]

It would seem, then, from an examination of the sociological and psychological literature that there appear to be a series of "rules" which, if followed, enable the group following them (albeit unaware of the explicit sociological implications) better to succeed in attaining its perceived goals, while, on the other hand, a group which for a series of historical and/or idiosyncratic reasons is unable to follow the "rules" will succeed in lesser degree. That is, some activities by a group engaged in community conflict are functional to the attainment of the goals of the group, while other activities are dysfunctional.

It should be possible, therefore, to suggest a series of those "rules" in the form of sociological propositions (in the manner of Coser) derived from the work of Coser, Boulding, and others, and, in the light of the data of the sit-in movement, see how valid these propositions are.

Three kinds of propositions will be suggested: (1) propositions dealing with the internal relationship of the parties involved in conflict situations; (2) propositions dealing with the interactive relationship of two or more groups; and (3) propositions dealing with the conditions of conducting and settling the conflict.

A. *General Propositions*

1. It has long been an established axiom in the field of race and ethnic minority relations that a group's internal cohesion (or in-group identification) is heightened by hostility from the outside. But for a successful conduct of the conflict there must also be a consensus within the group as to how to carry it out. In addition, the participant's self image can be heightened (or lowered) by conducting the conflict in terms of some super-individual goals, such as an appeal to religion or other values. These factors, however, are complicated by the factor of intragroup hostility. On the one hand, a

consensus is needed, a sense of group identification (morale) is required, and an ideology must be created. But on the other hand, the more totally an individual participates in the group (in terms of involving his personality), the more tensions tend to arise; hence mechanisms must be supplied to get rid of these tensions in a constructive rather than a destructive way. Finally, if the group is to survive as a group, a new threat must be found once the old one has been taken care of.

2. Another well-established axiom is that conflict may be latent; that is, the absence of conflict does not mean there is an absence of hostility. In fact, the longer the hostility remains suppressed, the more violent it will tend to be once it does break out into open conflict. Frequently, however, the acting out of hostility will depend more upon the relationship (or lack of relationship) between the groups in conflict than on the amount of hostility the individual participant thinks he feels. That is, a channel must be supplied before the feelings can come out. If these channels can be regularized so that hostility can be acted out in little bits, this may prevent the accumulation of frustration and, hence, of greater violence. While on the one hand the acting out of hostility depends on the availability of channels, on the other hand the channels (including the structures of the contending groups) depend on the group or groups' expectations of conflict, which may or may not be realistic. In turn, this factor depends in part on communication between the groups (partly dependent on the acceptance of some common values or goals), and on the existence of institutions suitable to solve community conflicts, if any.

3. While the conducting and settlement of conflict on the one hand (suggested above) depends on the existence of a common set of assumptions by the conflicting groups, the conflict itself creates new relationships between these groups. Within each group the conflict creates new coalitions between previously quite unrelated forces; between the groups the conflict may cause new norms and new sets of rules to develop. Conflict itself is often a necessary prerequisite to finding out, realistically, what the opponent's strength is, a prerequisite in turn to realistic negotiations. Hence it performs a positive function on the road to settlement. Additionally, the very process of combat is such that each contender wishes to use methods consistent with his internal structure, and at the same time wishes to have his opponent's command centralized for bargaining purposes. In any case the normal processes of running a bureaucracy force this centralization, so that both

internal need and external wish coincide to produce an ever more formalized structure within each group.

It can be seen that the positive conditions tending to heighten group identification and hence causing the group to function more positively toward its particular conflict-goals are going to be related to other components of group identification mentioned in earlier sections of this paper. (The negative conditions which need to be eliminated as being internally stressful will be dealt with in a separate section.) Any history of civil rights activity will itself create some degree of group identification and hence increase any specific group's (or movement's) morale. As has been pointed out earlier, the organization of counteractive moves on the part of the segregationist elements immediately after the Supreme Court decision of 1954 certainly served to make Negroes aware of their identity as a group even if they had not been aware of this just by being Negroes. It would also seem obvious up to a point that the morale and self awareness of any group would increase proportionally to the amount of hostility perceived and felt by the group.[116] The very fact that the students sitting in at various lunch counters in the South did not immediately obtain service, but rather faced varying degrees of opposition, probably enhanced their self images, and created the precondition for their awareness of themselves as a "movement."

These factors are just as true for the segregationist groups as they are for the Negro student organizations. Without the Supreme Court decision, and without the sit-ins, the white groups interested in maintaining the status quo with respect to segregation were weak, if they existed at all. They were not required as groups. The rise of Negro protest functioned to modify the white counteraction, create new organizations, revive old ones, and bring about, at least in some communities, a consensus among the whites as to how to conduct the conflict. One example of consensus in this respect is the use of the "Alabama method" versus the "Mississippi method" in terms of police action—the former indicates a failure to enforce the law, thus leaving the Negro Freedom Riders at the mercy of local extra-legal methods; the latter indicates positive police action against the Riders, action precluding the presence, or necessity, of mobs.[117]

The need for the movement to develop new goals once it has either succeeded in achieving its initial goals, or has run into insurmountable obstacles has been discussed earlier. As Boulding points out:

"Organizations frequently organize themselves against something, and, in the absence of a perception of conflict, their reason for existence is weakened or disappears, and they suffer from internal disorganization or even dissolution."[118]

Again, the white side of the conflict has just as much a functional need for this as the Negro. This has been pointed out above in the discussion of the apparent need of the Southern white segregationist for an "enemy" in terms of the Northern agitator. The scapegoat mechanism functions to alleviate in the segregationist the need to grapple with the reality of the Negro students' demands by enabling him to find an exterior "villain" upon whom he can place the blame for the social dislocations caused by the demonstration. This fear of villain and Negro, "far from deriving from the Negro's actual behavior, is a means of keeping the status system intact, of rallying all members of the white group around its standards . . ."[119] The segregationist, by assuming that the Yankee agitator or radical is really the person responsible for the Negro's protest activity, strengthens this fear and enables himself to rationalize his own new activities. These fears do not have to be real, for imaginary threats serve the same group integrating function as real threats.

The interactive relationship of the groups involved—in this case the sit-in movement on the local level, and the community power structure, composed usually of the government, the white merchants, and the segregationists (to a degree)—is going to be important in setting the limits and forms of the conflict. Actually no empirical data are obtainable to show whether or not the further, continued suppression of the interracial conflict in the South would have increased the intensity of conflict at a later point, as there are no controls available. But it does seem that where parties to a conflict were able to come to an agreement on a common end (namely, law and order and a return to business normalcy), the sit-in demonstrations did lead in the long run to a more integrated, more solidified community, at least based on the index of not continuing the interracial strife. As Boulding puts it, in slightly different terms, "Reconciliation will presumably be easier if reconciliation itself is highly valued as a process by the contending parties."[120]

In part a group's expectations of the other group's behavior will depend on the existence of this kind of consensus; in part (and this is related to consensus, too) it has to do with the group's perception of the opposing party. Realistic measures to conduct the conflict in a winning manner will be undertaken in proportion to a realistic appraisal of the forces at work. In turn this is at least in part determined by the earlier history of the group, and by the general socio-political conditions of the area in terms particularly of the Negro-white population ratio. Contact between the groups (as with the existence of a consensus arrived at through negotiation) alone is not enough if this contact merely strengthens previously conceived and stereotyped images. Contact can aid in realistic perception only if members of the opposing parties see each other as persons capable of conducting a rational conflict, and rational negotiations. In the Southern context this is a difficulty.

In terms of the conditions which modify the conducting and settling of conflict situations, we must deal first of all with the assumption that the conflict itself will tend to create, as a byproduct, or latent function, a new set of values and behavior patterns within the community if it is resolved successfully. That is, the sit-ins have in the places where they have succeeded, resulted in new laws, new mechanisms of dealing with community patterns (such as Human Relations Committees), and new ways of conducting behavior at lunch counters and in other places of public accommodations. Even when they have not succeeded, new relationships have developed—even though in some cases they might be evaluated as dysfunctional. An example of this might be the breakdown of communication between the dominant and subordinate groups in some areas. Another example might be new techniques developed by law enforcement officials to deal with the nonviolent movement. This in turn would create a counter-strategy among the student groups, and so on.

These two points, one the possible breakdown of communication between the groups concerned, the other the development of counter-strategies on both sides in response to the other, have been discussed by Boulding in terms of what he calls the "Richardson Processes."[121] These processes suggest that parties to a dispute tend to react to an increase in the perceived hostility of the other party by increasing their own hostility so that, depending upon how much initial hostility there was, we may actually reach a point of hostility where no equilibrium (negotiating point, or even, in a sense to be developed below, a detente) is possible. This possibility in turn is related to the basic idea of the Richardson Processes, namely that movements on the part of one party so change the field of conflict that the other party is forced to react, which so changes the field again that the first party must react again, and so on. This may, then, depending on the hostility (or degree of resistance by the white community) result eventually in some kind of negotiation, or it may not.

The next point is one akin to an earlier assertion that the attacking group always has some choice of weapons, while the defending group has a choice only if the attacker uses nonviolence. The internal structure of the conflicting elements both reflect, and help to create, the ideology and methods of the groups involved. In the current situation, the dominant group also has a monopoly of the means of violence, i.e. arms. Hence the weaker subordinate group is forced to seek methods of conflict which will take the dominant group by surprise, and force the dominant group to modify its tactics. Once the groups have tested each other out, and negotiations become the order of the day, it is of course necessary to find a power center within each group in order to conduct the negotiations. Confusion and delay has been created in cases where the white community power structure (through, say, a merchants' association) deals with the traditional Negro community leadership only to find that it no longer speaks for the group with which the merchants are locked in conflict.

The conflicts generated by the interracial situation in the South and heightened by the sit-ins have created new alliances among the Negro, as well as the opposing white, groups. The better morale and higher level of self-consciousness of the groups have in many cases forced them to make peace with other elements within the same group, for dissention is perceived as treasonable in the struggle. But perception of the strength of the opposing group is often clouded by preconceptions derived from an outworn past. In case after case the white community leadership has been unable to recognize the seriousness of the student efforts. That is, they have underestimated their opponents' strength. Early rounds of negotiations can be seen in proper perspective in this light. The merchants have often felt that if the students could be called off by an offer to negotiate, they would not resume their activities once the negotiations had fallen through. It was only when the students demonstrated their staying power after the first, and sometimes later, rounds of negotiations had failed, that the merchants and city officials realized the real strength of their opponents, and, in the light of a new and realistic appraisal, came to terms.

Here an additional observation can be added to Coser's: once the opposing sides in this kind of conflict have tested each other in actual conflict, the future type of combat, if any, can be interpreted in the light of whether or not the opponents have some common acceptance of common aims. Here the relative sizes of the groups seem to be crucial. Where the white group is dominant and the Negro group is large, but subordinate, the white group continues to regard Negro protest activity as though the Negroes wish to eliminate the white status quo altogether (and have the numbers to do so, should they have access to, and utilize the ordinary implements of violence). On the other hand, where the white group is dominant and the Negro group is small, the Negro protest is not a real or perceived threat to white status, power, and resources. Hence it becomes far more probable that a common acceptance of aims can be arrived at, in terms of "stopping trouble," an aim which cannot totally exclude either group from some measure of victory, and in terms of which compromise is possible. Aiding in this acceptance of common aims are the good examples set by other communities which have stopped trouble by opening counters to all regardless of race; the respectable demeanor of the students; and their espousal of nonviolence. In the case of a large Negro proportion in the population, compromise becomes difficult if not impossible; in the other instances, compromise is not dangerous, and is desirable for the business community.

The problem of common aims again refers back to the willingness of both parties to a conflict to create a "moral" situation, one in which business can be conducted as usual, or nearly so. Compromise is made easier if some mechanisms for negotiation are available, such as biracial committees. As Boulding points out

> ". . . when there are no institutions for procedural conflict, violence is likely to result . . . violence in itself prevents the conflicts from being resolved and indeed perpetuates them . . . (Violence) creates an atmosphere in which reconciliation is difficult . . . It likewise makes compromise difficult."[122]

B. *The Mechanism of Internal Hostility Release*

Let us now examine some of the internal workings of the sit-in protest groups in terms of Coser's general propositions. He suggests, in line with much of the psychoanalytical literature, that the more organized a group is, the more in-group aggression there will tend to be, and that the accumulation of aggressive energy, or hostility, between an individual and various frustrating agents, will be greater in primary groups, in situations involving more individual participation, and in cases where the individual's personality is involved. In brief, then, the more an individual's life is involved in the group, the more in-group hostility will be generated because of the multiplication of conflict factors. This hostility will somehow be acted out, for it cannot simply be bottled up or repressed. Even if it is temporarily suppressed, it will break forth in a more severe manner later, sometimes in terms of individual breakdown or malfunction. Obviously this would be even more the case where the "cause" of the group is serious and righteous, rather than merely peripheral or of little consequence. The self-image of the participant is involved to a great degree.

Now the sit-in protest group, or, for that matter, any group confronting great danger physically, and in a subordinate status, fits the description outlined above closely. This "just cause" has in advance enhanced the participant's self image, thus propelling him into a close relationship with the group which has given him a new sense of pride and worth. The very nature of the activity requires careful organization and planning, and involves a great deal of the participant's time, energy, and ego; that is, his personality becomes involved to a high degree, and "the movement" assumes a central place in his activity. At the same time that the movement gives him an opportunity to release a lifetime of frustration, the frustration is often increased by confronting the participant with a blatantly negative response—a failure to be served at the counter—while this response is accompanied by great hostility and feeling on the part of white persons around him.

This condition is further complicated by the fact that the participant cannot simply give vent to his pent up frustrations, hostilities and aggressions in physical or vocal acts of violence because his tactics and strategy are based on a philosophy of nonviolence. Thus the tendency must be to turn the hostility inward, either upon himself and/or upon the group. Unless measures were taken to provide a channel for this in-group or personally turned-in aggression, the individual would rapidly be rendered useless by his feelings in the situation (a kind of "battle- fatigue" which has been observed in some cases), and the group would quickly break apart under the strain (which has also taken place). Some mechanism for the release of internal hostility must be provided, even unconsciously, if the group is to continue to function.

Three devices have turned up which to one degree or another appear to function to release tensions: singing, joking, and the "workshop."

As one observer has pointed out, this is not the only function of song.[123] First, "what cannot be said in words without extensive emotional retraining is said in music," not only to the white opponent, but even within the group to other persons, or to institutions and ideas which must be criticized but cannot be criticized in the normal way without creating the appearance of diversion. Second, song inspires morale and group identification by expressing the movement's ideology as it is universally perceived by the participants. Third, it unifies the group in a stress situation through both the morale-building and the tension-releasing functions. Finally, and for our purpose most important, song permits a release of emotion which has been pent up in circumstances of conflict where emotion, particularly of the violent kind, cannot be permitted.

Thus the songs of the sit-in movement have become famous, have now been adopted (or adapted) by various non-Southern student political groups, and have been recorded and written down. Many, such as the following example, which is the "theme song" of SNCC, have religious origins and others have been adapted from various songs of protest of the 1930s. Others have been expressly written by the participants to meet a local situation.

We shall overcome
We shall overcome
We shall overcome some day . . .
Oh, deep in my heart
I do believe
We shall overcome some day.

This song has other verses, including "The Truth Will Make Us Free," "Love Will Conquer All," "We'll Walk Hand in Hand," "The Lord Will See Us Through," etc. By this time there are probably at least two dozen songs widely known throughout the South by various Negro students involved in protest activity.

Joking, or humor, has long been recognized as an indirect way of expressing hostility toward an object, as Coser points out. Political jokes in totalitarian countries are only one example of this, for jokes, like song, permit one to drain off hostilities without the danger of a direct confrontation. Thus the jokes of the sit-in movement have taken two primary forms: those directed against the white opponents, and those directed against the in-group, or members of it. One example of each will follow:

Several Negro students, in the course of a sit-in, take seats at a lunch counter, then the white manager approaches. The manager says, "I'm sorry, but we don't serve Negroes here." The spokesman for the Negro students replies politely, "That's all right, sir, we don't eat them, either."

After the successful termination of sit-ins in one city, one of the Negro students went to the newly integrated lunch counter.
"I understand you're integrated now," he said.
"That's right," replied the waitress.
"Well, I'll have an order of chitlin's and greens."
"I'm sorry, sir, we don't have that here."
"Oh. Well, then I'll have some hog maws."
"Sorry, we don't have that either."
"Well!", exclaimed the shocked Negro student. "How much picketing do we have to do to convince you we're serious about this integration stuff?"

As in the case of songs, there are now dozens of jokes which had their origin in the current wave of demonstrations. A side phenomenon to this has been the rise to fame of a series of Negro comedians who perform mainly in Northern night clubs, and whose brand of humor, poking fun at Negroes and white liberals alike, is understandable only to those having a closer acquaintance with the Negro community and its behavior patterns. The best-known of these, Mr. Dick Gregory, originated the tale of the white liberal who invited not one, but two Negroes to his "integrated" party—in case the first one didn't work out. Another, Mr. Bill Cosby, worked out a routine following Attorney General Kennedy's remark that there would be a Negro president some day. He envisioned a telephone conversation by the first Negro president:

"Hello. Yes, we're making out fine. Yeah, we broke the block. For sale signs going up everywhere." etc.

The "workshop" is probably the most formal device associated with tension releasing mechanisms, one which has been traditionally associated with CORE, and one which has become inseparable from most nonviolent direct action campaigns in recent years. The workshop is a socio-drama in which the participants, Negro students who plan a demonstration, play a variety of roles including white parts. On the surface this merely functions to prepare the students emotionally on what to expect—and, in case of violence, on how to react. It is perceived in the main as simply practice in the perfection of control of oneself in stress situations.

One latent function of the workshop is as morale-builder. The students who go into a conflict situation after the socio-drama are not only prepared emotionally to deal with violence in nonviolent ways, but also (a) know each other, having already experienced mock combat with each other, and hence trust each other. (b) Know that the group expects them to behave according to the "code" with which they have been indoctrinated; thus, as the "American Soldier" series pointed out, loyalty to one's buddies is often more important than hatred of the opponent, or knowledge of why they are fighting.

As far as tension release is concerned, one has to watch a socio-drama in motion to be aware of the intense feeling invested in the roles being played. The Negro students are able to play white roles of policeman, store manager, University administrator, etc., with a degree of accuracy and depth of understanding quite astounding at first impression. They imitate the actions of hoodlums with a vehemence which actually gives rise to violent reaction by Negroes playing the role of Negro students, even though the actors are actually their own peer group associates. Words are thrown about as if the actor had been waiting all his life for a chance to use the words as others have used them in relation to himself. But, solidified by the exclusiveness of membership in a group which has undergone treatment somewhat akin, one supposes, to fraternity hazing, and having drained off latent hostility through play-acting, the group goes forth functioning positively in terms of its goals.

In cases where the socio-drama is lacking the group can quickly disintegrate. This is true first because the conflict creates situations of constant surprise which the group is unfamiliar with. Secondly, the members of the nonviolent group have not seen each other in action of any kind before, and hence do not know what to expect of each other in the stress situation. Third, there is no group solidarity, no loyalty to one's buddies which would dominate feelings of fear; individuals will tend to run. Finally, the group, thrown intimately together for the first time in a situation of constant stress and hostility, and faced with constant frustration, releases its aggression upon its own members in the form of bickering, arguments on everything from tactics to the minutiae of daily living, and explosions of temper, and hence becomes immobilized for action.

These latent functions of the workshop, as well as other morale-building and tension-releasing mechanisms should not be taken to denigrate the real security engendered by the group's ideology, training, and feeling of fighting in a just cause. While it is true that such a feeling will tend to intensify the struggle with the opponent and perhaps make compromise less likely, as Coser points out, it is further true that the individual draws a great deal of self-confidence from the power he ascribes to the movement as a whole—a movement which is often perceived as being the servant of not only God but history. This is one reason for the oft-described aura of dignity and pride with which the Negro students (also the Black Nationalists, Muslims, and others) conduct themselves. The movement has contributed to that number of Negroes

"who, in spite of the handicaps of race, have developed mature personalities marked by courage and dignity. Their ego defense lies in the security of their knowledge and feeling that nothing that is done to them can make them inferior, and that they are not alone in their search for human decency."[124]

C. *The Stages of Local Conflict in the Light of Intergroup Dynamics*

It should now be possible to examine a series of concrete examples of the sit-in movement as it developed in some communities, and attempt to find out if any of the propositions of inter- and intra-group conflict, and the propositions of a stage theory of social movements make sense. Let us now draw these two strains together in terms of a set of manageable hypotheses or propositions which can be examined in the light of the data of some communities in which the sit-ins have taken place.

The constituent part of a social movement (the microcosmic or community-level components) go through a series of stages which unfold partly in terms of the dynamics of intergroup conflict:

1. An *incipient* stage similar in many ways to the beginning stage of the overall movement and characterized by a great deal of spontaneity and lack of formalized mechanisms or organization. Both the attacking and defending groups are scarcely organized at all, and are unfamiliar with each other's strengths and weaknesses. There has been no opportunity as yet to gauge their relative positions. Reactions tend to be swift and uncontrolled, unplanned and not thought through in terms of their realistic functions or latent possibilities. This is the stage in the sit-in movement of the first sit-in, the early growth of the organization, and the relatively unplanned reaction to the movement by the police in terms of arrests, by the managers of stores in terms of unstructured and varying counter-tactics which may vary

from day to day ranging from closing the stores altogether, roping off lunch counters, removing seats from stools, etc.

2. A *counteractive* phase characterized by the centralization of the white power structure in methods of dealing with the demonstrations. Here patterns begin to develop, resulting in centralization of the Negro student organization, further training by the Negroes, the establishment of a chain of command on both sides, and initial efforts by store managers to end the dispute without changing the current pattern. At the close of this phase, in part due to a failure of the contending forces to come to really full-scale grip with each other, the dominant power structure offers to negotiate, or accept student offers to negotiate, at the price of calling off the demonstrations.

3. A stage of *detente* or stoppage of action, a standoff point in the conflict during which there is no action, but the opponents engage in negotiations, during which they size each other up. Students gradually realize that they have misapprehended the purpose of the negotiation and underestimated the staying power of their opponents: some of them become impatient and call for a resumption of direct action in the face of a failure to settle. Others advocate this also, recognizing that delay will undermine the rank-and-file's faith in themselves and in their leaders to accomplish anything. The end of this phase is often marked by handing a deadline or ultimatum to the store managers naming a date for the resumption of action. Meanwhile the managers, also recognizing the seriousness of the situation, but still unprepared to make compromises that might be acceptable to the students, prepare for a concentrated counterattack in the event of renewal of action.

A qualifying statement in terms of this development must be interjected at this point, however, before going on to the next stage. There are situations, as will be seen in the material to be presented below, where no detente ever takes place. It is the contention of this paper that when, because of their consensus, the defending group is prepared to utilize violence despite its consequences to the community (that is, when the defending group is not prepared to share some of the basic assumptions of those working for change), no detente will take place, and the counteractive phase tends immediately to go over into a reorganizational phase and a showdown phase; these two may last indefinitely.

In other words, the situation may approximate those suggested in an earlier section in terms of our discussion of nonviolence: a series of conditions making nonviolence a difficult tactic to put through, as with Kuper's analysis of South Africa, exists, despite the fact that the overall culture of the country or world may support, at least verbally, the value of the attacking subordinate group. It may even be suggested that at times the overall culture may choose to retreat in the face of opposition by the local segregationists, even though they are a minority in the country, in order to minimize conflict and violence, as the leadership of the nation sees it. Or it may not retreat, but rather move more cautiously, as in the case of Meredith at the University of Mississippi, in the autumn of 1962.

Thus the unity of the white community in the face of a threat to the status quo (particularly when augmented by disunity among the Negroes) serves in some cases to eliminate the later stages of the movement altogether. It can, in fact, be suggested here that the greater the amount of violence utilized by the dominant group, the less it is likely that any developed detente, reorganizational, or show-down phase will take place at all. In effect, then, a continuum of resistance on the part of the white dominant group can be pictured: where, for various historical and social reasons, resistance is small, the movement will tend to follow through a normal series of stages to victory; where there is greater resistance, the movement will bog down in the show-down phase; still greater resistance will tend to eliminate a detente and the movement will go into the reorganizational and show-down phases and stay at that point; the most severe kind of resistance will result not only in no detente, but in counteraction so intense as to preclude any developed reorganizational or show-down battle by the integrationists. Let us go on now to discuss the last two stages for those cases where they do take place.

4. A *reorganizational* phase marked by retrenching by both sides for a long struggle. The Negro students enlist new numbers in their campaign, train them, obtain legal assistance, sit-in and picket, make liaison in the Negro community, whose aid they obtain for auxiliary action such as boycotts or selective buying campaigns, etc. The white merchants and the city officials make wholesale arrests, obtain anti-picketing ordinances, and injunctions, and, on the negotiating level, urge upon the students one or another compromise either directly, or through the medium of a human relations committee, a biracial mayor's group, a ministerial group, or the like. In this phase the action often moves from the student level to the adult community as arrests and other law enforcement tactics weaken the students; the economic boycott often assumes serious proportions at this point.

5. A *showdown* phase follows, basically involving a test of nerve on both sides, a do-or-die situation in which, if the white community wishes to, it can dominate the situation and crush the movement (typical in the Deep South

states, and in communities with Deep South population characteristics, for reasons suggested earlier in this paper). In other cases (typical of Middle and Upper Southern states or of communities sharing their population characteristics, e.g. Atlanta, Georgia) the white community leaders may split, enabling the students to settle with some, hence giving them an economic competitive advantage; or, more commonly, may await the coming of summer, hoping that the departure of the students will take the steam out of the campaign. Meanwhile, however, as a side-effect of earlier stages, there now exists a mechanism for settlement: a group which has conducted, or attempted to conduct, negotiations. As the divisions among the white merchants increase, the interracial commissions or committees increasingly move to the side of law and order, or resumption of business as usual, and urge acceptance of the students' conditions. The merchants, weakened by a continuing boycott by the adult community, a boycott which does not stop with the summer, surrender to the interracial committee, which quietly and without publicity arranges a truce with the Negro leaders, and provides tests on a predetermined date for the newly integrated facilities.

This development of stages is in line with the propositions suggested by Coser. In particular the construction of a new framework of relationships among the parties to the conflict proceeds as the conflict itself develops, so that one can see these stages in terms of the gradual development of such a framework. In addition, the stages also unfold themselves in such a way as to enable the parties to find out their own, and their opponent's strengths, and hence come to a realistic understanding of the relative power situations in the community. Thus the conflict functions (1) to create a changing and new set of relationships among the contending forces; (2) to enable the parties to gauge each other's strengths as a prerequisite to realistic negotiations; and (3) to centralize the commands of the conflicting sides so that negotiations and mediation can take place.

Ten communities have been selected to illustrate some varying patterns suggested by the above general proposition. The varying patterns can be seen in terms of a rough continuum of the factor of white resistance to integration, a factor which is ultimately responsible for the outcome of the "show-down" stage in the development, as well as the development of earlier stages. The communities range from one in the Upper South presenting many of the sociopolitical and economic factors leading to a "successful" outcome of the movement, to one in a Deep South county which presents a series of extreme factors which precluded even the development of a movement, much less its success. An important index in placing any community within this continuum was the degree of community violence present in the course of the sit-ins. It is assumed that violence directed at integrationist forces is a rough index to the amount of resistance which a community is prepared to mount against integration—particularly when the activities of law enforcement agencies (Mississippi Method) or their lack of activity (Alabama Method) serve to support segregationist activity, or obstruct the integrationist movements.

In all but two instances the outcome of the student movement was unsuccessful during the period under study; in two other cases, success was attained as a result of later action. Some more detailed reasons for choosing a particular community will be suggested in analyzing each one. It should be emphasized that these are not in any way necessarily "typical" or "average" communities in any statistical way. With the exception of Jacksonville and Montgomery, the author personally visited each one in the spring of 1961. Following a descriptive analysis of each community will be a section of analysis in terms of the proposition under discussion. The communities are:

Community	*Population*	*Location*	*% Negro in County*
Charlotte, N.C.	210,000	upper south	24.6
Nashville, Tenn.	347,000	upper south	19.2
Atlanta, Ga.	768,000	deep south	34.8
Jacksonville, Fla.	373,000	"upper" south	23.4
Rock Hill, S.C.	29,000	deep south	28.7
Columbia, S.C.	163,000	deep south	32.6
Tallahassee, Fla.	48,000	"upper" south	32.9
Montgomery, Ala.	143,000	deep south	38.3
Orangeburg, S.C.	14,000	deep south	60.1
Lawrenceville, Va.	1,941	"upper" south	58.7

Charlotte, North Carolina

Charlotte forms one extreme of the resistance continuum in terms of the sit-in movement. It represents, for the integrationists, the optimal condition of least resistance to change. Charlotte, an upland city, is a large (209,551) commercial center in which Negroes constitute 27% of the population

(24.6% of the County, 25.4% of the State are Negro). While on the one hand the city is only a few miles removed from South Carolina's northern boundary, on the other that particular section of South Carolina is itself the most industrialized, and most liberal, portion of the state. Charlotte, home of the renowned Harry Golden, is widely regarded as one of the more advanced commercial centers of the South. Since 1947, 152 new firms have moved to the county area. A total of 26,150 workers are now employed at 465 manufacturing concerns, the chief of these being in the textile and food processing industries.[125] Many of these are unionized. In addition, Charlotte hosts one of the South's finest newspapers, the Charlotte *Observer* (same management also operates the *News*); Johnson C. Smith University (Negro Presbyterian), Queens College (white Presbyterian women); nearby Davidson College (white Presbyterian men); and two junior colleges run by the city, Charlotte (whites), and Carver (Negroes). Charlotte also has several liberal church groups, notably a Unitarian Church and a Quaker group.

Prior to 1960 Negroes did vote and in fact were influential to a considerable degree in local politics through the NAACP's pressure and through the (later) formation of a West Side Consultative Council, which was a coordinated pressure group of the Charlotte Negro community. Most parks, recreational centers, balloting places, and buses, were integrated at least to some degree. No Klan or White Citizens Council existed. Only the junior college, the city owned swimming pools, the restaurants, and theaters were segregated; Negroes were not admitted to theaters at all, not even in the balconies.

The idea of the sit-ins came to students at Smith University from activity in Greensboro. The incipient stage of the movement was initiated on Thursday, February 9, 1960, when some hundred students staged orderly sit-ins at eight different stores on downtown Tryron Street. At most of them the lunch counters were soon closed. Only Kress' downstairs stand-up cafeteria remained open; it had served Negroes for some time.

A leader with considerable experience in organizing and in handling public relations quickly appeared: twenty-two-year-old Joseph Charles Jones, son of Rev. J.T. Jones, supervisor of Sunday School Missions in the Atlantic and Catawba Synods of the United Presbyterian Church, U.S.A.; the student's mother was a faculty member at J.C. Smith. Jones, a theological student, had long been active in USNSA, has served as secretary of the Southeastern Region, and had attended, as part of his NSA interest, the Seventh World Festival of Youth for Peace and Friendship (The Vienna Youth Festival) in the summer of 1959. Subsequently Jones appeared as a witness before the House Committee on Un-American Activities, at the instigation of some newspapermen, including the Washington correspondent of the Charlotte *Observer*, in order to counter the appearance of Paul Robeson, Jr.[126]

On February 10, the incipient stage developed further. Groups of students continued to range from three or four to more than forty in the downtown area. The Negro community appeared to be divided at first as to whether or not to support the movement. Dr. J.S. Nathaniel Tross, publisher of a Negro weekly, the *Charlotte Post*, said the sit-in approach

". . . only increases tensions. Bitterness between the races will be increased manifold unless something is done immediately to clarify the atmosphere and restore sanity in the minds of those who are caught up in the fire and fury of this ill-advised movement."

But the campaign picked up student support. At a meeting on February 9 of 650 of J.C. Smith University's 800 students, the campaign received overwhelming endorsement. Dr. Tross was hanged in effigy, labelled "Uncle Tom," in the gate of the college, an act quickly condemned by Jones. The latter, apparently extremely public relations conscious, also was quick to point out that the local development had no contact with outside groups, particularly with the Congress of Racial Equality, which had become identified with the movement elsewhere.

The incipient stage lasted only four days. Students then held off further activities as the mayor sought discussion with merchants and student groups. But on the following Monday, after receiving official backing from the Catawba Presbytery, the group which supports the University, the students picked up their demonstrations again. On February 19, demonstrations were again halted pending the mayor's efforts to begin conversations between students and merchants. On the 20th, the Negro Methodist Ministerial Alliance came out in support of the students. The *Observer*, on the same day, called for a conference, implying strongly that lunch counters don't make much difference in the profit-and-loss statements of stores, hence implying further that the stores' financial fear of integration was not justified.

At this point the counteractive phase of the movement began. On Tuesday, February 23, three Negro students and one white person were arrested in the course of a demonstration at Belk's department store. Shoving and bumping had resulted from a blocking of door as students chanted in low voices, "Freedom, freedom, everybody likes freedom." The white was

119

held as a witness. Four days later another Negro was arrested during more picketing—the final arrests to take place in Charlotte.

On March 1, Negro students protested to City Council, charging that a girl had been knocked down and an arrested student called "nigger" and threatened at a police station. The Council voted to send a copy of the complaint and a record of the discussion to Police Chief Jesse James. The movement became better organized at this time; a week later Jones was elected the official president of the Student Protest Movement, as it was now called. A week after that, as Jones informally broached the idea of a boycott of stores, Mayor James Smith proposed a special study group on race relations. This group was quickly set up and became the Mayor's Committee on Friendly Relations, headed by John R. Cunningham, Executive Director of the Charlotte Presbyterian Foundation and President of Dickinson College. This foreshadowed a later detente phase, but for the present the forces involved were still testing each other; in particular both the merchants and the students were still lining up their allies.

Within a few days of the founding of the Mayor's Committee, the 400 members, representing 300 churches, of the Mecklenburg (County) Christian Ministers Association called unanimously for an end to racial discrimination in both city and county. On March 18, to remind community leaders that there was another force still to be reckoned with, the students staged their first sit-in since February 27. That week and the following one saw continuing demonstrations, mass meetings, and picketing in the face of editorial and mayoral comments terming the demonstrations at this point "regrettable." The *Observer* felt that resistance to integration was bound to increase.

Early in April, sociology students at Belmont Abbey College, a Catholic institution in Belmont, N.C., did surveys in Charlotte, Greensboro, and Atlanta, asking 1,300 persons their views as to patronizing stores and lunch counters if Negroes were to be served. The Charlotte survey, taken of persons as they left stores under boycott, indicated that 58% of the persons asked (varying with age; the older, the more resistant to integration) would not patronize an integrated lunch counter; but 65% would patronize a store's other facilities even though counters were integrated. The results were published in Charlotte on April 2.

Meanwhile the counteractive stage continued as merchants refused meaningful negotiations. The students elaborated their strategy to include an Easter shopping boycott. On April 14, the first white person, a Northerner, joined Negro pickets. Jones immediately issued a statement that the individual was merely a reporter. "The students keep themselves free from all groups which are considered 'outsiders,'" Jones said, in what seemed a strategy to project the Movement as young, Southern, and concerned strictly with local problems. The Movement's image was, as far as he could help it, a "family" one, that is, the struggle was one involving Southerners only. This may have been in part to lessen local fears of outside intervention and thus increase the likelihood of merchants being willing to come to terms with strictly local Negroes.

In this connection it is interesting to note that Jones from the very first disclaimed any connections with any outside group, including CORE and NAACP. The latter group, which had a local branch, aided the Movement with legal help, but financial assistance was kept in the hands of a local Negro civic group, the forerunner of the West Side Consultative Council. Field secretary Gordon Carey of CORE did make a trip to Charlotte and issued some statements on the subject of demonstrations. Local students claim they asked him to go back to New York; from Greensboro in early February Carey had stated that students were prepared to be arrested. Said Charlotte Movement leaders, "He is perfectly welcome to get himself arrested, that's his prerogative . . . this movement has no intention of reconstructing social history, nor economic factors in Charlotte. All we want to do is sit down and eat when we are tired . . ." Jones' tactic of reducing antagonism to the Movement by reducing the prejudice attached to "outside interference and agitation" in the South seemed to work.

In May the Mayor's Committee began to try to open talks with merchants, and the students called their sit-in off. This was the detente stage of the Movement, the phase of truce which accomplished nothing on the surface, at least. This phase continued until June 22, approximately. The Mayor's Committee, composed of fifteen members (four of them Negroes), at first tried in vain to involve the seven merchants under attack in discussion. The Chairman called in person on each merchant, and found that the chain variety stores were in general willing to negotiate, but that they were holding off until a decision by the two local department stores, Ivey's and Belk Brothers. The mayor himself was in charge of all public relations, with the understanding between himself and the Committee that nothing would be made public. The detente lasted about a month; the students waited, assuming progress was under way. On June 22, having waited long enough, they resumed sit-ins. A boycott by Charlotte Negroes of the entire downtown shopping area, emphasizing the variety and department stores, continued, with merchants feeling a decided reduction in business, according to later reports.

The resumption of activity after the lack of results of the detente phase marked the initiation of what can be called the reorganizational phase of the conflict. The University semester ended, but, unlike the situation in other communities, a busy summer session began, with heavy attendance by the leaders of the previous period. Boycotts and sit-ins continued under this leadership and organization improved. On June 23, a group of ministers attending a meeting of the Catawba Presbytery joined pickets. On the 26th, a mass meeting was held in which all adults, including whites, were invited to join demonstrations. On the very next day, Rev. Sidney L. Freeman, white pastor of the Charlotte Unitarian Church and president of the North Carolina Chapter, Unitarian Fellowship for Social Justice, marched with the pickets. Two days later, twelve out of sixty demonstrators were white, and these proportions were maintained. The whites were mainly Unitarians.

The merchants then asked for consultation with the Mayor's Committee. The students were planning a major demonstration for July 4. On July 2, in what can be described as the final, or show-down phase of activity, the chairman of the Mayor's Committee informed the demonstrators that if they would hold off he was sure an agreement would be forthcoming. On the 4th, the Committee met and agreed to recommend settlement based on integration of the lunch counters. This was reported to all parties concerned and on July 9, fifteen students, by a prearranged plan, were served at seven stores where sit-ins had in the past taken place. Police were on hand and there were no incidents. News of the event was released to the press, and was reported, but only after it had all taken place.

In Charlotte the reorganizational and show-down stages of the struggle were marked by a clear division among the white forces in the community. It became a matter of the students and the adults of the Negro community showing the merchants, in the last phase of conflict, that the Mayor's Committee was right and that, regardless of the "moral" issues involved, they might as well give up. Hence the conflict, extended though it was, enabled the merchants to see the strength of the Negro community, gauge it realistically, and then the Mayor's Committee was ready to channel the reaction (surrender) to the proper and appropriate command (the Negro student and adult leadership) while at the same time being able to rationalize this surrender as being one actually engineered by other white forces (the Mayor's Committee). The merchants were, in a sense, off the hook.

A number of significant factors in the outcome can be suggested. First, the economic pressure of the Negro community in the form of a boycott to support the movement seemed to have played some role. Second, Negro voting strength in two recent local elections, one municipal and one gubernatorial, had been made evident; Negro precincts in the vicinity of the University had participated heavily for the more liberal candidates. Third, the more or less idiosyncratic or accidental factor that the college was open during the summer, hence affording the student movement an ongoing, trained leadership cannot be ignored. Fourth, partly a factor related to the city's generally more progressive atmosphere, was the assistance given at the crucial moment by the white Unitarians who by their presence hinted a beginning of what might have been an even bigger white swing to the Negro cause.

After the settlement on July 4, a number of public parks and swimming pools were opened that same summer, even though the Mayor's Committee, which had been intended to be permanent, was disbanded. (It was reassembled after the theater stand-ins began in Charlotte in January, 1961.) On October 28, 1960, Sears, Roebuck announced that its dining room in Charlotte had been integrated for two months, and Sears thus became the eighth store to integrate. The student movement then broadened its attention to include movie houses and the suburban shopping center lunch counters; both kinds of activity were still in progress when this writer visited Charlotte in April, 1961. In January of that year pressure by the Charlotte Mecklenburg Council on Human Relations (Negro) forced token integration of Charlotte and Carver Colleges.

The integration of counter facilities in Charlotte did not come without a movement which created the kind of pressure that could not be ignored by the white merchants. The subordinate group had to engage the dominant group in a community conflict which had to be fought through a series of stages before the conflicting groups could come to a consensus. That this consensus was actually arrived at is probably due in large measure to the fact that lunch counters represented to the majority group no major threat to their social, political, or economic power. In any case, this segregated facility was a minor remaining pocket of resistance—many other facilities had long ago been integrated. Thus the resistance to change was relatively slight, and the student movement was enabled not only to work its way through all of the normal stages, but also to achieve victory in the final stage.

The general atmosphere of the state, as well as the positive atmosphere of the specific community, also played a role in the factor of resistance, or the relative lack of it. This was the year in which Governor Terry Sanford defeated an arch-segregationist in the run-off election in the Democratic Party primary, and went on to win the governorship with the backing of the organized labor movement and many Negro community groups as well—not hitherto a typically Southern development.

Nashville, Tennessee

The situation in Nashville is one step removed from that of Charlotte, in terms of a continuum of resistance to integration. While success was ultimately achieved (even to the point of becoming the classical "Nashville Settlement" plan for other areas), it did not come easily. There was considerably more violence than in Charlotte. Students were expelled from local institutions of higher learning, faculty members resigned. Yet the convergence of a number of positive variables did result in a settlement which influenced others later, and hence marks a turning point, in a limited sense, for the sit-in movement. Here one of the first settlements of the South took place.

The next community under discussion, Atlanta, had quite a different outcome. Yet, because on the surface it would seem that these two large cities are in many ways comparable, it might be well to set forth important differences: Nashville, with a total population of 346,729, is 21% Negro, and 19.2% of the county's population is Negro. Atlanta is more than twice as large, with a population of 768,125, of which 27% is Negro. The county percentage is 34.8% Negro. Both cities are centers of learning, each with a complex of Negro colleges. Both have sizeable Negro communities, with complex Negro leadership structures, and Negro community organizations. But the fact is that Atlanta's Negro community is larger, older, and financially more developed. The implications of this will be discussed in the next section.

In Nashville, as in Charlotte, a leader emerged quickly—even prior to the sit-ins—to help create a public image for the student movement. He was James M. Lawson, who entered the Divinity School of Vanderbilt University as a transfer student from the Graduate School of Theology, Oberlin, Ohio, in September, 1958. In 1951 he had gone to prison as a conscientious objector, but had been paroled to the Board of Missions of the Methodist Church, and had served in India with that group. Sometime in November, 1959, Lawson held a series of workshops on nonviolence in a Negro Methodist Church as part of his work for the Fellowship of Reconciliation. This assignment was recognized for field work credit by the University. On November 28, 1959, a small group of students who had participated in these workshops tried a sit-in at Harvey's Department Store, a prominent downtown establishment. The newspapers missed it, as well as another tried on December 5. This activity initiated the incipient phase of the movement in Nashville, which thus predated the actual outbreak of the general movement by several months. On February 10, 1960, according to a correspondent from the *New York Herald Tribune*, Lawson got a telephone call from a group of students in North Carolina asking him to initiate some supporting action in Nashville. That night he called a meeting of some fifty students and this group became the core of the Nashville Student Movement.

Nashville, however, also had a series of other interested community groups; the Nashville Community Relations Conference, the Nashville Christian Leadership Conference, headed by Rev. Kelly Smith (Lawson was its Project Director) and a local CORE chapter all formed a nucleus of organizational support generally united in sympathy for the Movement.

On February 13, the incipient phase of the Movement was formally initiated with more than 100 students from Fisk, A&I, and the Baptist Seminary staging the first large sit-in at three downtown five-and-ten stores. All the stores closed. On the 15th, some 200 students came again, and included a fourth store. On the 20th, a Saturday, there were some incidents including jeering and arguing between demonstrators and whites. Police did not interfere, but merchants called on Mayor Ben West and asked him to stop the sit-ins. The counteractive phase began and a week later police were in the downtown area in force. There was considerable harassment of the Negro students, and eventually eighty-one Negroes and no whites were arrested that day. Within two hours bail for all eighty-one had been arranged. Two days later all were found guilty of disorderly conduct and fined $50 each and costs. According to one of the participants, "at one point (in the trials) Z. Alexander Looby, a well known NAACP attorney and city council member, threw up his hands and commented, 'What's the use!' Some 3,000 Negroes thronged the courtroom and, upon leaving, sang the Star

Spangled Banner and the Battle Hymn of the Republic. That same day there was a bomb scare at Fisk University.

In the last incident during this counteractive phase, sixty-three students were arrested at Greyhound and Trailways bus stations on Wednesday, March 2. Seventy-nine students, all of whom had previous records of sit-in arrests, were subsequently rearrested on a charge of conspiracy to commit acts injurious to public trade and commerce.

The detente began on the next day. Mayor West appointed a seven-man committee to try to work out a solution, and the sit-ins were discontinued. The committee included the head of the Community Relations Conference, a vice chancellor emeritus of Vanderbilt, the presidents of Fisk and A&I, and three businessmen. It was interracial. To replace the sit-ins, a general boycott of all downtown stores, including those without lunch counters, was initiated. Again it might be well to compare this strategy to that of Atlanta, in the next section, where the boycott hit only specific stores; the general boycott thus put the pressure of stores without counters onto stores with counters so that the former began to urge the latter to settle.

Three weeks later, on March 25, the student movement decided that the Mayor's Committee had had enough time, and called the detente off. The reorganizational phase thus began on March 25, sit-ins were resumed and full scale demonstrations began again on April 11. On April 5, the Committee had come out with its recommendations: that merchants divide their lunch counters into two sections, one for whites and one for those who wanted to eat in an integrated fashion. This was to operate on a 90-day trial basis, but was rejected by both sides.

Meanwhile the governor of Tennessee, Buford Ellington, charged publicly that a sit-in on March 25 had been instigated and staged for the benefit of the Columbia Broadcasting System, which network had been filming a television program in Nashville based on the Movement for some two weeks. The charge was denied by both CBS and the student movement.

The reorganizational phase quickly developed into a show-down, but parallel to all of this came the Lawson-Vanderbilt Affair, which deserves to be reviewed because it forms part of the resistance to integration in the Nashville community.

In an early meeting between the mayor and various Negro church leaders, Lawson had been quoted as saying he would urge students to violate the law. This was denied, but local newspapers began to play up Lawson as a "ringleader of disruption and lawlessness." To correct this image, Lawson and his Dean, J. Robert Nelson (white) met and prepared two statements for the Chancellor and for the Executive Committee of the Board of Trust of the University. On March 2, however, the Executive Committee voted to ask Lawson to withdraw from the University, implying that he would be dismissed if he refused.

On the next day, March 3, in the course of a student meeting at which Lawson was present, the Chancellor of the University came, and advised Lawson (although he did not recognize him, for they had never met) that he was dismissed in general for practicing and advising civil disobedience in a tense social setting. The student meeting, generally rebellious, spent six hours formulating a protest to be sent to the Board of Trust. The following day the faculty of the Divinity School officially protested the action at its regular meeting. At this very moment the downtown Nashville area was in an uproar and Lawson was under arrest. The faculty then and there raised $500 bail and set up a legal defense fund. A group of professors, including the Dean of the School, went to the jail, paid Lawson's bail, and drove him home.

A few days later, the faculty voted again to ask the Chancellor to review the expulsion. The Board of Trust was to take up the case on May 21. Meanwhile the stores opened in Nashville and all legal charges against Lawson were dropped as part of the agreement. On the 21st the Board of Trust upheld the dismissal. Lawson was going to apply for admission to summer sessions, but on May 30 the admissions committee of the Divinity School was informed that their readmission of Lawson was denied by the University. That same night Dean Nelson resigned his post. On June 2 and 7, Dr. Walter Harrelson, Dean of the Chicago Divinity School, who had agreed to join Vanderbilt's faculty, attempted to negotiate an agreement. Upon his failure, he also resigned. On the 7th, at a general faculty meeting of the whole university, Chancellor Branscomb presented what ex-Dean Nelson later called a "grossly distorted and biased" version of the events. The following day, at an open meeting of the AAUP Chapter, much discontent was voiced. It became clear that more than 25 professors other than Divinity School faculty were ready to resign.

This was too much for the administration, and negotiations were renewed once more. It was agreed that Lawson could return to receive his interrupted degree, and that all resignations would be returned. But the Executive Committee of the Board of Trust, meeting on June 9, abruptly reversed the recommendation of the president and chancellor to that effect. By the evening of the 10th, 161 signatures of faculty people had been secured urging the Executive Committee to accept the terms. That weekend, Dr. Branscomb exercised his prerogative in the matter and decided that Lawson would be permitted to return to earn his B.D., that Dean Nelson would be relieved of his duties effective June 13, and that other professors would have ten days to withdraw their resignations if they chose to do so.

Given what he considered a discriminatory decision against the dean, Lawson decided, from Boston where he was completing his work, that he could not return to Vanderbilt. Eleven had resigned; nine, feeling that the way had been opened for Lawson to return to earn his degree, withdrew their resignations. Two, plus Nelson, never returned. Lawson finished his degree in Boston, and went on to take a church of his own near Nashville, from which location he continued to play an extremely active role in Nashville integrationist affairs, in the later Freedom Rider campaign, and the like.

By this time, however, the initial Nashville sit-in movement had succeeded. On April 12, a day after demonstrations had been renewed in the face of the failure of the Mayor's Committee to obtain agreement, riot squads had to be called out twice to quell minor disturbances in the downtown area. Four Negroes and two whites were arrested, bringing the total arrests in two months up to 158. Further, the state board of education ordered the dismissal from state colleges of students convicted of misdemeanors. A few days later, twelve white (including two foreign exchange) students, all from Minneapolis by a "Motorcade for Civil Rights," met in Nashville with sit-in demonstrators and leaders. Demonstrations continued, and in the course of one of them a group of fifty white youths attacked a Negro bystander who was alleged to have thrown a pop bottle into the crowd. Police arrested seven more, including five Negroes, and then claimed that 98% of all persons arrested during sit-in demonstrations were from out of the city.

Climaxing the tension of this show-down stage, on April 19, the home of attorney Z. Alexander Looby was bombed, without casualties. Inside of a few hours, more than 2,000 Negroes, mostly students, marched on city hall to protest the failure of police to halt the violence, and crowd leaders talked to Mayor West—who then and there took a public position against lunch counter discrimination. This violence and the reaction to it marked the turning point of the Nashville situation. A few days later Rev. Martin Luther King, Jr. addressed a rally in Nashville in which adult members of the Negro community voiced their support once again for the sit-ins, emphasizing by their physical presence the economic boycott which was still underway.

The result of these dramatic events, plus the powerful boycott (estimated as affecting business from 5% to 15%, plus the unrest that was cutting down shopping by people normally traveling to the city from the nearby countryside, plus the general effect on all downtown shops, including those without lunch counters)—especially effective in the pre-Easter "Extra-Value Days"—was that negotiating committees between the merchants and the Negro community were quickly set up. On the new four-men negotiating team for the Negroes were two student leaders of the sit-ins—not the members of the former Mayor's Committee. Merchants objected to the Mayor's Committee's Negroes as not really being representative of Negro community feeling! After three formal sessions, lasting into early May, a plan was evolved. Merchants would prepare their employees in advance, and carefully watched tests would take place for a few weeks. Then controls would be taken off and a normal situation of integrated facilities would develop. In the case of one store, Grant's, which withdrew from the agreement, it was decided to withhold sit-ins, but maintain the boycott. On May 11, the rest of the stores desegregated, and on June 8th Grant's followed suit. This was the first successful desegregation due to the sit-in movement in the South, outside of Texas. It became the model on which numerous other communities in the Middle and Upper South patterned their own negotiated settlements.

Numerous factors contributed to the success of the plan, and to its acceptance in advance. (1) The decisive tactic was the successful boycott. In Atlanta the boycott was aimed only at specific stores; in Nashville at all. Thus some stores pressed the others for a settlement. (2) The Nashville Negro community is smaller in numbers, and more compactly located, than in Atlanta. Further, its own business class is less developed, thereby making the Negro community more dependent on white downtown stores—and vice-versa. In Atlanta the downtown area is not so dependent on Negro shopping in the first place, since many Negroes prefer to shop locally in that spread-out city, rather than travel so far. Local shops are "integrated" in the sense that they cater to Negroes almost exclusively, including at lunch counters. (3) Combined with this is the suburbanization of the Nashville whites, who tend to shop more, nowadays, at suburban shopping centers, hence making the compact downtown Nashville shopping area more dependent, relatively, on those who live nearby—the Negroes. Nashville lost population between 1950 and 1960, while the county almost doubled. (4) Politically, this situation is mirrored in the fact that there is a fight going on between city and county. Mayor West's support comes from within the city, and he is in conflict with the county governmental apparatus, which is supported by the "silk-stocking set." Hence the mayor is much more dependent on the Negro vote than he was in previous years.

Finally, it can perhaps be suggested that while merchants in some areas of the South form part of a consensus in which violence as a tactic is condoned in order to prevent integration, in other areas where no clear consensus exists merchants tend to see their interest as being poorly served by violence and continuing business unrest. The ending of the dispute, even though a victory for the subordinate group, is less of a threat than a continuation of conditions of unrest. This lesser threat was probably perceived as lesser at least in part due to the care taken by the Nashville students to present a respectable image of a group taking its nonviolent philosophy very seriously. The Movement in Nashville was probably more consciously oriented to nonviolence, due to the leadership of Lawson, than in many other localities.

Atlanta, Georgia

The very fact that Atlanta is so much larger, and older, than many other Southern cities, presents the observer with a Negro community structure that is therefore much more complex, more stratified, and more divided than in many other communities.

Atlanta is the leading commercial city in the Southeast, its largest city, and financially its most stable, broad-based, powerful. There are six Negro schools in Atlanta: Atlanta University, Clark College, Morehouse College, Morris Brown College, Spelman College (girls), and the Interdenominational Theological Center. In 1953 Rufus E. Clement, president of Atlanta University, was elected a member of the Atlanta Board of Education, defeating his white opponent by 10,000 votes, many of them from whites. In the same election two Negroes were elected to the city Democratic Party Executive Committee. Negro policeman have been hired, extremist segregationist groups curbed, court rooms made more courteous, and various separate facilities—such as schools—made more modern. Atlanta is the center of many successful Negro financial institutions. The city symbolizes the tendencies in race relations summarized by Henry Bullock:

". . . the tendency for cities to aggregate protesting personalities and tolerate their protests . . . Southern leaders express their discontent through an aggressive corps of Negro leaders found in every Southern city . . . (aided by the settlement pattern which gives Negroes) the spatial proximity necessary for collective expression. This proximity serves as a basis for the development of a common cultural heritage and a common institutional structure,"[127]

which includes such things as a Negro press, proximity to Southern liberals, who also tend to gather in big cities, citizens and voters' clubs, progressive newspapers, in some areas, the chance of coalition with other minority groups (not, however, in Atlanta).

While Atlanta has seen Negroes make much progress, this progress remains limited, and has often been accomplished only despite the outbreaks of violence. Mobs and bombings have accompanied Negro attempts to expand real estate holdings into "white" areas. In a city where a multiplicity of interracial betterment groups exist (NAACP, Urban League, Coordinating Committee on Housing, CORE, SCLC, Southern Regional Council, many others), there have been seven bombings, none of them solved, since December, 1960, alone. (December 12, 1960: bombing of a Negro school; February 26, 1961: a private home; January 27: a vacant home in a white neighborhood about to be sold to a Negro family; January 18: a house under construction in a Negro area; February 27: a Negro home; March 26: the Pine Grove Baptist Church; April 24: a labor union official's home. There were three other explosions in the last six months of 1960—two homes in disputed areas and a Negro car-for-hire business. None of the bombers was ever caught.)

The Negro community is geographically spread out, with centers existing at good distances from the downtown shopping center both East and West (East being the center of the old Negro upper class). The Negro aristocracy is well-developed in the city, stemming back to the 1890s, and centered in a number of "respectable" churches, the University Center, and some social clubs. Many of the older fortunes were built from catering to white people; the newer elite has its roots primarily in the Negro community, within a segregated society. This newer group was already well established by the First World War.[128]

On February 16, 1960, in response to a wave of sit-ins throughout the South, the Georgia State Legislature by a vote of 137-0 adopted a bill making it a misdemeanor to refuse to leave a place of business after being ordered out by management. It was signed promptly by Governor Vandiver.

The incipient phase of the Atlanta movement was confused, ridden with internal strife, and concentrated in its activities mainly within itself rather than in action to promote integration. This initial phase saw the deep divisions within the Atlanta Negro community transferred to the integration struggle, hence presenting at once a divided and decentralized front, a front making it difficult to negotiate and bargain even had the white merchants desired to do so. When students, after a lengthy time, finally got to the lunch counters, they found the counteractive phase confronting them, the governor, local police authorities, and store managers united in solid opposition.

Some adult members of the Negro community had been talking about sit-ins for some time. Miss Ella Baker, active with SCLC was for them; Rev. King was dubious; CORE in the city was weak. A CORE member reported the disgusted comment of one disappointed Negro: "Ella Baker says the whole South will arise and Atlanta will be the very last, and I believe it." Meanwhile, on March 4, and again on March 5, an informal group of students, later termed "mavericks," accompanied by at least one white youth, were served at Rich's Department Store. This was repeated on the 7th, but on the 8th, the group was refused service, and again on the 9th it was refused. On March 10, an unassociated group, part of the cast of "Finian's Rainbow" at Atlanta University, composed of five Negro men and one woman, attended a matinee performance of "My Fair Lady" at the Municipal Auditorium. The manager immediately designated the orchestra section where they were sitting (in reserved seats) as a Negro section. At intermission he asked if white persons around the section wanted to move. Six did. There was no commotion, and police were not involved.

The initiating "maverick" group was apparently connected with, or had been seen in the company of Dr. Lonnie Cross of Atlanta University's mathematics department. Cross, who is known nationally as a prominent figure in Black Nationalist circles, had also been associated with a splinter Trotskyite group which publishes a newspaper, *Workers World*. Thus he had been tagged locally as a "communist," and the maverick element got labelled by other elements more dubious of the value of sit-ins. On March 8, therefore, a group of administrators from the Atlanta University complex called a series of meetings, first with the "maverick" group, then with a larger group of students including the "mavericks." The president of Atlanta University managed to cool the students off so that some 150 ready to go downtown did not do so. Meanwhile behind the scenes another meeting apparently had taken place between the "mavericks," Rev. King, CORE representatives, and some observers from USNSA in an effort to iron out differences. This grouping advocated a downtown boycott. As a concession to the "mavericks," CORE, and other action-oriented elements, and as a compromise between this grouping, the larger student body, and the college administrators, there appeared in the local white press on March 9 a paid advertisement, the famous "Appeal for Human Rights," signed by representatives of student government bodies at all colleges of the university complex. It was basically a protest at segregation, and a call to abolish it—without teeth. Local students thought it a very radical move, and were later surprised to hear that sit-in leaders elsewhere didn't think much of "The Appeal."

On Thursday, March 10, picketing was scheduled to continue, but again college administrators attempted to get it called off. Rev. King, on whom the students had counted for support, did not come out forthrightly for sitting-in. At a student meeting that day, the word "communist" seems to have been used rather freely, with representatives of the "maverick" group being asked to dissociate themselves from Dr. Cross. As a result, no picketing took place, but the lack of activity provided the impetus to get CORE off the ground. Meanwhile, however, the downtown stores had taken advantage of the inactivity of the students to have police posted at the stores.

On Tuesday, March 15, some 200 students swarmed into the downtown area at ten different eating places including the State Capitol, the County Court House, City Hall, two bus stations, two railway stations, and two buildings housing federal offices—the first hint of the superb organization of which Atlanta students were capable. The students confronted united counteraction. From his sickbed Governor Vandiver labelled the students subversive, and ordered arrests; seventy-seven were arrested. At one cafeteria Negro employees refused a manager's order to pull the food off the steam table when the student group entered. Two days later, at a closed mass meeting of some 1,400 students, the sit-ins were temporarily cancelled! At this point CORE entered the picture to pick up the campaign.

These initial counteractive measures succeeded in blocking further demonstrations, particularly when combined with the deep division on tactics and strategy within the Negro community. The counteractive phase, initiated at this point, lasted without significant changes in pattern from the middle of March, 1960, to the following October, marked from time to time by larger demonstrations and further arrests, which can be seen in terms of premature attempts to organize a reorganizational phase in the face of severe opposition. Finally, in October the counteractivity was no longer able to halt developments altogether and, following the SNCC Conference, a detente came.

A brief word might be appropriate at this point as to the role played by Rev. King in this, and later, events. King came to Atlanta to work for SCLC only shortly before the sit-ins began. As one observer put it, "he was not exactly greeted with palm leaves" by the Negro elite of Atlanta. He supported the administrators in their go-slow policy at the March meetings, and publicly supported the "compromise" agreement of March, 1961. Based on the views of a number of observers (Rev. King himself was not available for comment) it seems to be clear that his ambivalent role is in part based on his view that unity is needed in the Negro community. This is complicated by the fact that SCLC is to a large degree dependent on the Atlanta Negro power structure, which tends to be conservative, and on the other hand by the fact that King, as a symbol of progress, needed to have his home town come up to par. Thus he walked a tragic tightrope, aggravated by the disappointment of the more militant Negro students in his lack of leadership in their struggle with the conservative elements. This dilemma confronts any Negro coming to Atlanta. To maintain militancy means to confront the Atlanta power elite directly, and in combat. King seems frequently to play the role of a pacifier and unifier. Observers agree that political infighting is not part of his stock in trade.

Picketing and large-scale leaflet distribution by CORE became the active component of the Movement after March, 1960. Due to restrictions of municipal law, batches of leaflets (some 20,000) were distributed surreptitiously in brown paper bags, demanding a boycott and an end to discrimination. CORE's activities, however useful in terms of embarrassing the official Negro leadership, and in training white students who later demonstrated on their own as the first all-white pro-integrationist student group, were dependent on the ups and downs of the semester; when examinations came, students left the picket lines (which had long replaced sitting-in, due to police surveillance), and on some occasions the CORE lines had not a single Negro. One Negro CORE member did, on April 26, bring suit against Atlanta's chief judge, and the mayor, to end discrimination in courtroom seating. April 15, five of the six original signers of the "Appeal," and two more students not originally arrested March 15, were also indicted, bringing the total up to eighty-three, who now faced maximum sentences of forty years and $27,000 each. On the 6th, Mayor Hartsfield had turned down requests for an interracial committee to negotiate the lunch counter situation; on the 14th a newly acquired Negro home in an all-white neighborhood was bombed; on the 27th crosses were burned at a Negro housing development, and on Rev. King's lawn. On May 6, three more misdemeanors were added to the totals facing the eighty-seven students.

The students, under their "official" organization, the Committee on Appeal for Human Rights, now headed by a student, Lonnie King (no relation) then planned a pilgrimage to the State Capitol for May 17, on the anniversary of the Supreme Court's school integration decision. A "rally" sponsored by NAACP as a prelude to the pilgrimage took place the Sunday prior to May 17; about 200 attended in a hall set up for nearer 900. On the 17th, however, between 2,300 and 3,000 students did begin a march toward the Capitol. They were diverted by police officials (exactly which later became a matter of controversy among the various police forces and Mayor Hartsfield and the Governor) and on order Lonnie King led the group to a nearby church. Rev. King addressed the group prior to beginning the walk.

As the summer began, the bulk of activity still lay with a small group of CORE members, who continued their picketing without major support from Negro leaders. On May 29, the Klan held a rally with 500 in attendance; the next day an endorsement of "The Appeal" appeared over the signatures of most groups in the Negro community—two and one-half months after its appearance originally. Signers included the Negro Voters League, the African Methodist Episcopal Ministers Union, the Baptist Ministers Union, the Interdenominational Ministerial Alliance, NAACP, etc. On June 23, Lonnie King and some others attempted the first sit-in in months; the counters were closed. In early July a small group of students placed wreaths on the steps of the Capitol in connection with Independence Day. They were held by police, but later released.

On August 7, a Sunday, students of the "Appeal" group initiated a new campaign: the Kneel-In. Some twenty-five students visited six churches, and were turned away from only one. Two weeks later, in another attempt, they were turned away from three churches. On August 8, the State Capitol cafeteria was closed to avoid a suit filed to end segregation there. Later, in September, city aldermen met a similar threat by closing the city cafeteria to the public and opening it on an integrated basis to employees. There were a number of sporadic and more-or-less spontaneous sit-ins, which all failed, throughout this time, but they were not part of any organized campaign.

During the summer months, internal bickering continued. Various attempts were made to get the "Appeal" group to initiate action despite attempts by the power elite to prevent it. Said one participant in these events, "Everywhere one turns there is evidence of the position of the power structure in Atlanta against moving and doing anything that will disturb Atlanta's peace of mind." One meeting, to try to coordinate the various efforts of different factions, was cancelled because a delegate charged that a CORE member belonged to the Communist Party. The delegate had received this erroneous information from the "Citizen's Committee," an organization of some Negro businessmen, who accused a CORE member on the sole ground that he had been spending time with Dr. Lonnie Cross.

On October 14-16, 1960, SNCC held its second conference in Atlanta at the University complex. The conference (discussed in detail on pages 45-46) closed on a Sunday. Then, by plan, two days later a mass of student demonstrators finally got downtown, officially under the leadership of the Committee on Appeal for Human Rights. Two department stores and eight variety stores were hit. Four stores were picketed. Sitters moved promptly from stores where counters closed to other stores, in prearranged hit-and-run tactics. Fifty-one demonstrators, including Rev. King (who was involved by accident, it turned out) were arrested. On the next day, twenty-three others, including Rev. King's brother, were arrested. Fourteen, including Rev. King, refused bond and went to jail on ten-day sentences, the first day, and twenty-two refused bond the second day.

Following this heightened activity, a detente was arranged on Saturday, October 22, when the mayor and Negro leaders agreed to a thirty-day truce. The mayor, who has powers of pardon in city offenses, immediately released those remaining in jail. Students were reported confident that this time the barriers would fall. Meanwhile, however, Rev. King himself was ordered to serve four months in prison on the grounds that his participation in the illegal sit-ins had violated a condition of a suspended traffic sentence. He was shortly released in part as a result of intercessions by a member of the family of presidential candidate John F. Kennedy, probably Robert Kennedy.

Immobilized by the truce period, Negro students in Atlanta were unable to participate in Election Day demonstrations. But twelve white students from Emory College picketed in an all-white demonstration, since they were not involved in the truce talks. This was despite the fact that a news leak developed and that the Dean called in twenty-five students, talking to them for some two and one-half hours, in an attempt to dissuade them.

136

The truce failed. While it had been underway, some Negro leaders approached the mayor to assure him that they would keep students from demonstrating, and that future boycotts could be ignored. The students set a 72-hour limit after the end of the truce, then moved into the reorganizational phase of the movement, which did not let up until the following April, after what can be termed a show-down. On November 25, picketing was resumed. On the 26th, about 100 Klansmen counterpicketed. A stepped-up boycott was announced. Rich's Department store took its segregated signs from wash rooms for one day; it was reported that 1,600 whites turned in their charge plates as a result. In early December, Georgians Unwilling To Surrender (GUTS) also joined in counterpicketing. On December 12, a Negro grammar school was bombed; that same day four Negroes were arrested for trespassing at the Greyhound Terminal.

On November 30, the only desegregation of the year in Atlanta had taken place. Five Negroes were served, accompanied by two whites, at the YWCA. Another arrived alone later and was also served. Said the management: ". . . we rejoice that in this instance we have been able to base our practice on our principles." The matter had not been prearranged.

Meanwhile the sit-in issue in the city began to be tied, in the minds of citizens in general, to the issue of school desegregation, ordered for September, 1961, by a Federal Court. Segregationist groups began to focus attention on Atlanta as a key to the maintenance of segregation throughout the Deep South. A variety of groups flocked to the city: GUTS, various KKK groups, National States Right Party members, etc. Moderates, already suffering a Negro boycott, began to fear the outbreak of violence in the city. However, on December 15, Chamber of Commerce officials turned down a request for new exploratory meetings, calling instead for an end to demonstrations.

Negroes marked the first anniversary of the Greensboro sit-in on February 1, 1961, with a march into downtown Atlanta. Over 500 participated. Dr. Rufus Clement, head of Atlanta University, informed Lonnie King that what the students needed to do was to negotiate, not create disturbances; but he couldn't think of any way to go about it. On February 7 Lonnie King and twelve others were held for trespassing at two lunch counters, and the next day twenty more were arrested. Only King and a girl, Herschelle Sullivan, posted bond; they were needed outside.

On Thursday, February 9, thirty-nine more were arrested during sit-ins, bringing the total to seventy-six. The increased tension marks a typical showdown development. The Chief Jailer said he had only three mattresses left in the jail. All were refusing bond. Lonnie King was arrested for contempt of court while challenging seating arrangements in the segregated courtroom during the hearing for the first group of thirty-nine. Said one student, "Reckon they have space for the 30,000 others that are coming?" Said the Judge to King, after he had failed to heed the constable, "Don't you know the constable, as often as you've been in here, Lonnie?" Replied King, "You know all white folks look alike to me, judge."

By February 11th the grand total was eighty-two; store managers were now turning students away at the doors. Fulton County Criminal Court Solicitor John I. Kelley said no special effort would be made to rush trials; he suggested prisoners sleep in shifts if conditions got too crowded. The following Wednesday, February 15, eight ministers were arrested while staging a sympathy sit-in; the next day three more students were held.

Meanwhile the Negro leadership group was trying to reopen negotiations, although the official student group had not requested the adults to intercede. That same Wednesday, Rev. King addressed a support rally of 1,900 adults. The ministers went out on bond; a rally set for the jail house on Sunday, the 19th, was changed to a local church at the request of the county commissioners. In another incident eight Negro doctors attending the Atlanta Graduate Medical Assembly were arrested when they tried to eat at the hotel's segregated restaurant. They said lunch was included in the registration fee. They accepted bond.

A new detente was then accomplished; on February 20, eight students put up bond and went out of jail. The next day, firmly believing that meaningful, genuine negotiations were under way, the remaining fifty-four students, twenty-five women and twenty-seven men, came out on bail arranged by a prominent Negro attorney, A.T. Walden. Involved in the negotiations were the attorney, the head of the student-adult liaison committee (a minister), Rev. King, Sr., and some others. For the businessmen, the president of the Chamber of Commerce, Mr. Ivan Allen, acted as spokesman. On March 8 the agreement was announced—it appeared to tie desegregation of lunch counters to successful integration of Atlanta's schools the September to come. Rev. King, in Detroit at the time, did not sign the agreement, but urged its support. Some thirteen stores signed, and the Negro students agreed to call off all demonstrations and boycotting.

In point of fact, reaction to the agreement among many students, adults, and many liberal whites in Atlanta ranged from disappointment to riotous dismay. The students in jail had been prepared to stay there, and many had come out reluctantly only with the understanding that something immediate would be forthcoming. As a result of the "compromise" agreement, schisms were further deepened in the Negro community, and it is still split and confused today as a result. On the extreme end of the protesters against the compromise were the Black Nationalists—whose influence correspondingly grew due to the slowness of "moderation."

> "The recent sell-out by the black middle class leadership of Atlanta is so dreadful that it is worse than the sell-out by that biblical character, the Rev. Mr. Judas, who betrayed his God for a measly thirty pieces of silver. (Here the leadership) betrayed their Atlanta brethren for a nebulous *promise* . . . nothing could be so tragic as the repeated betrayals of the black 'handkerchiefhead' leadership here . . ."[129]

At a meeting on Friday, March 10, to discuss the compromise agreement, there was constant cat-calling, calls of "tell us the truth," and the like. Attorney Walden was booed and hooted. A minister tried to get the floor to speak against the agreement and was refused the floor until the audience chanted its demand to hear him. One of the chief student leaders also opposed the agreement. As the *New York Times* correspondent, Claude Sitton, put it (March 12)

> "Only an impassioned speech by the Rev. Martin Luther King, Jr. saved the older men from an outright repudiation of their leadership . . . The crowd gave an unenthusiastic response to such prominent elderly statesmen as the Rev. Martin Luther King, Sr. . . . at one point they shouted down Mr. Borders (a minister) when he urged them to hear one explanation of the negotiator's actions. . ."

King, however, turned the tide. The students felt that they had to go along for the sake of unity, sacrificing the immediate gain. Later, trials of the students involved were indefinitely postponed, in effect acting to "blackmail" the students away from future action on penalty of punishment for past action.

The original news release of March 7 began a controversy since the Chamber of Commerce would not officially support the contention of Negro leaders that lunch counter desegregation was not actually tied to school desegregation. Another news release had to be issued later to "clarify" the matter. Negroes insisted in it that desegregation would take place regardless of what occurred in public school desegregation. But the original release, signed by the merchants, said only that ". . . the leading merchants have stated that it is their decision to carry out in lunch rooms and other facilities the same patterns as have been recognized and evidenced by (various Georgia and Atlanta school integration rulings) . . ." Later the Chamber of Commerce, in *its* clarifying statement, said that the lunch rooms would be opened "pending a final decision on the Atlanta school issue and that they will follow the pattern of that decision." The Chamber of Commerce subsequently did not withdraw that, but also did not contest the clarifying statement of the Negro group. Following school integration in the fall, counters were opened on an integrated basis.

While success was ultimately attained, it was not done during the first year of sit-ins. Furthermore, the victory came during the detente stage, a unique development. Thus the victory is not perceived by students as being primarily due to their own efforts, rather it is due to efforts of normal negotiating channels. Hence the self-confidence of the student movement was shaken and the next steps may be more difficult. In the light of the weakness of militant integrationist groups the Black Nationalists may correspondingly grow in Atlanta.

This unusual and perhaps unique conclusion marks one of the few cases on record in which the show-down phase of the conflict did not actually bring about immediate results one way or the other. Instead, a state of confusion was created as to what to expect in September, 1961. This state of confusion probably stems from the fact that (a) the Negro movement had no centralized chain of command, and therefore the white representatives were at most times dealing with persons who were not necessarily representatives of the student movement. There were a number of groups, always, who felt that they were not tied down to the "compromise" arranged by the self-appointed leaders of the Negro community. (b) The white leadership had long been accustomed to dealing with a specific stratum of Negroes who spoke for the Negro community and this same stratum managed to keep its hand in during the period under discussion, thus influencing and dividing the students. The division aided the confusion and decentralization. In many other communities this was avoided effectively when the traditional Negro leadership either abstained from the current conflict, or joined it but permitted the younger element to assume command. In such circumstances it is difficult if not impossible for both sides in the conflict to make accurate and realistic judgments about their opponent's strengths and weaknesses. Realistic appraisal is impaired by the emotions involved in the intra-group rivalries. The rivalries force each faction to make judgments which correspond to its needs in the factional situation, and these may be, and often are, at variance with the real situation. Thus Coser's point that nonrealistic conflict takes place to relieve tension, rather than to solve the problem, is well taken with regard to the Atlanta situation. So is his argument that outside hostility increased internal cohesion only if a consensus already exists as to how to conduct the conflict. If no such consensus exists, as was the case in Atlanta, the outside conflict serves only to split the group.

This is especially true if the various factions differ widely in their expectations of conflict; a widely disparate series of views as to what is likely to happen, and as to the potential actions and reactions of the opponent can serve only to disorient the approach to tactics, particularly if status is involved in making correct appraisals. It is probably true that if factions are based on a series of indices of status characteristics, as seemed to be the case in Atlanta, one's status within the Negro community helped in determining one's tactical approach (that is, one's appraisal of the situation), as well as being later affected by one's membership in any particular faction. These two considerations would not help any individual make a clear and unemotional analysis of the relative strengths of conflicting forces.

Jacksonville, Florida

Jacksonville, in Florida's most northeastern corner, was once located in what was a Black-Belt county, but in the last ten years or so there has been heavy migration out of the county, or into the city itself, so that today the percentage of the city's population which is Negro is 27%, and in the county (which is scarcely larger than the city) 23.4%. Jacksonville is a large city (372,569), with one of the largest Negro populations in the South (just short of 100,000). It is the only city in which juvenile gangs played any significant role in the sit-ins, and one of the few which saw disturbances to the point of "race riot." It is for that reason (that is, the unusual variables of gangs and race riot) that a brief report of the Jacksonville sit-ins is included here. This report is based largely on a Special Report of the Florida Council on Human Relations (affiliated with the Southern Regional Council) entitled *The Jacksonville Riot*, and published in September, 1960. Subsequently it was reported that while no integration of lunch counters had taken place, the bus terminals and most city-owned facilities, such as swimming pools, and the stadium, had been integrated. Observers have suggested that what little was done came about as the result of the riots (merchants' fear of repeats), and as a result of Negro voter pressure (the Negro vote seemed to be in part responsible for defeating the mayor of Jacksonville, Haydon Burns, in a run-off race for the governorship).

The first sit-ins in the city took place on March 13, when a group of students were ousted from a Kress store by seven police officers on penalty of violating a state law just passed giving eating establishments the right to refuse service. Sporadic activity characterizing the incipient phase of the situation continued from this time, but the Movement proper began only in July. About July 15 a survey was started by the Program and Research Committee of the NAACP Youth Council, composed in part of students from Edward Waters College, an African Methodist Episcopal-sponsored school, and in part of high school students. All-white Jacksonville University took no part in the movement. The survey came just a few weeks after the mayor's office had once again turned down a request for a bi-racial committee to help tone down what was felt by Negro leaders to be mounting racial tensions. Over the previous four years various individuals and groups, including the Northeast Florida Council on Human Relations, had made similar requests, all turned down on grounds that such a committee would foster rather than alleviate tension.

This phase of activity lasted until the events of late August. On August 13, 1960, after careful consideration and planning, the Youth Council sent some thirty demonstrators to Woolworth's department store. The counters were closed and the demonstrators continued to sit for some three hours. Demonstrations of this type continued without incident until the 18th. On that day the counteractive phase began when managers hit upon the policy of permitting only two demonstrators at a time into a store. On Friday, August 19, demonstrations continued without further incident, but that evening the "grapevine" reported to the Youth Council that the Klan planned to have its members downtown to cope with the sitters. The next day, Saturday, a demonstrator was nearly pushed off the counter stool, and was beaten with a stick. The stores again closed down, and picketing began.

On Wednesday, August 24, a knife was pulled on a demonstrator; another demonstrator reported the incident to police, who took no action. The individual who had pulled the knife then complained to the same officer, who went across the street (where demonstrators had tackled another store in the meantime) and arrested the complaining demonstrator. He was searched. The white complainant, according to the report of the Florida

Council on Human Relations, then took his own knife out of his pocket and said, "Here is the knife, I've found it." The demonstrator was jailed.

On Thursday, August 25, a white youth, Richard Parker, joined pickets for the first time. A crowd of whites immediately gathered, and Youth Council members hustled Parker out of the area, followed by a mob of about 300 persons. Nine Negroes were arrested that day, but all were subsequently released. One Negro boy, age fourteen, was kicked and beaten by a jail superintendent before his release. The following day, after nearly two weeks of demonstrations and sit-ins, Parker again joined pickets, and again he was rescued from possible violence by Youth Council members. Parker, a student at Florida State University (all-white) in Tallahassee had come to the city, he said, on his own.

During this week police indicated to the citizenry what their approximate reaction would be to violence; and in particular indicated that they were prepared to leave the resistance to private persons. This counteractive phase reached its high point on August 27, and gave way, finally, to a crucial decision as to whether or not there was to be a final showdown just a few weeks later.

Saturday morning, August 27, about 8:30, the adult adviser to the Youth Council received a telephone call telling him that a number of white men with baseball bats, clubs and axe handles were downtown. He went to the chief shopping area and saw about twenty whites armed with axe handles topped with Confederate flags at Woolworth's; a few blocks away another 100 or so men were lined up with similar weapons, "standing like soldiers." Other handles were being distributed in a nearby park by men who had on gray Confederate uniforms. Police did nothing to interfere.

Near noon on that day the demonstrators arrived at Grant's store. Parker had been asked by students not to come. Grant's then closed its counters after demonstrators sat-in for about five minutes. The sitters then left. As they proceeded toward other stores, a group of about 350 armed white men and boys began running down the street toward the store. Some Negroes broke and ran. The majority, however, proceeded in good order, until four or five members of the Youth Council also panicked and ran. At this point the mob caught up to the demonstrators. A girl was hit with an axe handle. Fighting then began as the demonstrators retreated toward the Negro section of town. A running battle proceeded, with injuries on both sides. A boy was pushed and hit by an automobile. One group passed a group of Negro juveniles at a street-corner close to "Little Harlem," and these joined in the fray. Police then came. By 12:50, only an hour after the first sit-in that day, Police Inspector Bates reported the downtown situation completely out of hand. A series of individual incidents of mobs catching Negroes and beating them took place during this time.

A few minutes after 1:00 p.m., a gang of between twenty and fifty Negroes, armed with sticks and bricks, marched out of Little Harlem, and a mob from one of the department stores moved out to meet them. When they were thirty-five feet apart, police formed a skirmish line to keep them apart. A Negro boy, age sixteen, was shot by a white man who fired at a gang of Negroes. The boy was an innocent bystander. By this time other gangs of Negroes were stoning cars with white occupants driving through Little Harlem. A Negro police sergeant drew a revolver on a white officer, claiming the officer was manhandling a Negro citizen.

That evening, with disorder still going on, a Negro man was shot in the head. A series of shootings and individual attacks continued into the night. Eleven acts of vandalism were reported to police between midnight and 8:00 a.m. Sunday, August 28.

A rally by the NAACP was held on schedule Sunday, but picketing and sit-ins set for Monday were cancelled in view of the tense situation. But immediately after the Youth Council had announced this decision on Sunday night, the Council received word that a series of Negro juvenile gangs were going to unite and assume the role of protector of the Negro community. Rumors of Klan raids on the community Monday night impelled the gangs to begin preparation for massive retaliation on the white community.

This situation was not altered by municipal court actions on Monday. Some eighty persons, mostly Negroes, had been arrested. Parker had also been arrested, and was sentenced to ninety days for vagrancy as the "chief instigator" of the riots, though no charges of the sort had been lodged. After receiving sentence, Parker was put into the city jail, alone with other white men, some of whom had been part of the white mobs. One of these men struck Parker and fractured his jaw. The assailant and Parker were both charged with disorderly conduct and each received a $25 fine.

All-out efforts then proceeded to set up communication between Negro community leaders, Youth Council members, and the gangs. These attempts succeeded and all but one gang agreed not to attack. The mayor then stated publicly that the gang activity was not a race riot, and had nothing to do with the Saturday incidents!

By Tuesday calm had been restored—but a boycott, effective in some cases up to 50%, was begun by the Negro community.

Thus a very tense situation during the counteractive phase gradually cooled down at least on the surface. On Tuesday, as a final burst of energy, Negroes threw fire-bombs into four white-owned stores. The Negro community seemed for a time to be divided as to which tactics to pursue. In the terms of this paper, at least some Negroes (the gangs and the fire-bombers) were intent on an immediate showdown, in which further counteraction would be mounted to retaliate against the forms of counteraction decided upon by sectors of the white community. Other parts of the Negro community, particularly the more traditional leaders and the Youth Council, determined upon a retreat, which was a de factor detente, paralleled by a reorganizational move to the field of economic boycott. The latter groupings managed to dominate the situation.

On Monday, August 29, fifty-seven Negroes and twenty-five whites were sentenced in municipal courts, with 140 persons remaining to be tried. As for the dead Negro, it was established that his car had been flagged down by a police officer; three white men shot at it, hitting the victim, and the car crashed. Following all of this a group of white clergymen issued an invitation to a wide list of people to create an interracial committee for the city. The mayor refused to participate in the effort. Extensive police precautions at all public interracial gatherings were taken; at a football game a week later, with attendance half that of the year before, no incidents took place.

Here was a case, the first in our series of studies, where the white community (or at least its effective leadership) seemed to be united to preserve segregation, and prepared to permit violence in order to achieve this goal. The specific decision-making process in such situations is not known—possibly there were no formal decisions taken, but it appears from the description of the riot that the segregationist elements were organized.

In comparison to this it is instructive to look at Chattanooga, Tennessee, where riots also took place, but where the outcome was rather different, very possibly because the city administration fully participated in attempts to settle the situation and return the city to normalcy, particularly from the commercial viewpoint. There the mayor early made it evident he would enforce the law with vigor; after a series of conferences stores served Negroes.

On the other side of the conflict, the Negro leadership was not prepared to deal with the extreme nature of the opposition, and was not cognizant of the implications of its plans. The reality of the situation came to this group only in the test of battle, and rather than risk further violence, a retreat was made in order to reorganize for a longer struggle. Tactically therefore the choice was in the hands of the Negro leadership, which might have chosen to rely on the manpower of the juvenile gangs in an immediate showdown of further violence. But such a choice might have been lost, and a nonviolent direct action campaign under those circumstances was equally unlikely, due to lack of preparation.

Rock Hill, South Carolina

Atlanta and Jacksonville, for various reasons, approximate Deep South social conditions, but it is only when we arrive at Rock Hill and Columbia that real Deep South conditions permeate the atmosphere. Atlanta, while in Georgia, a Deep South state, nevertheless has a large population, a significant Negro population, and is a center of Southern commerce and industry. Jacksonville is similar. But Rock Hill, with a population of merely 30,000, of whom just over 7,000 are Negroes, presents the observer with a different problem.

As a consequence, we find that a full flowering of the normal phase of a local community conflict and its subsequent settlement is no longer possible. Instead, as we shall see, the incipient phase of the Movement is quickly followed by a variety of counteractive measures which so overwhelm the local students that they are forced either to give up, or to enter at once the reorganizational phase and gird themselves for a long struggle.

Yet, while in South Carolina, Rock Hill is no Deep Southern community. Sociologically it belongs in North Carolina, the border of which is a scant sixteen miles to the north; and it shares many of the cultural and economic problems of Charlotte, only a few more miles away. Geographically it belongs to the Piedmont Carolinas, a part of the Piedmont plateau, which contains 53% of all the counties of the Southeast where manufacturing plants employ more than 10,000 persons per county. York County, which contains Rock Hill as one of its principal cities, employs over 12,000 persons in manufacturing, mainly in fabric, textiles and the printing of fabrics. Rock Hill has the world's largest fabric finishing and printing plant, the Rock Hill Printing and Finishing Company, a division of M. Lowenstein and Sons.

These factors prove an attractive asset to the city. The local Chamber of Commerce boasts that 99% of the population is native-born, that they think alike, act alike, are predictable and dependable; of some twenty manufacturing plants in the area, only four are unionized. South Carolina has had a "Right to Work" law since 1954.

Nearby is an old Catawba Indian Reservation, many of whose inhabitants also work in the local mills. The city has increased by some 6,000 population in the last ten years. Local police force: forty-seven men, of whom three are Negroes.

During Reconstruction the city was a center of Klan activity. In 1895, Winthrop College, a state college for girls, was transferred there from Columbia; in 1891 Friendship Junior College, a Negro Baptist school was founded; and in 1894 the AME Zion Church followed suit by erecting its Clinton Junior College there.

A group of about four students at Friendship Junior College initiated the sit-ins at Rock Hill on Friday, February 12, 1960. They had heard reports from other cities about activity; one radio report said that Rock Hill was expected to be the first city in South Carolina to have sit-ins so they decided to do this. Nearly 200, just about the total enrollment of the school, jammed four lunch counters on Rock Hill's Main Street. An ammonia "bomb" was burst in one store, but otherwise there were no incidents. There were no arrests, and no one was served.

In the middle of the following week, Farley Smith, son of the former Senator "Cotton Ed" Smith, of South Carolina, advocated the formation of a local Citizens Council. Smith was executive secretary of the Association of Citizens Councils of South Carolina, and was invited to come to Rock Hill after local sit-ins broke out. Sit-ins again took place on the 23rd and 24th of February, with a variety of minor scuffles and other incidents.

That same week Governor Ernest F. Hollings promised his support to the mayor's handling of the dispute; and the membership of the York County Citizens Council had grown to a claimed 350. State Senator L. Marion Gresette, of Calhoun County, promised that present state laws would be sufficient to stop the sit-ins. On March 1, there was a bomb hoax at Friendship College, and the girl's dormitory had to be evacuated in the snowy night. That day a robed but unmasked Klansman visited four stores that had been sit-in targets. March 15, seventy FJC students were arrested in the course of sit-in demonstrations—sixty-five for breach of the peace, five for trespassing. Trials dragged on for some weeks, subsequently resulting in conviction for all, and appeals.

On March 22, a boycott of eight establishments was voted by nearly 850 Negroes in Rock Hill at a meeting. When meeting chairman Rev. C. A. Ivory, thirty-nine-year-old head of the local NAACP and leader of the Committee for Promotion of Human Rights asked for nay votes, only one person, Dr. H. A. Logan, well-known backer of many Negro improvement causes and prominent NAACP member, stood up. The crowd roared with laughter. On April 16, Negro leaders requested Rock Hill Mayor Hardin to call a meeting of officials, ministers and others to open the lines of communication between the races, but no action along these lines took place.

June 7, Rev. Ivory, who is restricted to a wheel-chair, and another Negro were both arrested when Ivory wheeled his chair into a lunch counter and sought service. An officer wheeled the chair a half-block to the city jail, where Ivory was released on $100 bond. He was eventually convicted, for trespass.

Sit-ins erupted again on June 3 when FJC dismissed classes for the summer; students operating through a coordinating group, the "Student Friendly Civic Committee" continued picketing in small numbers throughout the summer. The SFCC, officially the local affiliate of SNCC, coordinated the work of the NAACP Youth Council, the Friendship Junior College CORE and NAACP chapters (most of the campus belongs to the latter; about thirty activists belong to the former), and some unaffiliated persons.

Thus the Rock Hill students chose not to give up, but rather to enter a very long reorganizational phase immediately after the intense counteraction launched by the formation of a local Citizens Council in February, 1960, and marked by continued arrests after that time.

In the fall, when the students returned to school, sit-ins and picketing resumed on a regular basis. With more people, picketing was often supplemented with sit-ins. Meanwhile, the NAACP boycott continued.

On December 9, 10, and 11, about eight FJC students attended a CORE workshop at Claflin College, Orangeburg, where the idea of jail versus bail was discussed. After lengthy discussion, FJC students decided that in case of future arrests, they would not accept bail. Beginning on January 3, 1961, demonstrations increased in frequency: by police count there were nineteen that month. On January 31, ten Negroes including a visitor, Tom Gaither, a CORE field secretary, were arrested and charged with trespassing. One went out on bail because he risked loss of marks and a scholarship; the rest stayed in prison and refused bail.

On February 1, all ten were found guilty and fined $100 or thirty days. Meanwhile, both Woolworth and McCrory lunch counters remained closed (and were later converted to accommodate other displays). On February 6, following a SNCC call issued throughout the South for students to come to Rock Hill, sit-in, go to jail and refuse bond, four prominent leaders of SNCC arrived in Rock Hill and did just that. They were Charles Jones, leader of the movement in Charlotte; Charles Sherrod of Virginia Union University in Richmond; Ruby Smith of Spelman College in Atlanta; and Diane Nash, of Fisk University in Nashville. All were promptly convicted, and the two men joined the nine FJC students at the York County Prison Farm. The girls were imprisoned for their thirty-day term in the York County Jail.

On February 8, the first white person joined Negro pickets; and a white woman observer from USNSA also arrived on the scene. SNCC meanwhile scheduled a mass motorcade to visit the York County Prison Farm on Sunday, February 12. Some forty students arrived from Nashville on Saturday, the 11th, and staged a two-hour picket in town. Sunday they held kneel-in demonstrations at five churches. They were admitted to three. Then they participated in a motorcade of some 600 persons, of which some 100 visited the County jail. This was followed later by a two and one-half-hour rally at the Mt. Olivet Zion Church on the occasion of the fifty-second anniversary of the founding of the NAACP. On their way home that Sunday evening, the Nashville students staged their own sit-in at the Union Bus Terminal at Asheville, N.C. There were no arrests. Picketing resumed normally the next day, February 13.

At the prison farm the students quickly made friends with the other prisoners. They were forbidden to worship and sing, and ignored this order. Consequently they spent a few hours in solitary confinement. Later they proceeded to outwork all the other crews at the farm, but officials were not satisfied; one students was ultimately transferred to the County Jail as a "troublemaker," and as the remainder did not know of his whereabouts they staged a seventy-two-hour hunger strike until officials reassured them. This was on February 18, the same day prison officials decided to eliminate Sunday morning visiting hours (afternoon hours were maintained) and the same day that several girls from FJC, chauffeured by Rev. Ivory, picketed Winthrop College for admission thereto.

On the night of February 13, the newly elected executive secretary of the County Citizens Council, a Presbyterian minister, the Rev. L. B. McCord, told an audience of about 500 that "segregation is morally right and theologically right." Farley Smith also spoke. On the 19th, a day after the Winthrop College picketing, a fist-fight broke up a picket line which included two whites from Washington, D.C.'s SNCC affiliate, Paul Dietrich, and Joan Trumpower. Both had, by this time, long records of commando-type raids in the D.C. area; and both were considered "trouble-makers" even within the Movement in terms of inserting additional factors prone to create violence by their presence in areas where they had no normal jurisdiction. Dietrich was twice arrested while in Rock Hill.

Picketing activity was soon thereafter restricted due to a new local ordinance forcing pickets to leave the scene if police believe that trouble is developing, an ordinance that in effect put all picketing at the whim of the police.

In 1954, the Rock Hill City Council had set up a twenty-one-member Council on Human Relations, the first group of its kind in the state; there had been five Negroes on it. It met on April 18, 1954, for the first time, and ended its activities on October 25, 1955 after eleven meetings in all. Negro leaders, throughout the period of the sit-in, had attempted to get this group revived, without success. On April 11, 1961, the City Council rejected for the fourth time within a year a Negro request for such a group. Partly responsible for the past formation of the local council was the South Carolina Council on Human Relations, an affiliate of the Southern Regional Council, which also promoted an interdenominational ministerial council. But the South Carolina Council is weaker in Rock Hill, and both groups collapsed.

Several observers of the Rock Hill situation feel that the responsibility for the failure to recreate a local biracial committee to mediate the sit-in problem stems in part from the state political picture: Governor Hollings and Mayor Hardin are said to be personal and political friends, and the latter is said to have political ambitions. Governor Hollings, despite what may be his personal views, poses as a staunch segregationist, and authorities at Columbia regard Rock Hill as a crucial testing-point for integration. Thus the moment the sit-ins broke out there, representatives of the governor, and agents of the State Law Enforcement Division (SLED) were on hand. It was rumored that SLED agents personally asked the president of FJC to stop the demonstrations; that a state attorney was offered to Rock Hill officials to aid in the prosecution; that the governor's secretary, Harry Walker, had gone to Greenville, South Carolina, and used his influence to cancel the proposed biracial committee there; and that this in effect is what prevented a Rock Hill biracial committee from being set up. One prominent Negro believed that "Rock Hill is being dictated to by Columbia, by the state." Negroes, while they do vote and register freely in Rock Hill, and while they could control two out of the seven voting districts of the city, cannot do so now because councilmen are elected on joint slates. Hence Negro political influence is not sufficiently important to offset the presence of the Citizens Council.

Another example of state interference was the indictment of Dr. Frank Graham's speech at Winthrop College early in 1961. Graham, former chancellor of the University of North Carolina, addressed a sociology forum on the United Nations, and in the course of his remarks included two sentences referring to the sit-ins and connecting them with the Declaration of Independence and the Judeo-Christian ethic, rather than with Moscow. The State House of Representatives passed a motion condemning Winthrop College for inviting him.

Under these circumstances it is surprising that the Movement got going at all in Rock Hill, were it not for the fact that, as suggested above, Rock Hill really belongs in North Carolina. There has been integrationist activity here before. Some seven years ago a local baseball team refused to play a team with Negroes on it, and local Negroes instituted a boycott. About four years ago Negroes forced the city bus company out of business through a boycott when it refused to desegregate. They set up their own bus line which still exists, although in financial hot-water. The Catawba Indians have also been involved in earlier racial incidents, particularly in action against state miscegenation laws. Catholic elementary schools desegregated shortly after the 1954 Supreme Court decision.

The Rock Hill jail-in marked a stage during the reorganizational phase at which the Movement in that community nearly reached a show-down. But the conflict did not seem to confront merchants or city officials in such a way that they felt a need to alter their tactics. As we have been able to observe in the period since the Freedom Rides, it is possible that such a phase of prolonged and sometimes violent struggle, that is, a show-down phase in which there is no real show-down, or outcome, can go on for a long time, as in the case of Albany, Georgia. In Rock Hill, perhaps because of its size, the conflict never attained the proportions of Albany or other communities. It can therefore be said that the white counteractive measures were sufficiently strong, and unified, to neutralize the Negro movement. As in Jacksonville, the segregationists had the advantage of police power.

Rock Hill is therefore an example of a community on the continuum of resistance to integration in which, despite its consequences to the community, the defending group will nevertheless utilize violence; the counteractive measures taken are so severe that no detente ever takes place, and the counteractive phase immediately becomes one of reorganization by the subordinate group, a new phase which can last indefinitely.

Columbia, South Carolina

Since, from the account of Rock Hill, it seems apparent that integration cannot be achieved in a city which plays a dependent role in state policies, it seems appropriate to go on at this point to a discussion of events in the state's capital.

Columbia has an old and honorable tradition as a Southern city, and its history is symptomatic of the stresses which are often found within the Southern states, as between the up-country and the plantation belt areas. Except for the State House and the French Consulate, no structure on Main Street antedates the burning of the city by General Sherman in 1865. The very founding of Columbia as state capital, in 1786, was a compromise between up-country small farmers and the wealthier plantation dwellers, who wanted Charleston to remain the seat of the government.

By 1800 Columbia was an important cotton and textile center, with slaves producing cotton goods. South Carolina College, now University, was chartered in 1801. The legislature was divided between up-country and plantation-country people in 1860, and a goodly number of them were unionists; however, the official document of secession of the state was drawn up December 17, 1860, in Columbia's First Baptist Church. After the burning of the city contrary to Sheman's promise following its surrender February 16, 1865, Radical Republicans took control of the state until 1876 when federal troops were withdrawn. General Wade Hampton (whose statue still stands in the state capitol park) was elected as a white supremacist governor in that year with the aid of the night-riding "redshirts." Populists (upcountry) did, however, succeed in regaining the state for some years; in 1903 Governor "Pitchfork Ben" Tillman's nephew James H., then lieutenant-governor, shot and killed editor N.G. Gonzales, founder and editor of The

State (still rabidly segregationist and conservative) for his continued opposition to populist politics. A statue was erected to Gonzales, symbolizing the present political domination of the plantation elements.

Today textiles still are 40-45% of the city's industry, and 28% of the state's population growth was in the Columbia two-county area over the last ten-year period. The state boasts that only .00004 hours of the total hours worked were lost in 1960 due to work stoppages, though officials now are worried by a major organizing drive by unions in the Spartanburg-Greenville area. Businessmen are worried by downtown Columbia's loss of trade in the last year or so, but few know whether it is due to the sit-ins and boycotts, or due to competition from the growing number of suburban shopping centers.

Located in Columbia are the University of South Carolina (white), Columbia College (white women), a theological seminary (white), and Allen University (A.M.E. Negro), and Benedict College (Baptist, Negro). Columbia's buses are integrated, but not much else in the city—two movie theaters have balcony facilities for Negroes, the rest have none. There are a few Negro police and firemen, but their activities are mainly restricted to Negro sections of town.

Neither Allen University nor Benedict College have a distinguished record of academic freedom. Allen, in 1957, while it was on probationary accreditation by the Southern Association of Colleges and Secondary Schools, dismissed or failed to rehire three teachers. Two of these were white. They had supported some of the views of the now prominent civil rights lawyer Fred Moore, then just admitted to Allen after expulsion from South Carolina State College. He had led a group testing bus segregation in the city.

In Governor Bell Timmerman's January, 1958, message to the state legislature he charged that information from the House Committee on Un-American Activities had revealed both white teachers to have a "record." The State Board of Education the prior September had suspended Allen's approval for teacher training, and these combined circumstances were enough to pressure the trustees and the president of the University to support the firings. Governor Timmerman twice more charged Communist influence at Allen, and all three teachers were finally voted out on May 15, 1958. No charges had been proffered, nor had they had a hearing of any kind. The American Association of University Professors' Committee "A" on Academic Freedom and Tenure recommended censure, and Allen was listed on the AAUP's "black list" (list of censured administrations) until spring, 1962.

At Benedict similar events took place. Governor Timmerman, in January, 1958, charged that three Benedict faculty members were Communists, but mentioned no names. On January 30 of that year the President of the College interviewed three faculty members and requested their resignations, which were refused. The Governor was then said to have applied personal pressure on the Executive Committee of the Board of Trustees, which then reversed itself and requested a resignation once more. The three teachers, all whites, were finally not retained, apparently due to their anti-segregationist views and a rising tide of activity at the college, some of the students of which had just applied to the all-white University of South Carolina for admission.

The AAUP again recommended censure, and Benedict College remains on the list of censured admissions to this day.[130]

Columbia, then, presents us with our first really "Deep Southern" sit-in situation. Unlike Rock Hill, it really belongs to the tradition and culture of the Deep South. While it is true that the incipient phase came early for such a community, it is also true that the opposition moved as quickly into its counteractive phase, and that, in true Deep South style, this phase blended into a reorganizational one with Columbia becoming the center later on for an all-state coordinating student group. It might also be pointed out that, as in many other Deep Southern communities, the Movement took a longer time hitting its high-water mark of activity. During the first year, in fact, it barely got out of the incipient stage, and it was only with the beginning of school in September, 1960, that real organization picked up headway.

Mr. I. DeQuincy Newman, a field secretary for the NAACP, seems to have been instrumental in bringing the news of the sit-in movement to Columbia, after the news media had already alerted the students in early 1960. Both Negro schools spontaneously, and independently, planned sit-ins for February 14 and 15, and plans were coordinated finally so that both days were utilized. Several hundred students from both colleges participated. Community tension was such that a cooling-off period was immediately called until March 5. Late during the night of March 4, a number of white youths rode past Allen University, and threw bricks. A cross was burned in front of a building. Apparently angered by this, a group of Negro students attacked a white drive-in restaurant with clubs and bricks, then fled. Police picked up four students, but released them. Benedict was also attacked.

March 5 marked the founding date of the South Carolina Student Movement Association, which was intended to coordinate action among all

Negro schools for integration. A state-wide demonstration was scheduled for March 15 (the date of the major demonstration in Orangeburg) and sit-ins took place in Columbia as part of this. Nine students were arrested, two the previous day. That same week six Negroes attending an annual spring rally of the American Legion requested service at an all-white hotel, and were refused service.

There were a series of other smaller sit-ins and demonstrations, mainly by Benedict students, during the latter part of the spring semester, including one involving about thirty-five persons at the city hall, and another with over 150 participants, at the governor's mansion. The Columbia *State* generally blacked-out the news or played it down, and students had to read Charlotte and other out-of-state newspapers to know what was going on. Throughout the summer small-scale picketing continued from time to time.

Oganizational problems between the two colleges and the city's Negro power structure did not become resolved until the fall. There was no CORE chapter in the city, but there were NAACP chapters at both campuses, plus a local citizens' group which helped the students with funds. Initially the college administrations were no problem, but in the course of events the Benedict administration changed its mind and forbade students who are minors to participate, ostensibly on the grounds of the stabbing of a Benedict student; but students openly talk about store "pay-offs."

On October 15, 1960, the Student Committee for Human Rights was formed to coordinate city-wide activity, and Allen students took up the brunt of activity. A series of meetings was attempted between representatives of this group and the mayor, City Council members, store managers, and Chamber of Commerce officials throughout the fall, accompanied by a letter-writing campaign. This continued until March, 1961, with little sitting-in or picketing going on; contributing to the lack of outward activity throughout this period was a certain amount of demoralization resulting from the fact that the first chairman of the Student Committee was caught "with his hand in the till," and also with his hand out to the stores, who were paying him to slow the demonstrations down. He was ultimately exposed and a new chairman elected. This, however, did not take place until early 1961.

Meanwhile, one store had some twelve students arrested during sit-ins, which resumed in early February. Thirteen more were arrested when they gathered outside the city jail to welcome those previously arrested when they came out on bail. On February 24, 1961, there was a regional conference of the NAACP in Greenville; a strategy meeting of student leaders was held in connection with the conference, and a large-scale demonstration was planned for Columbia on March 2. Over 200 students, divided into groups of a dozen or so, marched on the State Capitol that day. They were met by the governor's aide, Harry Walker, who was wearing a SLED badge. They were permitted to circle the building once, single-file, but the group continued to march despite orders to disperse. One hundred and ninety-two students were arrested for breach of the peace; all went out on bail.

On March 5, two leaders of the Student Committee were out on a routine check of a Woolworth sit-in when one of them, Lennie Glover, was seriously stabbed by an unknown assailant. The other Negro student, David Carter, was subsequently arrested for contributing to the delinquency of a minor, and thus built up a record of three arrests within a year. The assailant was never captured, and his victim required a serious spleen operation.

Following this event a boycott of Main Street was arranged by the Student Committee in connection with a Negro teacher's convention just prior to Good Friday (March 24-25-26), which resulted in what the students considered a real blow to Easter buying. In addition, for the local community, an Easter Lennie Glover No Buying Campaign was instituted. Regular picketing every day, preceded around noon by sitting-in, then began and continued for the remainder of the spring, 1961, semester. This was supplemented with hit-and-run commando sit-ins and attempts to get served at various private restaurants by light-skinned Negroes (sometimes posing as foreigners) accompanied by white instructors or white Divinity School students.

Such a campaign, it was estimated, could conceivably go on for a long time without definite results unless the boycott of the shopping area brought the merchants to capitulation. The latter eventually would only come about, observers believed, if competition from the suburban shopping centers began to be felt—unless that strain were counteracted by the pressure from the governor's offices, the bright dome of which commands all of Main Street. Main Street is to a considerable degree dependent on trade coming from soldiers at nearby Fort Jackson; there, the commanding officer has forbidden the men to participate in the demonstrations, but some men have contacted the students anyway. In the case of Columbia, again, state politics seem to have a great deal of importance. The governor, forced to maintain a posture of segregationism in the interest of his political career, could hardly allow the city to become a crack in the Southern armor, despite what might be the common-sense desires of Main Street merchants.

One of the complicating factors in Columbia was that the Negro leadership lacked a clear consensus. This was at least in part due to the political pressures placed upon the two college administrations concerned, and also to some competition between the two student bodies, both factors being even further complicated by the idiosyncratic factors of the personalities of the college heads and of the leaders of the student groups as well. At the same time a certain tension within the white community also played a role. The students continued to try to negotiate with representatives of business elements, not realizing that the State Administration's weight was sufficient to negate any progress in that direction. As a result a semi-detente did take place from the fall of 1960 until March, 1961; activity was sporadic and numbers participating few. In March, again under the impetus of the state-wide NAACP, the detente was called off and full-scale demonstrations resumed, supported by a widespread boycott of the downtown area.

This resumption of activity, marked by the knifing, can be said to indicate the beginnings of the reorganizational phase, a phase which might be expected to stretch out indefinitely into the future. Unlike some other situations, the Rock Hill and Columbia sit-in movements and their careers were probably dominated by the political interests of the state-wide administration, rather than by the deep-set opposition of local business leaders. Here the problem seemed to be that despite the possible willingness of local white leaders to settle the conflict, the political situation in the state as a whole put the governor into the position to veto local progress in at least these two cases. Thus the outcome of the reorganizational phase here probably will not be determined by the nature of the forces opposing each other inside the city, but rather by state-wide considerations of the same sort. Possibly a significant increase in Negro voter registration would change the situation sufficiently to force the gubernatorial powers to withdraw their interference, thus leaving localities to work out their own problems in their own ways, i.e. on the basis of local forces.

Tallahassee, Fla.

Although Tallahassee is not in a Black Belt state (in fact, is the capital of what in the South is considered a progressive state) it is in a Black Belt county nicknamed "little Mississippi," and total segregation prevails. This mixed situation produced a confusing picture insofar as the sit-ins were concerned; but ultimately the Deep South characteristics of Tallahassee won out over the other part, and no success was forthcoming.

The city, over 30% Negro in a county also over 30% Negro, was, in 1960, surrounded by two counties over 50% Negro. It is the home of Florida State University (white) and Florida A&M University (Negro), both state-run. One of the chief problems of the city is that its primary industry is government, hence the Negro middle class, despite a Negro population of nearly 16,000, is very small. There is no local Negro newspaper, and for some time there was no Negro attorney in the city. The backbone of the Negro middle class consists of ministers, who lacked unity in terms of their approach to race relations.

In 1956 a bus boycott, patterned after the Montgomery one, took place in Tallahassee, but without the more or less definite victory of Montgomery. The boycott, primarily organized and led by Rev. C. K. Steele and the Inter-Civic Council, was called off after the court decision which also ended the Montgomery boycott. But in early 1957, the Tallahassee City Commission put into effect a "seat-assignment plan" which circumvented the court decision, and in the face of considerable violence, pending a decision on appeal of a case involving the new plan, the boycott dwindled out.

In the summer of 1959 two girls, Patricia and Priscilla Stephens, students at Florida A&M University (FAMU) happened to be in Miami, and more or less by accident wandered into a CORE workshop. They joined CORE then and there, and upon their return to Tallahassee that fall, organized a chapter at FAMU. This began the incipient phase of the Movement. A national field secretary, Gordon Carey, helped to set up the initial organization. In November of that year several Negroes participated in a CORE project in Tallahassee, in which six or eight buses were tested for integrated service. There was no incident. Later that same month, several CORE members purchased tickets in the "white" waiting room of a bus company. There was one successful purchase, and one unsuccessful effort. The latter incident was reported to the Interstate Commerce Commission and other federal agencies, and an investigator from the ICC came to Tallahassee to follow this up early in 1960. A series of other tests followed, including "sit-ins," but there was no publicity, and Negroes left when refused service.

Then a wave of sit-ins broke out in North Carolina. In response to these, eight FAMU and high school students, working under CORE auspices, sat-in at a Woolworth counter for two and one-half hours on February 13, 1960. The counter was closed. There were no arrests.

A week later, on Saturday, February 20, after extensive briefing and "socio-drama," the group, now eleven in number, returned. By this time counteractive tactics had been organized. A squad of police, led by the mayor, asked the group to leave and when they did not, all were arrested. They were instantly bailed out by a local minister, Rev. Daniel B. Speed. Arraignment followed that Monday, and the group was charged with disturbing the peace by riotous conduct, and unlawful assembly. Five other charges were dropped by trial time, March 17; each of the participants was found guilty and sentenced to sixty days or $300. All but three chose to serve the sixty days—the first incident of "jail-versus-bail." Sit-ins again took place on March 5 and 12, both times with white students from Florida State University (FSU) participating. On the latter date, some 240 students were arrested, of both races.

Later in the day, some 1,000 FAMU students in groups of seventy-five again headed downtown, with posters asking the release of those arrested. The local Citizens Council barred the approach to one store with a small group of white men, variously armed. The Negroes turned back. This march, not organized by CORE, was hastily recruited at the college. Six of these students were subsequently arrested. When the marchers reached the downtown area they were ordered to disperse by the mayor. Before their allotted time of three minutes was up, police began firing tear gas. Several of the girls were hospitalized with burns. The governor then ordered students confined to campus. Some of those out on bail due to the February 20 sit-in were rearrested this time. None of the armed whites were arrested.

The following accounts from the *Florida Flambeau*, student newspaper at white FSU, are indicative of what occurred: after one group of sitters left a lunch counter,

"They were met near the Florida Theater by a crowd of white men, some carrying clubs and sticks, who ordered them to stop and hurled insults. Chanting 'no violence,' the Negroes stood for a few minutes, then moved back up to the park across from the Police Department. Homer Barrs, local soda fountain operator and executive director of the Florida Citizens Council, was in front of a white group carrying a three foot long club. The air of tension continued until the groups gradually dispersed. Asked if any of the white men carrying clubs were arrested, Police Chief Frank Stotamire said yesterday (March 15-M.O.): 'Ain't no law against a man walking down the street with somethin' in his hands. It's what he does with it.'"

Another incident, from the same source, involved the later march:

"A man representing the mayor called through a megaphone, 'I'm giving you three minutes to disperse.' Within two minutes policemen were lobbing tear gas bombs into the center of the group, which had halted and was breaking up. The line receded and became small groups of still silent students. A cluster of six to eight had crossed the street and was standing there indecisively. 'Let's get a few,' shouted a policeman. Six FAMU students, including one girl, were deposited, unprotestingly, in cars and driven off. The tear gas fumes made our eyes smart. The Negroes were doing their best to ward off the fumes with handkerchiefs and scarves . . ."

"Scarcely had we gotten in the car when a police car drove up in back; its occupants, six sturdy officers, surrounded us. Then the harangue began. 'Your folks would be ashamed of you!' 'Them niggers are better than you are.' . . . 'You're worse than niggers—you're sons-of-bitches.' . . ."

Of the eleven convicted, six were Negroes and five whites. While the sitters spent Easter in jail, state officials persuaded the students to call a halt to demonstrations, partly on the ground that Florida's Interracial Committee would be in a weaker position to deal with Tallahassee officials, and partly also that further agitation would throw the state's Democratic gubernatorial primary to segregationist candidate Farris Bryant. He won anyway. A series of visits to city officials and merchants followed this detente, backed up by a general boycott (which continued well into 1961). Finally an interracial committee was formed by a group of private citizens under the auspices of the Interdenominational Ministerial Alliance. But rather than help the situation, this group failed to secure any results, and its presence was taken by some people as an excuse to drop out of actively supporting sit-ins.

CORE alone decided to continue a series of sit-ins about December, 1960, but this effort was not as generally supported as the previous activities had been. Instead, the community, under the leadership of NAACP, continued to boycott most downtown chain stores, and published every so often "Traitors Lists" of Negroes who had been "buying segregation." The pattern of picketing in the fall and winter, 1960-61 was that the pickets and sitters would assemble, the mayor would order them to disperse after hoodlums assembled to harass them, and would order arrests if pickets did not leave. Harassers were not molested by police.

The CORE chapter at FAMU is not a recognized on-campus group. The NAACP chapter is recognized, but only because it refrains from open activity. Two regional USNSA meetings during the course of these events, originally scheduled for FAMU, had to be cancelled or moved off the campus at the last minute because they involved interracial groups. FSU has had no less a problem. At least one white student there was expelled, partly due to his participation in the sit-ins. And the college is one of the mainstays of USNSA's opposition group in the South, the all-white Southern University Student Government Association, founded primarily because of USNSA's strong pro-sit-in stand.

In early 1961, the sit-ins and picketing were brought to almost a total standstill because of the dwindling strength of the FAMU chapter, and the lack of support in the community for more direct action than boycotting. Despite Governor Collin's liberal stand on the sit-ins, the local Negro middle class was not sufficiently strong and independent to sustain the student protests in the face of local government opposition and Citizens Council activity.

The detente called by the students at the insistence of state officials for political reasons had the important side effect of dividing the consensus existing up until that time, and in the face of continued severe opposition by authorities many Negroes dropped out of the struggle and the reorganizational phase took on a rather sporadic and weak form.

The class structure of the Negro community (in that no independent group of Negroes existed who could effectively support the students financially or in terms of legal aid) seemed to be a crucial factor in the development of this schism within the Negro community. The students, left on their own, were quickly subdued or discouraged by the hostility of the authorities plus the apathy or hostility of college administration and some members of the Negro community. Thus once again it can be seen that the hostility of the outside group can only build up group identification and morale provided that a consensus exists within the subordinate group as to tactics and strategy. The white group had such a consensus, and the Negro group did not. Several idiosyncratic factors in terms of the personalities of some of the CORE activists probably also aided in alienating not only the possible support of some liberal whites, but also that of some Negro community leaders.

So far in our discussion we have had only three communities which are located in Deep Southern states: Atlanta, Rock Hill, and Columbia. The former two were strictly speaking not characteristic of the Deep South. Columbia, on the other hand, was. And, despite its location in a liberal

Southern state, so is Tallahassee. We now proceed to three other communities—Montgomery, Orangeburg, and Lawrenceville (the last of which is located in an Upper South state, but in a Deep South-type county) to see even more extreme pictures of the resistance to integration, and conditions under which the sit-in movement did not succeed.

Montgomery, Alabama

Montgomery, the capital of Alabama, is situated in the heart of the Black Belt which crosses the center of the state, east and west. It is situated in a county which in 1950 had over 50% Negro population (it is now 38.3%), and borders on Macon County (Tuskegee Institute), which still has a Negro proportion of 83.5%.

Montgomery is the city of Alabama State College, of Maxwell and Gunter Air Force Bases (nearby) and of Martin Luther King, Jr. and the Bus Boycott. One out of every fourteen civilians in the city work at the bases, which contributed $58 million into the local economy in 1955; one out of every seven families was an Air Force family, either civilian or military. Aside from this, Montgomery remains primarily a market city for cotton and lumber. There is little heavy industry, as contrasted to Birmingham, roughly four times as large, only ninety miles to the north. The lack of local industry forces some 63% of the Negro woman workers to be domestics; 48% of the Negro men are laborers or domestics. Complete segregation was the pattern; even in the area of voting. In 1954, before the boycott, there were only 2,000 registered Negro voters in the county out of an estimated 30,000 eligible.

Under these circumstances it is easy to predict, in retrospect, that despite the size of the city, and despite the presence of a Negro college, given the general Deep South characteristics of the city—particularly the fact that no integration existed in any area—that no success would be immediately forthcoming. The city therefore appears in our continuum as a clear-cut case of a sit-in movement which developed along strictly Deep Southern lines, with the appropriate outcomes, due to the predictable resistance.

The sit-in first came to Montgomery, capital of the Confederacy, on February 25, 1960 when a group of thirty-five students from the all-Negro State College took seats in the lunch room of the County Courthouse. The shop immediately closed, the sheriff arrived, and the students were ordered to line up single file. They were photographed. The governor then ordered them expelled, and issued a further order the next day that the president of the College, H. Councill Trenholm, expel any student involved in a sit-in. That same day the students held a protest rally at the College threatening that if the school was closed by the government, they would seek mass enrollment in white schools. Thus the incipient phase of the Movement lasted only a few minutes before local authorities proceeded to take action to crush it. Police action, supplemented by mob violence a few days later, remained standard operational procedure from this point on.

On Saturday, February 27, about twenty-five white men with toy baseball bats (billie clubs) roamed around downtown Montgomery. A Negro woman was attacked and beaten. The police made no arrests, although a news picture of the incident, including the person swinging the bat, was available.[131]

The following Monday some 800 Negroes in the city held a rally addressed by Rev. King, to plan another demonstration the very next day. Tuesday, March 1, somewhere between 1,000 and 1,200 Negroes marched from the campus of the College to the state capitol building, assembled on the steps where Jefferson Davis had been inaugurated, and sang the Star Spangled Banner and the Lord's Prayer. They then marched back to the campus. Leaders announced that a prayer meeting would be held the next Sunday, March 6, on the capitol steps.

As a result of these events (followed on the next day by an announcement by more than 700 students that they would quit if any of the thirty-five in the first sit-in were expelled) Governor John Patterson relented; that is, he ordered the expulsion of only nine leaders, and put twenty others on probation pending good behavior. The students then voted to boycott classes in protest, and that week a number of examinations were boycotted. A mass strike was approved for spring quarter registration, scheduled for Monday, March 7, by a vote of about 1,000 students at the College.

On Sunday, the 6th, crowds began to gather downtown early. Many whites came in from the country. About 1 p.m., city, county and state officials arrived. Highway patrolmen began lining the streets. Negroes met at the Dexter Avenue Baptist Church, the last building on Dexter Avenue where the street dead ends onto the Capitol grounds. Led by Rev. Ralph Abernathy, one of King's chief aides in the SCLC and in the 1956 Boycott, the Negroes began to come out of the church and down the steep steps toward a crowd estimated by this time at 5,000. The police held the Negroes back, and, as the leaders stood fast, some behind them began to flee back into the church. The fringes of the white crowd struck out at some Negroes, and there was a general retreat back into the church. Two fire trucks drove up at this point and hoses were aimed at the already retreating Negroes. Twenty mounted deputies held the crowd back until all the Negroes were in the church once more, then dispersed the people. Later in the course of the day Negroes came out in small groups and went home.

Two days later, on the second day of school registration, students staged their own demonstrations on campus. As about 600 students and faculty prepared to walk to the Capitol, thirty students and one faculty member were arrested on charges of disorderly conduct and disobeying an officer. Two others were taken into custody while trying to get to see the arrested students. At Tuskegee Institute, when news of the Montgomery events arrived, some 700 students stayed out of their classes in a sympathy strike. The following day police put a cordon around the State College to prevent further demonstrations, and registration was extended a day. On the 10th another campus demonstration was held, with no effort to move out into the city; Governor Patterson ordered a full-scale investigation pending his decision on whether or not to close the school altogether. The next day Bernard Lee, leader of the student movement and one of the nine expelled, announced that students would return to school March 14 for at least a week, perhaps two, before resuming their walk-out. This was done so that visitors to a State Teachers' Association meeting at the campus would not become involved in violence.

(A UPI wire story datelined Montgomery, revealed that in addition to sheriff's deputies, city and state police, "mobile civil defense workers" had joined in controlling the demonstrations on March 6.)

A series of minor incidents, more or less anti-climactic, followed this week of activity. The County Courthouse snack bar, where the original sit-in had taken place, was subsequently leased to a private concern; only county employees were allowed in, and Negro employees were allowed to take orders out only. Thirty-two students and one expelled student were fined $200 and costs each, and a faculty member $10 and costs. Two students were acquitted.

More than a year later, on August 4, 1961, the U.S. Circuit Court of Appeals for the Fifth Circuit ruled that the expulsion of six students in the case mentioned had been illegal, and ordered an injunction to that effect granted.

On March 22, 1960, seven Negro students applied for admission to all-white University of Alabama, Montgomery extension, as a result of the expulsion from State College; on the 29th President Trenholm disclosed that about 100 students had been ordered to leave the College, but said these cases were not connected with the demonstrations. Yet a demonstration was held on the same day in protest against the dismissals. Thirty sympathizers from Tuskegee also participated.

Two days later more incidents took place. Eleven white college students and their professor, R.D. Nesmith, all of MacMurray College, Jacksonville, Ill., professor Nesmith's wife, and seven Negro students with whom they had been lunching in a cafeteria, were arrested. All were released on bond after spending several hours in jail. They were on a sociological trip. Police raided the cafeteria, which was then closed down as a "public hazard" due to "defective equipment."

About the same time Bernard Lee, expelled student leader, was arrested on a vagrancy charge although he was employed at the time. A series of arrests followed throughout May and June; in early June Rev. Ralph King, a white Boston University student in Alabama to stand trial along with seven local Negroes on an unrelated integration charge, was again arrested together with a guest, Rev. Elroy Embree, one of the State expellees, while eating in Rev. King's hotel dining room.

On May 28, Dr. L.D. Reddick, biographer of Rev. King, Jr., and head of the Alabama State College history department for six years, who had been prominently identified as a sympathizer of the sit-in movement, resigned because his request for a long-term contract had been denied by President Trenholm. The practice was to renew contracts a year at a time. The resignation was to take effect August 31. This apparently interfered with Gov. Patterson's plans to take punitive measures, and at the next meeting of the State Board that controls the College, Patterson moved that Reddick be fired that same day, June 14. This was done. Reddick then took legal action on a breach of contract, and also against the governor for defamation of character. (Gov. Patterson had charged Reddick with having communist connections.) Meanwhile, however Reddick was forced to secure other employment, and he subsequently joined the faculty at Coppin State Teachers College in Baltimore. A few weeks after being fired, Reddick flew to Ghana as guest of President Kwame Nkrumah.

From this point on the Movement was slowed down to occasional sporadic demonstrations and sit-ins as the counteractive phase deteriorated into a reorganizational stage which continues, sometimes at a slower pace and sometimes faster, to this day. It is therefore necessary once again to modify the original series of stages contained in our propositions in the light of local circumstances. As in a few previous cases the detente never took place and the extreme nature of the counteraction sufficed to prevent any serious reorganization by the Negro community in terms of alternative tactics until the Freedom Rides over a year later. Even then the white community, apparently united in a consensus that segregation was to be maintained at all costs, was able to continue its drive to keep the integrationist movement under severe restrictions, even though not actually underground. As in Tallahassee, Columbia, and a number of other Deep Southern cities, communications between Negroes and whites broke down; they shared few or no assumptions about the conflict situation, which continues unresolved.

Early in the fall of 1960, when expelled students from the College sought admission to some California schools, a "gentlemen's agreement" not to admit them was uncovered at San Jose State College. St. John Dixon, one of the expelled students, had applied there and was not admitted; he had no honorable dismissal, and the College had refused to send a transcript of his marks.

Considerable legal action apart from the demonstrations in the city also took place in Montgomery. The trials of Dr. King himself formed one part of this picture. He had been arrested in Atlanta on February 28 on a hearing for extradition into Alabama to confront perjury charges in connection with tax evasion. An all-white jury heard the case and on May 28 acquitted King. Other charges were dropped later. Prayer services were held on the courthouse steps and King was represented by a battery of six attorneys. From the witness stand King charged that the trials were reprisals for his civil rights activities.

In another action on April 19, the City of Montgomery filed a $500,000 libel suit against the New York Times, with four Negro clergymen as defendants, due to an advertisement placed by the "Committee to Defend Martin Luther King and the Struggle for Freedom in the South." The Times refused to retract. Later, Governor Patterson said he was going to file an additional personal suit against the Times and the four Negroes whose names appeared as signers in Alabama State Court. On November 4, in Montgomery, an all-white jury awarded $500,000, a record amount, to Police Commissioner L. B. Sullivan, who claimed he was libeled by the ad. The clergymen claimed in defense that they had no part in the publication of the ad, and had not given their consent to having their names used. In 1961 the cases were still on appeal.

Subsequently, in 1962, a Lawyers' Committee on the Alabama Libel Suits was formed. It sent a letter and summary of several of the suits to Attorney General Robert F. Kennedy and to heads of state and local bar associations in which the Committee charged that the suits "are fraught with danger for all Americans . . . We refer specifically to the indiscriminate use of the libel laws of the State of Alabama as a device to stifle truthful reporting and open discussion of conditions arising in the South."[132] The summary cited seven libel actions claiming damages of $3,100,000 against the *New York Times* due to a series of articles by reporter Harrison Salisbury, the advertisements mentioned above, and a later suit against the Columbia Broadcasting System for $1,500,000 following a television broadcast on difficulties experienced by Negroes in registering to vote.

The Montgomery events are much more complex than the above story would at first indicate. The chief factor in assessing the failure of the Movement at that point seems to be the complete opposition of the state apparatus to the student movement, to the point that a number of observers have suggested that the whites had been invited to violence by the demagoguery of state and local officials. Police had on previous occasions permitted, or closed their eyes to, or participated in, segregationist rallies. White mobs previously had not been controlled by police. The police commissioner and the mayor, as well as the governor, had, by their public statements and actions, indicated their deep-seated opposition to the student movement, and these could be, and perhaps were, interpreted by certain elements as invitations to proceed with actions outside the law, actions that would not be (and were not) punished. During the period of demonstrations, police intruded at meetings, and harassed campus centers. Negro homes were entered without warrant. Several expellees were arrested for vagrancy. So widespread was this activity that Rev. King, joined by Walter Reuther and Roy Wilkins, appealed to the Federal Government for intervention. (There was no response.)

The Safety Commissioner of Montgomery, L.B. Sullivan, has been the guest speaker at rallies of the Citizens Council, and has made his position—that the forces of the law will stand for the preservation of Southern "traditions"—clear. Such a speech was made by him for the WCC in April, 1960. The scars of bombings which took place during the Bus Boycott are still visible in the city.

Two representatives of the American Friends Service Committee's Southeastern Regional Office, in Montgomery to set up a summer voter registration project, were questioned by police, and one was photographed and fingerprinted in the process. They reported a "police state" atmosphere in which tapped phones were common, and repeated a remark made by a white minister that the majority of Montgomery policemen were members of the Klan. The project was cancelled as a result.

Under such circumstances the Movement was driven virtually underground.

Orangeburg, South Carolina

Orangeburg is Deep South in the traditional sense of that term. The seat of agricultural Orangeburg County (60% Negro), Orangeburg is one of the very few smaller cities (population 13,852, including 5,493 Negroes, or 42%) in the Deep South to experience a sit-in movement. The fact in itself is extraordinary; that it did not succeed, and was suppressed with the utmost resistance is not particularly surprising under these circumstances.

Orangeburg County has about 3,500 farms; less than half its operators are white. Nearly 30% are tenants. In the city itself there are eight firms which employ over 100 persons—none more than a plywood concern's top 508. The remainder include two meat packers, three textile concerns (cotton is raised in the area), a bakery, and a chemical concern. The county leads the state in the production of dairy products, meat products (hogs and beef), cotton, pecans, soy beans, and small grains such as oats, wheat, barley, and rye. Population, according to census and Chamber of Commerce figures, is dropping, again typical of many rural Deep South communities.

City Population

1930	8,776
1940	10,521
1950	15,322
1960	13,852

Orangeburg becomes notorious for its size only because of the presence in the outskirts of town of two Negro schools: South Carolina State College, a major institution of well over 1,500 students, and Claflin College, a smaller Methodist school of approximately 450 students (coeducational).

Action in the field of integration was not new to the community. In the summer of 1955, following various U.S. Supreme Court decisions on school integration, fifty-seven Negroes petitioned for local public school integration; in response to this a local Citizens Council was organized and subsequently a number of Negro merchants among the petitioners found their supplies suddenly curtailed. Various petitioners found credit hard to come by. Negroes then retaliated against white merchants prominent in the Citizens Council by circulating a list of twenty-three local firms to be boycotted. A $50,000 fund was set up to aid Negro victims of the white boycott, including some $20,000 donated by NAACP. Because of the involvement of South Carolina State College faculty people in this, State Representative Jerry M. Hughes of Orangeburg demanded and got an investigation of NAACP activities at the College. Parts of both student and faculty bodies protested this, and expressed approval of the NAACP. South Carolina's Governor Timmerman claimed to have information indicating that "subversive elements" were going to sponsor a demonstration against the government. A student protest strike followed; students presented the college president with a list of grievances, including protests against the investigation, and protests that the College was patronizing white merchants on the boycott list. The strike lasted one week; one student was expelled, 25 others were asked not to return, and the contracts of several faculty members were not renewed. Given these developments, the investigating committee held no further hearings.[133]

As result of this purge, South Carolina State College was for a time on probation with accreditation agencies because it did not have a sufficient number of holders of the Ph.D degree on the faculty, which is all-Negro. This atmosphere still holds; during the active spring of 1960, the student newspaper at SCSC, *The Collegian*, maintained a total silence on sit-ins in Orangeburg and elsewhere. Needless to say, there is almost total segregation in the city; in the movies, Negroes can get into balconies only. But Negroes have registered to vote, and have voted in fair numbers.

Sometime in February, 1960, after hearing of sit-ins elsewhere, a group of students tried unsuccessfully to negotiate with various variety store owners and managers. The original group quickly organized the Orangeburg Student Movement Association, which coordinated activities between the two colleges (which are geographically separated only by a fence anyway). At Claflin, an NAACP chapter headed by Tom Gaither (later a field secretary for CORE) formed the organized apparatus; at SCSC no such organizations are permitted.

On March 1, some 400 Negro students, organized into groups of seventy-five or so, marched from the campus area to the central plaza of Orangeburg. Police ordered them to put down their placards and they did. The students returned to campus without further incident. This was the first major demonstration; there had been small-scale sit-ins on February 25 and 26. An anti-picketing ordinance prevented further demonstrations of that kind, and large-scale training sessions in nonviolence were being held back at the campus of Claflin College. Thus incipient phase activity resulted in immediate countermeasures.

Following the march, lunch counters remained closed for some two weeks. A boycott of variety stores was begun. Mayor S. Clyde Fair warned that further demonstrations would not be tolerated without a permit. He said local demonstrations were "the outgrowth of a movement engineered by outside non-Southern organizations to force integration . . . to foment troubles that might be used to influence the current Senate debate in Washington on the so-called Civil Rights Bill," thus echoing the remarks made a few days earlier (and headlines throughout the South) by Senator Richard Russell of Georgia. Local editorial comment in the *Times and Democrat* echoed these sentiments again: ". . . those carrying out the march . . . (are) organized and directed by outside agitators . . . this pattern of mass demonstrations follows communist lines . . . further increasing tension and ill-will . . ."

On March 14, lunch counters reopened in the city. The next day, coinciding with major demonstrations at Rock Hill and Columbia, some twelve groups of seventy-five to one hundred students each headed by different routes to downtown Orangeburg. The first group was stopped by police, but when officials swerved to interrogate a second group, the first went through, the only one actually to stage sit-ins that day. The rest (with the exception of only one group, which turned back) were asked to return to campus, and when they refused and continued to march into town, fire hoses and tear gas were turned on the groups. The jails filled. Then police herded other students into a make-shift stockade. Other students, not able to be arrested, went back to college and brought dry clothes and blankets for those in the stockade. Over 500 were actually held; finally only 388 stood trial.

Aside from the gas and fire-hoses, it had been raining, and weather was cold. None had umbrellas. One coed, a blind girl, was knocked to the ground by a fire-hose. A few other students were arrested later while giving aid to those inside the stockade—throwing blankets over, etc. Those inside the jails were not much better off; one student reported his incarceration in a cell with seventeen others, six beds and one non-operative toilet. But within hours all were bailed out, many on strength of property put up by faculty members.

The first group was finally tried on March 17. Governor Hollings' ever-present aide, Harry Walker, was on the scene. Meanwhile the administration of SCSC was giving every assurance that further demonstrations would be discouraged, and the Chairman of the College's Board of Trustees said further participants would be expelled. The Student Activities Director a few days later read a statement to the court warning students (back on March 2) to be prudent and further warning of disciplinary action if anything happened. On the 19th, the first group of fifteen to be tried was found guilty, and fined $50 or thirty days. They appealed, as did all subsequently convicted. None have served sentence.

The trials continued in batches well into June. Ultimately 341 were convicted, and forty-seven were thrown out mainly due to lack of time on the court calendar. Most of these forty-seven had been arrested previously at one time or another anyway. In some cases, subsequent events and arrests made up for the temporary reprieve. Charges in all cases were breach of the peace.

While the trials were going on, sporadic sit-ins continued. One of these, on May 19, resulted in the closing down of Kress' lunch counter for the entire day, and the closing of the store for some forty-five minutes. Three anonymous bomb threats were received. But the manager refused to have the students arrested. On several other occasions small groups of four to six students were arrested.

On March 26, several Klansmen in full regalia posed before a burning cross alongside highway U.S. 301. The same day cross burnings were reported at Greenville, Columbia, Charleston, and Greenwood. The Klansmen, who identified themselves as members of Klavern number 829 of Orangeburg, had permission of the owner of the land to be there and were not interfered with.

On May 5, the State Senate held a second reading of a bill, already passed by the State House of Representatives, making it illegal for a person to refuse to leave a place of business when asked to do so by the management.

The Orangeburg events made the *Congressional Record* on March 18, 1960, when Senator Paul Douglas, debating the 1960 Civil Rights Bill, said: ". . . then the 400, still dripping wet after this experience, sang 'God Bless America.' How many of us . . . would have had the patience to sing 'God Bless America?'. . ."

When students returned to the local campuses in September, sit-ins were resumed on a small scale, but without effect. On October 12, six were arrested, the first to be charged with trespassing under the new state law. Due to a mix-up, four of these did a half-day on the work-gang before bond was posted. On Election Day some 150 students walked around the town square twice, then returned to campus without incident. Later in the month there were more arrests, including the student body president of SCSC. A march on the jail was cancelled at the last minute. The students asked the president of the college what he would do, now that the president of the student body was in jail. He made no reply.

In the spring of 1961, there were some negotiations with the mayor, and he at one time indicated he might appoint a biracial committee. But he changed his mind, stating that the student participation on March 2 in demonstrations at Columbia demonstrated the students' bad faith. In the opinion of some student leaders, this was merely an "out."

All of these events include the incipient and counteractive phases of the Orangeburg movement. A formal detente never took place, and, while some sporadic sitting did occur, no real resurgence of the movement during that year or the following year was apparent. In Tallahassee, Montgomery, and Orangeburg we have seen how a large degree of violence, condoned by the authorities, served to prevent such a resurgence of the movement. It has become apparent in the meantime that violence is not really needed to bring about this result—the "Mississippi method," as utilized during the Freedom Rides there in 1961, will do just as well—but perhaps it was only the danger of federal intervention which led to a reanalysis of tactics and a redefinition of a consensus along these newer lines. At this earlier point, during 1960, authorities apparently did not feel themselves deterred by either federal or commercial (loss of business) forces from permitting mob violence in these types of communities. In our discussion of the less resistant communities we have seen how some constraints were effective in various degrees in at least preventing mob violence.

Added to the difficulties facing the Movement in terms of local government was a certain amount of organizational bickering. One of the first leaders of the Orangeburg Student Movement Association, the representative from SCSC, had to be removed due to constant internal bickering. In the fall, a demonstration in Orangeburg was severely criticized by NAACP representatives, who alleged that CORE had acted irresponsibly. NAACP implied, or at least students inferred, that that group would not defend cases unless they had been initiated under NAACP auspices. Further damage was done by an NAACP official's statement that he would not support a jail-versus-bail campaign. This resulted in a degree of disillusionment with national organizations, and further local efforts were conceived independently, assisted by the Orangeburg Movement for Civic Improvement, a community group.

Lawrenceville, Virginia

Lawrenceville is the extreme: a community in which nothing very much happened, yet in which a Negro college, St. Paul's College (former St. Paul's Polytechnic Institute), finds its home. This writer went to Lawrenceville to find out why nothing happened. In a sense, then, Lawrenceville is a control, since it is one of the few communities with a Negro school, yet without any significant civil rights movement.

Lawrenceville is the County Seat of Brunswick County, which borders on North Carolina. According to both 1950 and 1960 census figures, Negro population in the county exceeds 50%, though inside the city limits it is now only 37%.

Both the city and the county are losing population:

	City Population	County
1950	2,239	20,136
1960	1,940	17,733

The population seems to be old; there have been steady drops in pre-school and first-grade registrations in past years. As to why, several reasons are possible contributors—many of the plantations in the county are now occupied by the owner only, and but one or two, or no, tenants; large portions of land have been put in the "soil bank" or bought by timber companies recently; the county tobacco allotment has been cut by the U.S. Department of Agriculture from 6,648 acres to 5,019 acres in ten years. In other words, it is the extreme case of a Deep South plantation county.

Lawrenceville is an isolated, small town. It is built away from U.S. Route No. 1 by some miles, and is not on a railroad track. The town is completely segregated. About 750 Negroes were registered to vote, having paid a poll tax, in 1960 for the whole county—somewhat low, considering that the county population, which is nearly 60% Negro, is over 17,000.

In 1960 the International Ladies Garment Workers Union lost an election at the Lawrenceville Manufacturing Company by vote of 147-68.

The Citizens Council exists in strength in nearby Blackstone, Va., but there is no active Council in Lawrenceville. Local Negroes believe, however, that in case of "trouble" the local police force would call on the Council in Blackstone.

There is no NAACP in the city; no Negro lawyer and no Negro bondsman. St. Paul's, a Protestant Episcopal school, has an enrollment of just under 500, with 400 living on campus, including some faculty. It abandoned trade courses just a few years ago, and graduated its first B.A. degree in 1959.

According to the *Student Journal* (May, 1960), a group of students, after investigating the Lawrenceville segregation situation, concluded that demonstrations would receive "inadequate police protection." In addition, they said, "there have been no active signs of community support. Under these conditions it is unwise and unsafe for us to stage an active sit-down strike. Since we do not give much patronage to the two small white drug stores, we have decided to hit where it hurts the most . . . Lawrenceville's segregated State Theater. We are now taking a recess from the movie until the management decides to let us sit where we please." Students also set up a Fund for Equal Rights. There was a complete blackout of this in the local newspaper, and it is considered quite possible that most of the white townspeople never knew that this was going on.

The idea of the "sit-out" was originally presented by a nucleus of seven students, who took it to the faculty-student council. This had been tried a few years earlier, when management waited the students out until summer vacation. Despite the fact that there was no picketing, students did not return in numbers to patronize the theater in the fall of 1960.

The administration, in view of the local atmosphere, was opposed to open sitting-in or picketing, and this factor, added to the police problem plus lack of Negro community support, convinced student leaders not to go ahead with anything more drastic.

The theater, in the course of the spring, 1960, was (for this or other reasons not determinable) in danger of closing, and put forward all kinds of incentives to visit the movies, including free passes, lower prices, and the like.

Some $200 to $250 was collected by students for support of activity elsewhere, but aside from that, there was no further action. The administration of the College finally established an on-campus movie theater which showed the same features as the town movie at lower prices.

Students at the College in 1961 reported that efforts to start an on-campus NAACP chapter were running into snags because there was a difficulty in getting 25 people to pay membership fees. Students had virtually no contact with the Movement elsewhere, although one student did attend the White House Conference on Youth, in 1960.

In Lawrenceville, therefore, the Movement died during its incipient stage. It never actually got to the point of being termed a "movement." It may be possible to suggest several tentative reasons for this. One is that the students at St. Paul's were unable to develop that degree of group identification and morale necessary to a movement, to the sacrifices entailed in it, and to the enthusiasm necessary to get it off the ground. Partly this may be due to the relative isolation of St. Paul's—even in isolated Orangeburg there were two schools, one of which was large; and while the students at Rock Hill were certainly few in number, they were influenced by strong adult leadership and a local tradition of integrationist activity. Partly, too, it may have been due to the apathy or even opposition of the college administration to a more active movement.

Another, and overlapping, factor was not the degree of violence, since there was neither action nor violence, but the perception in the minds of the students of what might have taken place in the counteractive phase had there been one. The students who might have taken the leadership of a sit-in movement perceived conditions as being so adverse that they hesitated to engage in direct action at all, and when they finally did so it was not the kind of action which confronted the white forces of the community directly—that is, it was a *withdrawal* from conflict (in the form of boycott) rather than an active engagement in conflict. This perception, then, realistic as it probably was given the general social background of the community, acted in the place of counteraction and functioned in the same manner, hence cutting off further development.

FIVE

Conclusions

A. *The Results of the Movement—An Overview*

At this point it might be valuable to summarize what the Southern Negro Student Movement accomplished during its first year of operation, the year which can be marked by the various stages of the "sit-ins." Demonstrations took place in approximately 104 communities, including marches, mass rallies, boycotts, sit-ins, stand-ins, etc., for the purpose of changing local customs of segregation. Of these 104 communities we have sufficient information on sixty-nine(analyzed in an earlier section) so as to be able to ascertain the result. In thirty-five other communities demonstrations were not sustained and/or information is not available upon which to make a judgment concerning success or failure. These thirty-five are listed alphabetically below (only 1960 included):

Annapolis, Md.	Jackson, Miss.
Bluefield, W.Va.	Jackson, Tenn.
Charleston, S.C.	Jefferson City, Mo.
Columbia, Mo.	Lenoir, N.C.
Columbia, Ga.	Monroe, N.C.
Covington, Ky.	Murphysboro, Ill.
Douglasville, Ga.	Myrtle Beach, S.C.
Deland, Fla.	Newport News, Va.
Denmark, S.C.	Orlando, Fla.
Dunn, N.C.	Pensacola, Fla.
Elizabeth City, N.C.	Rutherford, N.C.
Fayetteville, N.C.	St. Louis, Mo.
Florence, S.C.	Sarasota, Fla.
Fredericksburg, Va.	Shreveport, La.
Huntingdon, W.Va.	Starkville, Miss.
Huntsville, Ala.	Suffolk, W.Va.
Hyattsville, Md.	Whaleyville, Va.
	Xenia, Ohio

In fourteen of these thirty-five communities at least some facilities had been integrated by March, 1961, according to a CORE report dated March 10.

At least 119 integrationists had been arrested, and at least seventeen of these had been convicted.

Of the sixty-nine communities under study, there was some measure of success in forty, while results were negative in twenty-nine, a success rate of 56.5%

In the 104 communities concerning which figures were gathered for this study during the year 1960, a total of 2,875 integrationists were arrested. This figure, while probably not exact, is probably fairly close to the actual total. Of these, 991 were convicted, about 100 acquitted, and the remaining cases are either unknown as to outcome, or trial was postponed and demonstrators released on bail bond. Relatively few of those convicted, perhaps less than 200, actually served any part of a sentence; most are free on appeals.[134]

The "casualty" side of the consequences of social conflict was not, however, limited to arrests. During this first year about forty-five persons were expelled from schools, and about fifteen persons were fired from various positions, including about ten college teachers. One professor at Baton Rouge, Louisiana, died probably as a result of the strain imposed by local civil rights activities. One person in Houston, Texas, was mutilated, the letters "KKK" being carved on his chest. Dozens of Negro students and white sympathizers were beaten, physically harassed while engaging in sit-ins (by such methods as dropping lighted cigars on their clothing, throwing food and hot liquids on them, spraying them with insecticides and ammonia, and the like), and threatened with all manner of violence. Hundreds have been sprayed by fire-hoses, in at least one case in sub-freezing weather, and have suffered exposure to tear-gas and police dogs. Beatings and harassment have been accepted so much as a matter of course that incidents are no longer recorded by participants, hence records are no longer up-to-date or significant (particularly if one includes the period of the Freedom Rides and voter registration). Estimates at this point can at best be very rough.

State-supported institutions have been particularly quick to act. In Montgomery, Alabama State College expelled nine student leaders. At Kentucky State College in Frankfort, twelve students were expelled and two teachers fired. At Southern University in Baton Rogue seventeen students were expelled. At Alabama State College Professor Lawrence D. Reddick, chairman of the Department of History, was dismissed for his part in the sit-ins there. In Tallahassee a music instructor, Richard Haley, was fired by the Florida Agricultural and Mechanical University. Others may have been expelled or fired but, on grounds of expediency, never brought their cases to the attention of any agency, and hence remain unrecorded. Also unrecorded are instances of students and professors who have refrained from engaging in activity or research relating to civil rights as a result of local pressure.[135]

The cases of academic freedom and tenure coming to the attention of the American Association of University Professors increased from thirty-seven in April 1961 to fifty-five one year later; twenty-three of the current cases involve Southern institutions, and a majority of censured institutions are in the South. While much of this comes at a date later than the subject matter of this paper, the atmosphere pictured is an outgrowth of the sit-in movement, which stimulated the actions resulting in later infringements of academic freedom and civil liberties.[136]

By August, 1960, some twenty-seven Southern cities and counties had opened some facilities to customers regardless of race; about nine had been opened as early as June. These twenty-seven pioneering communities were: Miami, Chapel Hill, Charlotte, Concord, Durham, Elizabeth City, High Point, Greensboro, Salisbury, Winston-Salem, Frankfort, Knoxville, Nashville, Austin, Corpus Christi, Dallas, Galveston, San Antonio, Alexandria, Arlington County, Fairfax County (Virginia), Falls Church, Fredericksburg, Hampton, Norfolk, Portsmouth, and Williamsburg. Non-Southern cities of Xenia, Ohio, Las Vegas, Baltimore, Kansas City, Missouri, and Oklahoma City had also desegregated some facilities.

The majority of these cities integrated quietly during the summer, after students had gone home, in actions originally spurred by the student demonstrations. Almost all of the above-listed communities had some kind of local demonstrations.

On October 13, 1960, representatives of four variety store chains, Woolworth, Kress, Grant, and McCrory-McLellan, met with representatives of USNSA for a clarification of views. The chain stores later released a statement in which they claimed that they had negotiated in good faith, that facilities had been integrated by them in 112 cities in the South during 1960, in 75% of which no demonstrations had taken place, and further claimed that the stores concerned opposed arrests and prosecution of students involved in sit-ins. USNSA did not endorse the statement. Timothy Jenkins, former student sit-in leader at Howard University and then national affairs vice-president of USNSA pointed out in the *National Student News*, official USNSA newspaper (November 1960) that no progress at all had been made by the chains in Alabama, Arkansas, Georgia, Louisiana, South

Carolina, and Mississippi; and that USNSA had "some reservations about accepting at face value" the stores' claim that their people refused to order arrests. In fact, while some of the stores were following a fairly consistent policy of refusing to have arrests made, others were asking for arrests in some communities. The national chairman of CORE, Mr. Charles R. Oldham, who had taken part in other negotiations with Woolworth, Kress, and Grant Stores, also held that the boycott be continued at least until charges against students were dropped by store managers.

By March 10, 1961, CORE reported that 138 communities had integrated at least some facilities since February 1, 1960. In thirty-four other communities, CORE said, demonstrations had taken place, but without result. Of these thirty-four, seventeen were in the Deep South states of Alabama, Georgia, Louisiana, South Carolina; in Mississippi there were no demonstrations noted, and no integrated facilities by that date. Slightly under 60% of the 138 integrated communities had had no recorded demonstrations, not the 75% of the chain stores' 112 cities. Also, the basis of "integration" was not reported: all downtown stores serving on an equal basis is one kind of integration; a neighborhood cigar store in a Negro district agreeing to sell cigarettes to Negroes is another kind.

The effectiveness of selective buying, or boycott, in obtaining integration, is open to a wide range of dispute. Woolworth has 18% of its stores in the South; sales during the first five months of 1960 were up 11.8% nationally. Kress, with nearly 60% (151 out of 266) stores in the South, had sales running 4.6% below 1959 sales by May. Dividends dropped from $.50 a share to $.25 a share during the second quarter, and were eliminated for the third quarter of the year. Business in the South was down 15%-18%, the Kress public relations people admitted. But Kress earnings had been dropping anyway, and a decline in 1960 had been expected. Precisely how much of it was due to boycotts was not known; Kress admitted the picketing was not doing them any good.

Stockholders' meetings of Woolworth, Kress, Grant, and Greyhound were pressured by integrationist groups, primarily CORE. CORE picketed both Woolworth and Kress board meetings in 1960, and a former Florida A&M University student spoke to Woolworth stockholders at their meeting in Watertown, N.Y. Kress, however, declared stores would continue to follow local customs, and this policy was in general followed by the others.[137]

The above represent the tangible results of the sit-ins. The less tangible results, such as the effects upon the 1960 election, are open to more dispute.

180

Then there is a range of intangible results which cannot be measured or accurately observed. First, there were the pressures put on other communities to integrate before the demonstrations had a chance to spread; this included the formation of local biracial committees to bring integration about. Second, there was the "splash effect" of the sit-ins and the student organizations upon the Negro community locally and nationally, in terms of a new concern for social action, a broadening of interest for action in related fields such as employment opportunity, voting, etc., and a general raising of the level of morale, consciousness and pride among American Negroes in general. Included in this category would be the unanticipated growth in numbers and financial resources of all civil rights organizations, particularly NAACP, CORE, and local Negro betterment groups and civic improvement groups; and the renewed interest in civil rights by white liberal organizations of all types, particularly the churches.

Thirdly, after the demise of the more blatant forms of McCarthyism, the sit-in movement resulted in a reawakening of the American campus in general. As many as 50,000 American students have participated to some degree in the Movement or its support in the North—even if only to the extent of contributing money. Dozens of campuses which had seen no social concern since the 1930s or later 1940s, had committees formed, contributed students to local picket lines around Northern outlets of chain stores, and the like. A series of regional support organizations have been formed. And from the ranks of the supporters of civil rights in student circles have come new recruits for a host of other student causes which were, prior to the sit-ins, almost non-existent—abolition of the House Committee on Un-American Activities, abolition of capital punishment (the Chessman case), abolition of compulsory ROTC, liberal campus political parties, and peace action.

The subsequent development of the Southern Negro Student Movement in its semi-institutionalized stage has been discussed in terms of the problems confronting the Movement as to its direction. Following the initial successes, and the failures, the Movement developed a series of tentatively outreaching bridges toward what might be the next development. These tentative developments came about more or less by accident, to meet immediate needs of particular populations.

(1) The sit-ins as such continued mopping-up operations in those communities which had strong and persisting student organizations. In cities where some facilities had been integrated, sitters turned their attention to

181

suburban shopping centers and/or "stand-ins" at movie theaters. SNCC officially called for a "second phase" coordinated stand-in at theaters for February 1, 1961, the first anniversary of the sit-ins. Northern groups were urged to boycott and put other pressures on local outlets of theater chains. A sit-in took place at the offices of Paramount in New York City.

However, the initial glamour of the sit-ins had to a large degree worn off in the North, and response to these calls was not overwhelming. In the Deep South initial-phase sitting and picketing continued throughout the spring semester, 1961, but the continuing drain of this reorganizational phase-type struggle cut down on the number of students carrying on these activities. In the Upper South mopping up operations also did not require either the numbers or the continuing enthusiasm of the earlier campaigns.

(2) With the turn of the year (to 1961) the condition of Negroes in Fayette and Haywood Counties, Tennessee, came to the attention of both students and adults in liberal and civil rights organizations, and effort was turned in this direction in order to assist, financially and materially, these beleaguered people. Largely tenant farmers, share-croppers, and small-holding farmers, the Negroes of these two Mississippi River counties had been turned off their land as part of a campaign to discourage them from registering to vote. As a result hundreds of families faced the winter without food or shelter. Ultimately, a "tent city" was constructed. Students, both North and South, became involved in these efforts.[138] The campaign functioned to keep up the interest of students in the civil rights field, that is, as one of the tentative transitional campaigns which helped to sustain the Southern Student Movement.

(3) The most significant campaign serving to sustain the Movement pending a long-range strategic decision as to its direction was one more or less deliberately conceived to do just that: the CORE-sponsored "Freedom Rides." These also directed the attention of the civil rights movement to the field of interstate commerce, and, due to mob violence in Anniston, Birmingham, and Montgomery, Alabama, forced the intervention of federal authorities directly for the first time in the current developments. A new campaign of direct action followed the initial arrest of the twenty-seven original Freedom Riders, and by August, 189 persons had traveled to Jackson, Mississippi, and had been arrested. Most served some time at the State Prison Farm in lieu of bail. The Freedom Rider campaign served as a shot in the arm to civil rights groups just when interest on the part of Southern Negro students seemed to be flagging in the other channels in

Southern Negro students seemed to be flagging in the other channels in which they had been directing activity. The Freedom Rider campaign put the students into contact with adult members of the Negro community in the Deep South areas out of touch with Negro colleges for the first time; the Jackson community in particular maintained its contact with the student riders sponsored by SNCC. This organization subsequently shifted its focus of action to a field vaguely reminiscent of the student Populists who "went to the people" in Czarist Russia of the 1880s and 90s. SNCC organizers proceeded into the field in a very literal sense.

(4) As 1961 drew to a close the political side of civil rights, in the form of a campaign to increase Negro voter-registration in Deep Southern communities, began to occupy the attention of the student movement. SCLC and SNCC began to issue statements, supported by educational conferences and training sessions, suggesting that its member groups begin to concentrate on grass-roots political needs. The campaign of a Negro for Congress in Mississippi, the organization of a newspaper, *The Mississippi Free Press*, to speak for the Negro community, the sustained campaign of the white community against these efforts, including violence and even murder,[139] followed.

The voter-registration focus, while requiring personnel possibly as vast as the initial sit-in movement, did not attain such personnel, nor is it likely to do so. The personal risks faced by the SNCC voter-registration campaigner in the Deep South are much greater, hence requiring a far higher degree of personal commitment. Further, the time and place of these efforts often require that the student leave school, give up important summertime job opportunities which would ordinarily help him financially through the school months, and possibly interrupt his education permanently because of imprisonment—imprisonment under conditions far harsher than those faced by most students arrested in the course of sit-ins, and involving longer and more serious sentences and fines.

Nevertheless, with the voter-registration focus the student movement appeared to have found a new field of action not only likely to be long-term, but necessarily dangerous, hence militant. The semi-institutionalized student movement, forced to cope with this type of campaign, can be expected to become more institutionalized, for the nature of the campaign mechanically requires more formal organization and more efficient organizational work. In terms of the traditional literature of social movement, the agitator of large masses is likely to be replaced by the technician who, under the conditions of the Deep South, is able to engineer the registration of large numbers of Negro voters. One can, in fact, suggest that the semi-underground nature of this type of campaign may actually result in the type of over-organization discussed by observers of the Bolshevik type of political party—the vanguard party.[140] This highly conjectural point may of course never be proven or disproven, for the movement may shift its field completely one or more times in the next few years, just as it has shifted its field in the past few years. But it would require an extraordinary turn of events to resurrect the kind of mass enthusiasm and participation of the early months of the sit-ins in 1960.

B. *The Framework of the Study—Concluding Remarks*

By utilizing the literature of social movement theory, and combining it with the work of some of the theorists of the dynamics of conflict, the writer has sought to fill a theoretical gap between the data of Negro social movements in the United States, and social movement and conflict theory, though not fully. We share, in addition to a theoretical interest, the value of Dr. C. Wendell King that social movements

> "are one kind of agency for deliberately altering the social order and for attempting to predetermine events and situations of the future. To the extent that social planning operates on the basis of principles . . . it must draw upon scientifically established findings, some of which can be derived from the study of social movements."[141]

That is, one does not choose, fortuitously, to study a social movement. One studies it with certain sympathies if not for the movement, then at least for (and sometimes against) the values for which it seeks to conduct a struggle. So the student of, say, fascism studies the movement in an effort to understand its causes, processes, and results in order that he may, by a more ordered, precise and scientific understanding, engage in the kind of social action (or perhaps advise others who engage in social action) which will in the future prevent, forestall, or in some other way damage a movement the values and goals of which he deems harmful to society, and to his own value system.

Probably more frequent, in the literature, is the converse: the student of civil rights movements more often is sympathetic to the cause and, in seeking to bring to its study some scientific precision does this so that, in some way, he may help the movement understand itself better and by so doing carry out its goals in a more effective manner. This may result in disillusionment as the facts which present themselves undermine the student's preconception and prejudices; or the disillusionment may come later as the student finds the movement unwilling or unprepared to accept the suggestions coming from one who stands to a degree outside the immediate struggle. Or he may influence the movement or some of its participants to one degree or another. But all of these things are latent consequences, for the study is there and the scientific chips fall where they may, regardless of the wishes of the student. Who is to say, after all, that the opponent cannot learn from the findings of the sympathizer? Thus the sociological contribution must stand apart from the values of the sociologist, even though these same values directed the sociologist to his subject in the first place.

In the introductory pages to parts II (The Social Movement Concept and its Application to the Study of the American Negro) and IV (The Dynamics of Inter-Group Community Conflict) we have briefly summarized some of the more important trends of the two chief focii of this paper: social movements, and conflict theory. Let us summarize the particular place of our research within these two fields.

The two fields in question can actually be viewed as two parts of a more basic concept: social change, with the movement part as one outcome of certain kinds of social conditions, or prerequisites, and the conflict part indicating a certain framework of change, that is, one which encounters various modes of resistance. Not all change takes place through the format of social movements, but all social movements are responses to certain conditions which "require" (in a social sense) some change. These certain conditions have been discussed earlier in terms of such concepts as relative deprivation, group identification, and actionable social context. We have brought these concepts to bear upon a specific social movement and have attempted to show how they conditioned its birth and growth. Movements, as the literature has amply demonstrated, go through certain phases which on the one hand may be used to predict the behavior of these particular kinds of social organizations, and on the other form a convenient tool for the ordering of data about a movement so that such data is not a simple collection of haphazard information, but rather differentiates the wheat from the chaff. In turn this aids not only in making predictions, but also (on the basis of experience with earlier movements) to help us participate in the kind of social action which will translate our particular value systems with regard to the movement effectively.

The particular kind of social change which gives rise to social movements implies also a resistance to change. The social conditions which generate much resistance and help determine its forms and outcomes are obviously of crucial importance to the participant in social movements, and to the student of them. The second half of this paper is primarily devoted to this problem, both in terms of the party which resists (and what socio-economic and political conditions appear to affect this resistance) and of the party which is attempting to effect the change. Community conflict, just as movements in a more overall sense, goes through phases, the development of which is conditioned by the kind of resistance which a dominant group offers to the changes demanded by a subordinate group. In our study we have found this opposition to change to be highly related to the presence or absence of conditions commonly associated with the term "Black Belt," or "Deep South," the chief of which seems to be the ratio of population between the subordinate Negro group and the dominant white group. Ten communities have been examined in terms of the degree of resistance to integration present, and they have been ordered along a continuum of resistance which is related to the greater or lesser presence of these traditional "Black Belt" characteristics.

This paper has therefore attempted to synthesize from the literature of social movements, and conflict, in order to present the data of the Southern Negro Student Movement in such a way that it would on the one hand be data relevant to the field of sociology, and on the other, be useful in making predictions about the movements of the future. Additionally there is the latent function of enabling those oriented to social action (either on behalf of the values espoused by the Movement, or in opposition to those values) to bring a somewhat higher degree of precision to that action, whatever it may be.

Notes

1. Gunnar Myrdal, *An American Dilemma*, v. II, New York, Harper and Brothers, 1944, p. 775.
2. Professor Robin M. Williams Jr. in a lecture for the 10th Anniversary Series of the Albert M. Greenfield Center for Human Relations, Nov. 17, 1960.
3. C. Wendell King, *Social Movements in the United States*, New York, Random House, 1956, pp. 118-119.
4. Theodore Abel, *Why Hitler Came Into Power*, New York, Prentice-Hall, 1938, p. 348.
5. Anthony Wallace, "Revitalization Movements," *American Anthropologist*, 58:265 (1956).
6. Ralph H. Turner and Killian, Lewis M., *Collective Behavior*, Englewood Cliffs, N.J., Prentice-Hall, 1957, p. 308.
7. King, *Op. Cit.*, p. 27.
8. *Ibid.*, p. 86.
9. *Ibid.*, p. 87.
10. Turner and Killian, *Op. Cit.*, pp. 501-502.
11. Herbert Blumer, "Collective Behavior," in Alfred McClung Lee (ed.) *New Outline of the Principles of Sociology*, New York, Barnes and Noble, 1946, pp. 199ff.
12. Turner and Killian, *Op. Cit.*, pp. 308ff.
13. *Ibid.*
14. Wallace, *Op. Cit.*
15. Daniel Webster Wynn, *The NAACP Versus Negro Revolutionary Protest*, New York, Exposition Press, 1955, is a recent example.
16. Such as the work of Cantril, Abel, Davis, Heberle, etc.
17. Such as the work of Mead, Wallace, Worsley, etc.
18. For example, the work of Pirenne, Tawney, Weber, Marx, Turner, and others.
19. An exception is C.L.R. James, *A History of Negro Revolt*, London, 1938.
20. E.V. Stonequist, *The Marginal Man*, 1937, Charles Scribner's Sons.
21. Rudolf Heberle, *Social Movements—An Introduction to Political Sociology*, 1951, N.Y.: Appleton-Century-Crofts.
22. Thomas H. Greer, *American Social Reform Movements*, 1949, N.Y.: Prentice-Hall.
23. Turner and Killian, *Op. Cit.*, p. 309.
24. King, *Op. Cit.*, pp. 39-40.
25. Abram Kardiner et al., *The Mark of Oppression*, 1951, N.Y.: Norton Co.
26. King, *Op. Cit.*, pp. 13, 15.
27. *Ibid.*, p. 15.

28. Erich Fromm, *Escape From Freedom*, 1941; Robert K. Merton, *Social Theory and Social Structure*, Glencoe, Ill., Free Press, 1949, p. 126.
29. George Devereux and Edwin M. Loeb, "Antagonistic Acculturation," *American Sociological Review*, 8:133-147 (April, 1943).
30. Ralph Linton, "Nativistic Movements," *American Anthropologist* 45:232 (1943).
31. Samuel A. Stouffer and other, *The American Soldier: Adjustment During Army Life*, v. I, 1949, Princeton: Princeton University Press.
32. King, *Op. Cit.*, p. 23.
33. Lewis A. Coser, *The Functions of Social Conflict*, Glencoe, Ill., The Free Press, 1956, p. 37.
34. Arnold Rose, *The Negro's Morale: Group Identification and Protest*, Minneapolis, Univ. of Minn. Press, 1949, p. 7.
35. Rose, *Op. Cit.*, p. 4.
36. King, *Op. Cit.*, p. 89.
37. Peter Worsley, *The Trumpet Shall Sound*, London, MacGibbon and Kee, 1957, p. 255.
38. Hortense Powdermaker, "The Channeling of Negro Aggression by the Cultural Process," in Clyde Kluckhohn and Henry A. Murray, *Personality in Nature, Society, and Culture*. New York, Alfred A. Knopf, 1959, p. 598.
39. Leo Kuper, *Passive Resistance in South Africa*, New Haven, Yale Univ. Press, 1957, ch. III.
40. U.S. Commission on Civil Rights, *1961 Report*, Washington, 1961, v. I, *Voting*, pp. 5-6.
41. U.S. Bureau of the Census, *Current Population Reports*, Series F-50 (1957), nos. 66, 86, 89; Series P-60 (1960) no. 33.
42. Ruth Searles and J. Allen Williams Jr., "Negro College Students' Participation in Sit-Ins," *Social Forces*, 40:216 (March, 1962).
43. *Ibid.*, p. 219. A forthcoming dissertation at Harvard University (Dept. of Social Relations) by James H. Laue, dealing primarily with later aspects of the sit-ins and the Freedom Riders, deals with the concept of relative deprivation more extensively. Some other aspects of Mr. Laue's work parallel this one.
44. Howard Zinn, *Albany: A Study in National Responsibility*. Atlanta, Ga., Southern Regional Council, 1962, p. 16.
45. Martin Luther King, Jr., "Hate is always Tragic," in Robert P. Williams, *Negroes With Guns*, N.Y., Marzani and Munsell, Inc., 1962, p. 9.
46. Leslie W. Dunbar, "Reflection on the Latest Reform of the South," *Phylon* 22:251-252 (Fall, 1961).
47. Crane Brinton, *The Anatomy of Revolution*, New York, Vintage Books, 1957, ed., pp. 31-32.
48. E. Franklin Frazier, *Black Bourgeoisie*, 1957.
49. Brailsford Brazeal, *The Brotherhood of Sleeping Car Porters*, 1946; Horace Clayton and George Mitchell, *Black Workers and the New Unions*, 1939; Herbert R. Northrup, *Organized Labor and the Negro*, 1944.
50. The *Report* of the U.S. Civil Rights Commission for 1959 suggested that in Atlanta, as a result of the large Negro vote, "Negro policemen have been hired. Race-baiting groups such as the Klan and the Columbians have been

suppressed. City officials have been more courteous and sensitive to the demands of Negroes. Courtroom decorum has improved . . . a Negro has been elected to membership on the Atlanta Board of Education . . . " (p. 547). The integration of some Negro students into previously all-white Atlanta public schools in September, 1961, without serious incident and under police protection is well-known.

51. Margaret Price, *The Negro and the Ballot in the South*, Atlanta, Southern Regional Council, 1959, p. 11.
52. *Ibid.*, p. 13.
53. Donald J. Rogue, *The Population of the U.S.*, Glencoe, Ill., Free Press, 1959, p. 136.
54. Price, *Op. Cit.*, p. 9.
55. U.S. Commission on Civil Rights, *Report*, 1961. Book 3, "Employment," pp. 45ff. details the historical facet of Armed Forces integration; the further statement is based on personal observation and conversations with Negro servicemen. While very few of the current leaders of the student movement are ex-servicemen, this influence cannot be denied altogether. Of Southern Negro leaders with armed forces background the best-known is probably Robert F. Williams, an ex-Marine, who led Monroe, N.C., Negroes in armed defense against segregationist forces in 1961.
56. U.S. Commission on Civil Rights, *Report*, 1959, pp. 152ff.
57. U.S. Commission on Civil Rights, *Report*, 1961, v. 1, p. 6.
58. John B. Martin, *The Deep South Says Never*, 1957, pp. 1-4, 12, 137, 155.
59. Ira DeA. Reid (ed.), *Racial Desegregation and Integration, Annals*, v. 304 (March, 1956), pp. 44-52.
60. Herbert Garfinkel, *When Negroes March*, 1959.
61. Rayford Logan (ed.), *What the Negro Wants*, 1944, pp. 133-150.
62. Garfinkel, *Op. Cit.*, pp. 82-93, 137-138.
63. Maurice R. Davie, *Negroes in American Society*, 1949, p. 324.
64. Much of this account is based on Martin Luther King, Jr., *Stride Toward Freedom* (1958), which remains the definite statement of nonviolent ideology as it is expounded by its advocates in the Southern Negro Student Movement.
65. M.L. King, *Op. Cit.*, p. 89.
66. M.L. King, *Op. Cit.*, pp. 102-107.
67. Charles U. Smith and Lewis M. Killian, *The Tallahassee Bus Protest*, New York, Anti-Defamation League, 1958.
68. *I.F. Stone's Weekly*, May 27, 1957.
69. Data on the Marches is based on press releases, interviews, and personal observation.
70. Data based on CORE files.
71. Barbara Ann Posey, "Why I Sit-In," *Social Progress*, 51:8-10 (Feb., 1961). As Miss Posey put it, ". . . it was the most exciting trip of my life. Besides seeing New York and meeting all sorts of interesting people, I experienced some of the little things that I realized I had always missed. I ate in cafeterias. I sat in lunch counters with everybody else . . . When I returned to Oklahoma City, I knew that it was time to do something."

Even discounting the public relations aspect of the statement, it is not hard to see how this kind of influence, multiplied by the many acculturative agents suggested in an earlier section, served to help create an awareness of disprivilege, or a sense of the deprivation which prior to her trip may have been a relatively minor part of Miss Posey's life.

72. *The Southern Patriot*, publication of the Southern Conference Educational Fund, New Orleans, La., February, 1960.
73. Bruno Bettelheim, "Individual and Mass Behavior in Extreme Situations," *J. of Abnormal and Social Psych.*, 38:417-452 (Oct., 1943); Erik Erikson, *Identity and the Life Cycle, Psychological Issues* I (1959) Monograph 1, quoted by George R. Lakey, *The Sociological Mechanism of Nonviolent Action*, unpublished M.A. Thesis, University of Pennsylvania, 1962, p. 42.
74. Laue, *Op. Cit.*; Robert K. Merton and Paul F. Lazarsfeld, *Studies in the Scope and Method of "The American Soldier"*, Glencoe, Ill., The Free Press, 1950, pp. 41, 50-51, 61.
75. New York, Philosophical Library, 1954.
76. As quoted in J. Allen Williams' unpublished ms., *The Sit-Down: A Study of a Social Movement in a Southern City*, Chapel Hill, Univ. of North Carolina Institute for Research in Social Science, 1961, on which much of this initial account is based.
77. Confidential informant.
78. Interview with Joseph McNeill, one of the initial four students.
79. Three representatives from City Council including 1 Negro, 3 from the C. of C., and 3 from the Merchants Association.
80. James H. Laue, *The Sit-Ins: A New Decade and a New Generation?* Unpublished thesis, Department of Social Relations, Harvard University, Graduate School, May, 1960, p. 18.
81. Daniel H. Pollitt, "Dime Store Demonstrations: Events and Legal Problems of First Sixty Days," *Duke Law J.* #3 (Summer, 1960), p. 320.
82. *Ibid.*, p. 322.
83. Interview with Conference observer David Fineman, representative of the Philadelphia Civil Rights Coordinating Committee.
84. From NSA's *Proposal for an Emergency National Student Conference* . . .
85. This account is taken from USNSA releases, confidential informants, and an account by Susan Gyarmati in *Venture*, September, 1960.
86. Merrill Proudfoot, *Diary of a Sit-In*, Chapel Hill, U. of N.C. Press, 1962, pp. 185-186.
87. Southern Regional Council, *Report*, *L-20* (October 25, 1960) and *L-22*, (December 9, 1960).
88. *Ibid.*
89. Charles M. Grigg and Lewis M. Killian, "The Bi-Racial Committee as a Response to Racial Tensions in Southern Cities," *Phylon* 23:379-382 (Winter, 1962).
90. Southern Regional Council, *Report* L. 22, p. 4.
91. SCLC New York Office press release, June 27, 1960.

92. *New York Times*, July 2, 1960.
93. Ralph McGill, in his column of December 22, said it was Robert Kennedy, the President's brother.
94. *The Student Voice*, special supplement to SNCC's publication, Election Day, 1960.
95. Frazier, *Op. Cit.*; Wynn, *Op. Cit.*; Warren D. St. James, *The NAACP: A Case Study in Pressure Groups* (1958).
96. See, for specific instances, U.S. Commission on Civil Rights, *Report*, 1961, v. 5, "Justice."
97. Interview with Richard Ramsay, College Secretary who replaced Mr. Heirich.
98. William A. Nolan, *Communism Vs. the Negro* (1951) and Wilson Record, *The Negro and the Communist Party* (1951).
99. Powdermaker, *Op. Cit.*, p. 605.
100. H.M. Blalock, Jr., "A Power Analysis of Racial Discrimination," *Social Forces*, 39:56 (1960).
101. David M. Heer, "The Sentiment of White Supremacy: An Ecological Study," *AJS* 64:592-598 (May 1959).
102. *Ibid.*, p. 592; V.O. Key, Jr., *Southern Politics in State and Nation*, 1950.
103. Heer, *Op. Cit.*, pp. 592-593.
104. Thomas F. Pettigrew, "Desegregation and Its Chance For Success: Northern and Southern Views," *Social Forces* 35:342-343 (May 1957).
105. U.S. Department of Labor, *The Economic Situation of Negroes in the United States*, Bulletin S-3 (rev. 1962), p. 2, table 4.
106. Jacquelyne Johnson Clarke, "Standard Operational Procedures in Tragic Situations," *Phylon*, 22:325 (Winter, 1961).
107. Bureau of the Census, U.S. Dept. of Commerce, *1960 Census of Population*, Final Reports Series PC (1)-A; newspaper and other sources given earlier.
108. Population figures are based on Bureau of the Census, U.S. Department of Commerce, *1960 Census of Population*, Final Reports Series PC (1)-A, for the states concerned.
109. Coser, *Op. Cit.*; Jessie Bernard, "Where is the Modern Sociology of Conflict," *AJS*, 56:11-16 (1950).
110. For example, the work of Pareto, Mosca, Michels, Selznick and others.
111. For example, the work of Robin M. Williams Jr., *The Reduction of Intergroup Tensions* (1947) and various studies in the field of prejudice analysis.
112. For example, the work of K. Lewin, Bales, Borgatta, Hare, Homans, Moreno, Mayo and many others. See especially Kenneth H. Boulding, *Conflict and Defense*, New York, Harper & Bros., 1962.
113. Georg Simmel, *Conflict*, Glencoe, Ill., The Free Press, 1955; Theodore Abel, *Systematic Sociology in Germany*, 1929.
114. Rudolf Heberle, "The Sociology of Georg Simmel: The Forms of Social Interaction," in Harry Elmer Barnes, editor, *An Introduction to the History of Sociology*, Chicago, U. of Chicago Press, 1948, p. 257.
115. Coser, *Op. Cit.*, p. 8.

116. Gordon W. Allport, *The Nature of Prejudice*, New York, Garden City, Doubleday Anchor, 1958, pp. 145ff.

117. Charlotte Devree (ed.), *Justice?* (Excerpts from hearings by Committee of Inquiry into the Administration of Justice in the Freedom Struggle), New York, CORE, 1962, p. 31.

118. Boulding, *Op. Cit.*, p. 145.

119. Coser, *Op. Cit.*, p. 109.

120. Boulding, *Op. Cit.*, p. 312.

121. Boulding, *Op. Cit.*, pp. 25-28.

122. *Ibid.*, p. 323.

123. James Monsonis, "A Movement's Music Sings Out For Freedom Now," *New America*, September 28, 1962.

124. Seaton W. Manning, "Cultural and Value Factors Affecting the Negro's Use of Agency Services," *Social Work*, 5:13 (October, 1960).

125. These figures are derived from Chamber of Commerce releases in 1961.

126. According to a statement by Jones to the author in April, 1961. His testimony appears in Committee on Un-American Activities, U.S. House of Representatives, *Hearing on Communist Training Operations*, Part II, p. 1451, February 2 and 3, 1960. Washington, U.S. Government Printing Office, 1960.

127. Henry Allen Bullock, "Urbanism and Race Relations," in Rupert B. Vance, *The Urban South*, Chapel Hill, U. of N.C. Press, 1954, p. 222.

128. August Meier and David Lewis, "History of the Negro Upper Class in Atlanta, Ga.," *Journal of Negro Education*, (Spring, 1959), pp. 128-139.

129. Atmore T. Simpson, "From Sit-Ins to Sell-Outs," flyer distributed by the "Black Voice of Freedom."

130. Report of Committee "A" on Academic Freedom and Tenure, AAUP *Bulletin*, 46:87-104 (March, 1960).

131. George McMillan, *Racial Violence and Law Enforcement*, Atlanta, Southern Regional Council, 1960, p. 19.

132. Leonard E. Ryan, "Suits in Alabama Stir New Protest," *New York Times*, October 14, 1962.

133. Howard W. Quint, *Profile in Black and White* (1958), pp. 51-54. Washington: Public Affairs Press, 1958.

134. The Southern Regional Council, in a report released September 29, 1961, covering the period from February 1, 1960, until September, 1961, estimates that about 3,600 students and their supporters have been arrested in the course of the movement. Some 70,000 persons are said to have actively participated in behalf of the movement, including persons sitting-in, picketing, marching, and attending mass meetings.

   SRC goes on to state that "Numbers of students and faculty were dismissed, allegedly for sit-in activities . . . At least 141 students and 58 faculty members were thus involved . . ." (p.3).

135. Dorothy Dunbar Bromley and Susan McCabe, "Impact of the 'Sit-In' Movement on Academic Freedom," *Negro Educational Revue*, 12:63-71 (April, 1961).

136. C. Vann Woodward, "The Unreported Crisis in the Southern Colleges," *Harper's Magazine*, October, 1962, pp. 81-89.
137. *Time Magazine*, May 30, 1960, p. 68; *Charlotte Observer*, February 19, 1960; Phila. *Afro-American*, September 13, 1960.
138. Industrial Union Department, AFL-CIO, *Tent City*, n.d.
139. Tom Hayden, *Revolution in Mississippi*, New York, Students for a Democratic Society, January, 1962.
140. Philip Selznick, *The Organizational Weapon*, Glencoe, Ill.; The Free Press, 1960.
141. King, *Op. Cit.*, v.

Bibliography

A. *BOOKS CITED OR CONSULTED*

Abel, Theodore: *Systematic Sociology in Germany.* New York: Columbia University Press, 1929.

Abel, Theodore: *Why Hitler Came Into Power.* New York: Prentice-Hall, Inc., 1938.

Abramovitz, Jack: *Accommodation and Militancy in Negro Life, 1870-1915.* Ph.D Dissertation, Columbia University, 1951.

Allen, James S.: *The Negro Question in the United States.* New York: International Publishers, 1936.

Allport, Gordon W.: *The Nature of Prejudice.* Garden City, N.Y.: Doubleday Anchor, 1958.

Anglin, Robert A.: *A Sociological Analysis of a Pressure Group.* Ph.D Dissertation, Indiana University, 1949.

Aptheker, Herbert: *American Negro Slave Revolts.* New York: Columbia University Press, 1943.

Aptheker, Herbert: *Essays in the History of the American Negro.* New York: International Publishers, 1945.

Aptheker, Herbert: *Negro Slave Revolts in the United States, 1526-1860.* New York: International Publishers, 1939.

Ashmore, Harry S.: *The Negro and the Schools.* Chapel Hill: University of North Carolina Press, 1954.

Bardolph, Richard: *The Negro Vanguard.* New York: Rinehart and Co., 1959.

Barnes, Harry Elmer, and Becker, Howard (eds.): *Contemporary Social Theory.* New York: D. Appleton-Century Co., 1940.

Bogue, Donald: *The Population of the U.S.* Glencoe, Ill.: The Free Press, 1959.

Bondurant, Joan V.: *Conquest of Violence: The Gandhian Philosophy of Conflict.* Princeton: Princeton University Press, 1959.

Bone, Robert: *The Negro Novel in America.* New Haven: Yale University Press, 1958.

Boulding, Kenneth E.: *Conflict and Defense*. New York: Harper and Brothers, 1962.

Brawley, Benjamin: *The Negro in Literature and Art*. New York: Duffield and Co., 1918.

Brazeal, Brailsford: *The Brotherhood of Sleeping Car Porters*. New York: Harper and Brothers, 1946.

Brinton, Crane: *The Anatomy of Revolution*. New York: Vintage Books, rev. ed., 1962.

Brisbane, Robert H., Jr.: *The Rise of Protest Movements Among Negroes Since 1900*. Ph.D. Dissertation, Harvard University, 1949.

Broderick, Francis L.: *W.E.B. DuBois: Negro Leader in A Time of Crisis*. Stanford: Stanford University Press, 1959.

Brown, Sterling A. (ed.): *The Negro Caravan*. New York: Dryden Press, 1941.

Burgess, M. Elaine: *Negro Leadership in A Southern City*. Chapel Hill: University of North Carolina Press, 1960.

Butcher, Margaret Just: *The Negro in American Culture*. New York: Mentor Books, 1957.

Cantrill, Hadley: *The Psychology of Social Movements*. New York: John Wiley and Sons, 1941.

Carroll, Joseph C.: *Slave Insurrection in the United States, 1800-1865*. Boston: Chapman and Grimes, 1938.

Cash, Wilbur J.: *The Mind of the South*. New York: Alfred A. Knopf, 1941.

Cayton, Horace R., and Mitchell, George S.: *Black Workers and the New Unions*. Chapel Hill: University of North Carolina Press, 1939.

Clark, Thomas D.: *The Emerging South*. New York: Oxford University Press, 1961.

Coffin, Joshua: *An Account of Some of the Principal Slave Insurrections in the U.S. and Elsewhere*. New York: American Anti-Slavery Society, 1960.

Coser, Lewis A.: *The Functions of Social Conflict*. Glencoe, Ill.: The Free Press, 1956.

Cronon, Edward D.: *Black Moses*. Madison: University of Wisconsin Press, 1962.

Davie, Maurice R.: *Negroes in American Society*. New York: McGraw-Hill, 1949.

Davis, Jerome: *Contemporary Social Movements*. New York: The Century Co., 1930.

Davis, Robert E.: *The American Negro's Dilemma*. New York: Philosophical Library, 1954.

Davis, W. Allison, and Dollard, John: *Children of Bondage*. Washington: American Council on Education, 1940.

Davis, W. Allison, Gardner, Burleigh B., and Gardner, Mary R.: *Deep South*. Chicago: University of Chicago Press, 1941.

Dawson, Carl A., and Gettys, Warner E.: *An Introduction to Sociology*. New York: Ronald Press, 1935.

Dollard, John: *Caste and Class in A Southern Town*. Garden City, N.Y.: Doubleday and Co., 1957 (3rd ed.).

Drake, St. Clair, and Cayton, Horace R.: *Black Metropolis*. New York: Harcourt, Brace, 1945.

DuBois, William E.B.: *Dusk of Dawn*. New York: Harcourt, Brace, 1940.

Edwards, Lyford P.: *The Natural History of Revolution*. Chicago: University of Chicago Press, 1927.

Fauset, Arthur H.: *Black Gods of the Metropolis*. Philadelphia: University of Pennsylvania Press, 1944.

Franklin, John H.: *From Slavery to Freedom*. New York: Alfred A. Knopf, 1947 and 1957 (rev. ed.).

Frazier, E. Franklin: *Black Bourgeoisie*. New York: Collier Books, (rev. ed.), 1962.

Frazier, E. Franklin: *The Negro Family in the U.S.* New York, Dryden Press, 1948.

Fromm, Erich: *Escape from Freedom*. New York: Farrar and Rinehart, 1941.

Gandhi, Mohandas K.: *An Autobiography*. Boston, Beacon Press, 1957.

Gandhi, Mohandas K.: *Satyagraha*. Ahmedabad, India: Navajivan Publishing House, 1951.

Gandhi, Mohandas K.: *Towards Non-Violent Socialism*. Ahmedabad, India: Navajivan Publishing House, 1951.

Garfinkel, Herbert: *When Negroes March*. Glencoe, Ill.: The Free Press, 1959.

Ginzberg, Eli: *The Negro Potential*. New York: Columbia University Press, 1956.

Goodman, Mary E.: *Race Awareness in Young Children*. Cambridge, Mass.: Addison-Wesley Press, 1952.

Gosnell, Harold F.: *Negro Politicians. The Rise of Negro Politics in Chicago*. Chicago: University of Chicago Press, 1935.

Greer, Thomas: *American Social Reform Movements—Their Pattern Since 1865*. New York: Prentice Hall, 1949.

Gregg, Richard B.: *The Power of Nonviolence*. Nyack, N.Y.: Fellowship Publications (rev. ed.), 1959.

Grimshaw, Allen D.: *A Study in Social Violence: Urban Race Riots in the United States*. Ph.D Dissertation, University of Pennsylvania, 1959.

Guerin, Daniel: *Negroes on the March*. London: New Park Publications, 1956.

Hamell, Janvier L.: *The Hungarian Events of October-November, 1956 and the Revitalization Movement Concept*. M.A. Thesis in Anthropology, University of Pennsylvania, 1960.

Harlan, Louis R.: *Separate and Unequal*. Chapel Hill: University of North Carolina Press, 1958.

Heberle, Rudolf: *Social Movements*. New York: Appleton-Century-Crofts, 1951.

Herskovits, Mellville J.: *The Myth of the Negro Past*. Boston: Beacon Press, 1941 (and 1958 rev. ed.).

Hicks, John D.: *The Populist Revolt*. Minneapolis: University of Minnesota Press, 1931.

Hoffer, Eric: *The True Believer*. New York: New American Library, 1958.

Jack, Robert L.: *History of the National Association for the Advancement of Colored People*. Boston, Mass.: Meador Publishing Co., 1943.

James, Cyril L.R.: *A History of Negro Revolt*. London: Pact Monographs, 1938.

Johnson, Charles S.: *Growing Up in the Black Belt*. Washington, D.C.: American Council on Education, 1941.

Jones, Raymond J.: *A Comparative Study of Religious Cult Behavior Among Negroes with Special Reference to Emotional Group Conditioning Factors*. Washington: Howard University Studies in the Social Sciences, v.2, #2, 1939.

Kardiner, Abram, and Ovesey, Lionel: *The Mark of Oppression*. New York: Norton Co., 1951.

Kennedy, Louise Venable: *The Negro Peasant Turns Cityward*. New York: Columbia University Press, 1930.

Kephart, William: *Racial Factors and Urban Law Enforcement*. Philadelphiaa: University of Philadelphia Press, 1957.

Key, V.O., Jr.: *Southern Politics in State and Nation*. New York: Alfred A. Knopf, 1950.

King, C. Wendell: *Social Movements in the United States*. New York: Random House, 1956.

King, Martin Luther: *Stride Toward Freedom*. New York: Harper and Brothers, 1958.

Kuper, Leo: *Passive Resistance in South Africa*. New Haven: Yale University Press, 1957.

Lakey, George: *The Sociological Mechanisms of Nonviolent Action*. M.A. Thesis in Sociology, University of Pennsylvania, 1962.

Lambert, Richard D.: *Hindu-Moslem Riots*. Ph.D. Dissertation, University of Pennsylvania, 1951.

Lee, Alfred McC., and Humphrey, Norman D.: *Race Riot*. New York: The Dryden Press, 1943.

Lewis, Edward E.: *The Mobility of the Negro*. New York: Columbia University Press, 1931.

Lewis, Hylan: *Blackways of Kent*. Chapel Hill: University of North Carolina Press, 1955.

Locke, Alain: *A Decade of Negro Self-Expression*. Charlottesville, Va.: John F. Slater Fund (Occasional Papers No. 26), 1928.

Locke, Alain: *Negro Art: Past and Present*. Washington, D.C.: Associates in Negro Folk Education, 1936.

Locke, Alain: *The New Negro*. New York: A. and B. Boni, 1925.

Logan, Rayford W. (ed.): *What the Negro Wants*. Chapel Hill: University of North Carolina Press, 1954.

Logan, Rayford W.: *The Negro in American Life and Thought: The Nadir, 1877-1901*. New York: Dial Press, 1954.

Lomax, Louis E.: *The Negro Revolt*. New York: Harper and Brothers, 1962.

McCormick, Thomas C., and Francis, Roy G.: *Methods of Research in the Social Sciences*. New York: Harper and Brothers, 1958.

Martin, John B.: *The Deep South Says Never*. New York: Ballantine Books, 1957.

Mathews, Basil J.: *Booker T. Washington*. Cambridge: Harvard University Press, 1948.

Merton, Robert K.: *Social Theory and Social Structure*. Glencoe, Ill.: The Free Press, 1949.

Merton, Robert K., and Lazarsfeld, Paul F. (eds.): *Studies in the Scope and Methods of "The American Soldier."* Glencoe, Ill.: The Free Press, 1950.

Mitchell, Glenford E., and Peace, William H. III: *The Angry Black South*. New York: Corinth Books, 1962.

Moon, Henry L.: *Balance of Power*. Garden City, N.Y.: Doubleday and Co., 1949.

Myrdal, Gunnar: *An American Dilemma*. New York: Harper and Brothers, 1944.

The Negro Handbook. New York: W. Malliet, 1942, 1946/47, 1949.

Nolan, William A.: *Communism Versus the Negro*. Chicago: Henry Regnery Co., 1951.

Northrup, Herbert R.: *Organized Labor and the Negro*. New York: Harper and Brothers, 1944.

Ottley, Roi: *New World A-Coming*. Boston: Houghton-Mifflin Co., 1943.

Powell, Adam Clayton: *Marching Blacks*. New York: Dial Press, 1945.

President's Committee on Civil Rights. *To Secure These Rights*. Washington: U.S. Government Printing Office, 1947.

Price, Hugh D.: *The Negro and Southern Politics*. New York: New York University Press, 1957.

Proudfoot, Merrill: *Diary of A Sit-In*. Chapel Hill: University of North Carolina Press, 1962.

Quint, Howard: *Profile in Black and White: A Frank Portrait of South Carolina*. Washington: Public Affairs Press, 1958.

Ramsey, Paul: *Christian Ethics and the Sit-In*. New York: Association Press, 1961.

Record, Wilson: *The Negro and the Communist Party*. Chapel Hill: University of North Carolina Press, 1951.

Reddick, Lawrence D.: *Crusader Without Violence*. New York: Harper and Brothers, 1959.

Redding, J. Saunders: *The Lonesome Road*. New York: Doubleday and Co., 1958.

Rose, Arnold: *The Negro's Morale: Group Identification and Protest*. Minneapolis: University of Minnesota Press, 1949.

Rudwick, Elliot M.: *W.E.B. DuBois: A Study in Minority Group Leadership*. Ph.D Dissertation, University of Pennsylvania, 1956.

St. James, Warren D.: *The NAACP: A Case Study in Pressure Groups*. New York: Exposition Press, 1958.

Selznick, Philip: *The Organizational Weapon*. New York: McGraw-Hill, 1952.

Simmel, Georg: *Conflict*. Glencoe, Ill.: Free Press, 1955.

Spero, Sterling D., and Harris, Abraham: *The Black Worker*. New York: Columbia University Press, 1931.

Stonequist, E.V.: *The Marginal Man*. New York: Charles Scribner's Sons, 1937.

Stouffer, S.A., Suchman, E.A., DeVinney, L.C., Star, S.A., and Williams, R.M.: *The American Soldier: Adjustment During Army Life*, (v.1). Princeton: Princeton University Press, 1949.

Thomas, W.I.: *Source Book for Social Origins*. Boston: Gotham Press (6th ed.), 1909.

Thompson, Warren S.: *Population Problems*. New York: McGraw-Hill, 1942.

Tumin, Melvin M.: *Desegregation: Resistance and Readiness*. Princeton: Princeton University Press, 1958.

Turner, Ralph H., and Killian, Lewis M.: *Collective Behavior*. Englewood Cliffs, N.J.: Prentice-Hall, 1957.

U.S. Commission on Civil Rights: *Report*. Washington: U.S. Government Printing Office, 1959.

U.S. Commission on Civil Rights: *Report*. Washington: U.S. Government Printing Office, 1961.

U.S. Department of Commerce, Bureau of the Census: *Current Population Reports*. Washington: U.S. Government Printing Office, 1958, 1959, 1960, 1961.

U.S. Department of Health, Education, and Welfare, Office of Education: *Statistics of Negro Colleges and Universities: 1951-52 and Fall of 1954*. Washington: U.S. Government Printing Office, 1955.

U.S. Department of Labor: *The Economic Situation of Negroes in the United States*, Bulletin S-3 (rev.). Washington: U.S. Government Printing Office, 1962.

U.S. Department of Labor, Bureau of Labor Statistics: *Labor Unionism in American Agriculture* (Bulletin #836). Washington: U.S. Government Printing Office, 1945.

Vance, Rupert B. (ed.): *The Urban South*. Chapel Hill: University of North Carolina Press, 1954.

Wakefield, Dan: *Revolt in the South*. New York: Grove Press, 1960.

Warner, William L., Junker, Buford H., and Adamas, Walter A.: *Color and Human Nature: Negro Personality Development in A Northern City*. Washington: American Council on Education, 1941.

Wehr, Paul E.: *The Sit-Down Protests*. M.A. Thesis, Department of Sociology and Anthropology, University of North Carolina, 1960.

Williams, J. Allen: *The Sit-Down: A Study of A Social Movement in A Southern City.* Chapel Hill: University of North Carolina Institute for Research in Social Sciences, 1961 (unpublished manuscript).

Williams, Robert F.: *Negroes With Guns.* New York: Marzani and Munsell, 1962.

Williams, Robin M., and Ryan, Margaret W. (eds.): *Schools in Transition.* Chapel Hill: University of North Carolina Press, 1954.

Williams, Robin M.: *The Reduction of Intergroup Tensions.* New York: Social Science Research Council (Bulletin #57), 1947.

Wolff, Kurt: *The Sociology of Georg Simmel.* Glencoe, Ill.: The Free Press, 1950.

Woodson, Carter G.: *The History of the Negro Church.* Washington: Associated Publishers (2nd ed.), 1921.

Woodward, C. Vann: *Origins of the New South.* Baton Rouge, La.: Louisiana State University Press, 1951.

Woodward, C. Vann: *The Strange Career of Jim Crow.* New York: Oxford University Press, 1955.

Worsley, Peter: *The Trumpet Shall Sound.* London: MacGibbon and Kee, 1957.

Wynn, Daniel W.: *The NAACP Versus Negro Revolutionary Protest.* New York: Exposition Press, 1955.

B. *ARTICLES AND SHORT WORKS CITED OR CONSULTED*

Adams, Walter A.: The Negro Patient in Psychiatric Treatment, *Am. J. Orthopsychiatry,* 20:305-310, 1950.

Abramowitz, Jack: Agrarian Reformers and the Negro Question, *Negro Hist. Bull.,* 138-139, 1947.

Barth, Ernest A.T., and Abu-Laban, Baha: Power Structure and the Negro Sub-Community, *Am. Sociological Review,* 24:69-76, 1959.

Bernard, Jessie: Where is the Modern Sociology of Conflict? *Am. J. of Sociology,* 56:11-16, 1950.

Bettelheim, Bruno: Individual and Mass Behavior in Extreme Situations, *J. Abnormal and Social Psych.,* 38:417-452, 1943.

Blalock, H.M., Jr.: A Power Analysis of Racial Discrimination, *Social Forces,* 39:53-59, 1960.

Blumer, Herbert: Collective Behavior, in Lee, Alfred McC. (ed.), *New Outline of the Principles of Sociology*. New York: Barnes and Noble, 1946.

Bullock, Henry A.: Urbanism and Race Relations, in Vance, Rupert B. (ed.), *The Urban South*. Chapel Hill: University of North Carolina Press, 1954.

Bunche, Ralph: *An Evaluation of the NAACP*. New York: NAACP (n.d.).

Bunche, Ralph: The Programs of Organizations Devoted to the Improvement of the Status of the American Negro, *J. of Negro Ed.*, 8:539-550, 1939.

Bunche, Ralph: A Critical Analysis of the Tactics and Programs of Minority Groups, *J. of Negro Ed.*, 4:308-320, 1935.

Burgess, J. Stewart: The Study of Modern Social Movements as a Means for Clarifying the Process of Social Action, *Social Forces*, 22:269-275, 1944.

Davis, W. Allison: American Status Systems . . .; and Social Class and Color Differences . . ., in Kluckhohn, Clyde, and Murray, Henry A. (eds.): *Personality in Nature, Society, and Culture*. New York: Alfred A. Knopf, 1959.

Devereaux, George, and Loeb, Edwin M.: Antagonistic Acculturation, *Am. Sociological Rev.*, 8:133-147, 1943.

Dunbar, Leslie W.: Reflection of the Latest Reform of the South, *Phylon*, 22:349-357, 1961.

Grimshaw, Allen D.: Lawlessness and Violence in America and Their Special Manifestations in Changing Negro-White Relationships, *J. Negro Hist.*, 44:52-72.

Hayden, Tom: *Revolution in Mississippi*. New York: Students for a Democratic Society, Jan., 1962.

Heberle, Rudolf: The Sociology of Georg Simmel: The Forms of Social Interaction, in Barnes, Harry Elmer (ed.): *An Introduction to the History of Sociology*. Chicago: University of Chicago Press, 1948.

Heer, David M.: The Sentiment of White Supremacy: An Ecological Study, *Am. J. Sociology*, 54:592-598, 1959.

Hoffman, Edwin D.: The Genesis of the Modern Movement for Equal Rights in South Carolina, *J. Negro Hist.*, 44:346-369, 1959.

Industrial Union Department, AFL-CIO: *Tent City*, Washington, D.C. (n.d., prob. 1961).

Jackson, James B.: Theoretical Aspects of the Negro Question in the U.S., (Supplement) *Political Affairs*, (Feb.) 1959. New York, Communist Party, U.S.A., 1959.

Johnson, Guy B.: Negro Racial Movements and Leadership in the United States, *Am. J. Sociology*, 43:57-71, 1937.

Linton, Ralph: Nativistic Movements, *Am. Anthropologist*, 45:230-240, 1943.

Makdisi, Nadim: The Moslems of America, *Christian Century*, Aug. 26, 1959.

Manning, Seaton W.: Cultural and Value Factors Affecting the Negro's Use of Agency Services, *Social Work*, 5:3-13, 1960.

Meier, August: Boycotts of Segregated Street Cars, 1894-1906: A Research Note, *Phylon*, 18:296-297, 1957.

Meier, August: The Emergence of Negro Nationalism, *Midwest J.*, Part I:96-104, (Winter 1951-52); Part II:95-111, (Summer) 1952.

Meier, August, and Lewis, David: History of the Negro Upper Class in Atlanta, Ga., *J. of Negro Ed.*, 28:128-139, 1959.

Mitchell, George S.: The Negro in Southern Trade Unionism, *Southern Economic J.*, 2:26-33, 1936.

Monahan, Thomas P., and Elizabeth H.: Some Characteristics of American Negro Leaders, *Am. Sociological Rev.*, 21:589-596, 1956.

Morgan, Shubel: The Negro and the Union, in Cochran, Bert (ed.), *American Labor in Midpassage*. New York: Monthly Review Press, 1959.

Ovington, Mary W.: The National Association for the Advancement of Colored People, *J. Negro Hist.*, 9:107-116, 1924.

Pettigrew, Thomas F.: Desegregation and it Chance for Success: Northern and Southern Views, *Social Forces*, 35:339-344, 1957.

Powdermaker, Hortense: The Channeling of Negro Aggression by the Cultural Process, in Kluckhohn and Murray, *Personality in Nature, Society, and Culture* (1959).

Price, Margaret: *The Negro and the Ballot in the South*. Atlanta: Southern Regional Council, 1959.

Price, Margaret: *The Negro Voter in the South*. Atlanta: Southern Regional Council, 1957.

Record, Wilson: The Development of the Communist Position on the Negro Question in the United States, *Phylon*, 19:306-326, 1958.

Record, Wilson: Negro Intellectuals and Negro Movements in Historical Perspective, *Am. Qu.*, 8:3-20, 1956.

Record, Wilson: Social Stratification and Intellectual Roles in the Negro Community, *Brit. J. Sociology*, 235, (Sept.) 1957.

Reddick, Lawrence D.: Critical Review: The Politics of Desegregation, *J. Negro Ed.*, 31:414-420, 1962.

Reddick, Lawrence D.: A New Interpretation for Negro History, *J. Negro Hist.*, 22:17-28, 1937.

Reid, Ira DeA.: Negro Movements and Messiahs, 1900-1949, *Phylon*, 10:362-369, 1949.

Rudwick, Elliot M.: The Niagara Movement, *J. Negro Hist.*, 42:177, 1957.

Segregation and Desegregation. Annals of the American Academy of Political and Social Science, 304 (March) 1956.

Smythe, Hugh H.: Negro Masses and Leaders—An Analysis of Current Trends, *Sociology and Social Research*, 35:31-37, 1950.

Spirer, Jess: Negro Crime, *Comp. Psych. Monographs*, 16, No. 2, 1940.

Standing, T.G.: Nationalism in Negro Leadership, *Am. J. Sociol.*, 40:180-192, 1934.

Stone, I.F.: *I.F. Stone's Weekly*, May 27, 1957.

Vander Zanden, James W.: Accommodation to Undesired Change: The Case of the South, *J. Negro Ed.*, 31:30-35, 1962.

Vander Zanden, James W.: Resistance and Social Movements, *Social Forces*, 37:312-316, 1959.

Wallace, Anthony: Revitalization Movements, *Am. Anthropologist*, 58:264-281, 1956.

Wish, Harvey: American Slave Insurrections Before 1861, *J. Negro Hist.*, 22:299-320, 1937.

C. *ARTICLES AND SHORT WORKS ON THE SOUTHERN STUDENT MOVEMENT*

American Civil Liberties Union: *Annual Reports*, July 1, 1958-June 30, 1959; July 1, 1959-June 30, 1960; July 1, 1960-June 30, 1961. (Nos. 39, 40, and 41).

Baldwin, James: The Dangerous Road before Martin Luther King. *Harper's Magazine*, 33-42, Feb. 1961.

Bodan, Susan: *Miami Interracial Action Institute—Summary and Evaluation.* New York: Congress of Racial Equality, 1960.

Bromley, Dorothy, and McCabe, Susan: Impact of the "Sit-In" Movement on Academic Freedom, *Negro Ed. Rev.*, 12:63-71, 1961.

Clarke, Jacquelyne Johnson: Standard Operational Procedures in Tragic Situations, *Phylon*, 22:318-328, 1961.

Committee "A" on Academic Freedom and Tenure. Report, *AAUP Bull.*, 46:87-104, 1960.

Committee "A" on Academic Freedom and Tenure: Alabama State College, *AAUP Bull.*, 47:303-309, 1961.

Committee on Un-American Activities, U.S. House of Representatives, *Hearings, Communist Training Operations*, Pt. 3, Feb. 5, 1960, pp. 1451-1461.

Constable, John: Negro Student Protests Challenge N.C. Leaders, *New South*, 15:3-10, 1960.

Congress of Racial Equality, *It Can Happen In Missouri*. New York: CORE, n.d.

CORE-lator, Fall 1959-Dec. 1961 (monthly).

Collins, LeRoy: *The South and the Nation*. Atlanta, Ga.: Southern Regional Council, 1960.

Cothran, Tilman C., and Phillips, William, Jr.: Negro Leadership in a Crisis Situation, *Phylon*, 22:107-118, 1961.

The Crusader, November, 1959.

Current, Gloster B.: 51st Annual NAACP Convention—Accent on Youth, *The Crisis*, 67:405-420, 1960.

Devree, Charlotte (ed.): *Justice?* New York: Congress of Racial Equality, 1962.

Florida Council on Human Relations. *The Jacksonville Riot*. Miami, Fla.: FCHR, 1960.

Fuller, Helen. We Are All So Very Happy, *New Republic*, April 25, 1960.

Fuller, Helen. Southern Students Take Over, *New Republic*, May 2, 1960.

Gaither, Thomas: *Jailed-In*. New York: Congress of Racial Equality, 1961.

Golden, Harry: Negroes New Tactics Winning Struggle, *Life*, 24-25, March 14, 1960.

Grigg, Charles M., and Killian, Lewis M.: The Bi-Racial Committee as a Response to Racial Tensions in Southern Cities, *Phylon*, 23:379-382, 1962.

Gyarmati, Susan: N.S.A. Conference on the Sit-In Movement, *Venture*, Sept., 1960.

Hedlund, Joan: Students for Integration, *The Crisis*, 67:345-348, 1960.

Highlander Folk School. *Considerations by Southern White Students of their Roles in the Struggle for Democracy in the South*. Monteagle, Tenn., 1961.

Highlander Folk School, Myles Horton, May Justus and Septima Clark v. State of Tennessee. Assignments of Error, Brief and Argument of Plaintiffs-in-Error (1961).

Hope, John II: The Negro College, Student Protest and the Future, *J. Negro Ed.*, 30:368-376, 1961.

Industrial Union Department, AFL-CIO: *The Civil Rights Fight: A Look at the Legislative Record.* Washington, IUD, 1960.

Jones, Charles: Negro Voting in the South, *New University Thought*, 1:39-47, 1960.

Jones, Lewis, and Smith, Stanley: *Tuskegee, Alabama: Voting Rights and Economic Pressure.* New York: Anti-Defamation League, 1958.

Kahn, Tom: *Unfinished Revolution*, New York: Socialist Party-SDF, 1960.

King, Martin Luther: *Our Struggle.* New York: Congress of Racial Equality, 1956.

Kinkhead, Katharine T.: It Doesn't Seem Quick To Me, *The New Yorker*, April 15, 1961.

Knoxville Area Human Relations Council. *A Chronology of Negotiations Leading to Lunch Counter Desegregation in Knoxville, Tennessee.* Knoxville: Knoxville Area HRC, 1960.

Laue, James H.: *The Sit-Ins: A New Decade and A New Generation?* Cambridge: Harvard University Department of Social Relations, 1960 (unpublished manuscript).

Leonard, George B., Jr.: The Second Battle of Atlanta, *Look*, April 25, 1961.

Life, Sept. 19, 1960, pp. 40-43.

Lomax, Louis R.: The Negro Revolt Against "The Negro Leaders," *Harper's Magazine*, pp. 41-48, 1960.

McMillan, George: *Racial Violence and Law Enforcement.* Atlanta: Southern Regional Council, 1961.

McMillan, George: Sit-Downs: The South's New Time Bomb, *Look*, pp. 21-25, July 5, 1960.

Monsonis, James: A Movement's Music Sings Out for Freedom Now, *New America*, Sept. 28, 1962.

Morland, Kenneth: *Lunch-counter Desegregation in Corpus Christi, Galveston, and San Antonio, Texas.* Atlanta: Southern Regional Council, 1960.

National Association for the Advancement of Colored People. *The Day They Changed Their Minds.* New York: NAACP, 1960.

Nelson, J. Robert: *The Lawson-Vanderbilt Affair: Letters to Dean Nelson.* Privately published, 1960.

Nelson, Stuart: Sit-Ins: Non-Violence in America. *Gandhi Marg.* no date.

New University Thought. Sit-Ins and Pickets. 1:16-27, 1960.

Olds, Victoria M.: Sit-Ins: Social Action to End Segregation, *Social Work,* 6:99-105, 1961.

Patrick, Clarence H.: *Lunch-Counter Desegregation in Winston-Salem, N.C.* Winston-Salem: Good Will Committee, 1960.

Peck, Jim: *Cracking the Color Line.* New York: Congress of Racial Equality, 1960.

Peck, Jim (ed.) *Sit-Ins: The Students Report.* New York: Congress of Racial Equality, 1960.

Phillips, William, Jr.: The Boycott: A Negro Community in Conflict, *Phylon,* 22:24-30, 1961.

Pollitt, Daniel H.: Dime Store Demonstrations: Events and Legal Problems of First Sixty Days, *Duke Law J.,* 1960:316-365, 1960.

Posey, Barbara Ann: Why I Sit-In, *Social Progress,* 52:8-10, 1961.

Price, Margaret: *Toward A Solution of the Sit-In Controversy.* Atlanta: Southern Regional Council, 1960.

Reddick, Lawrence D.: The State vs. The Student, *Dissent,* 7:219-228, 1960.

Rich, Evelyn: Room 400 B—Shoreham Hotel, *Venture,* Sept., 1960.

Searles, Ruth (ed.): The Sit-Down: A Study of A Social Movement. *Research Previews* 7, no. 3, (May) 1960. Chapel Hill, N.C.: University of North Carolina Institute for Research in Social Science.

Searles, Ruth, and William, J. Allen, Jr.: Negro College Students' Participation in Sit-Ins. *Social Forces,* 40:215-220, 1962.

Shannon, William V.: Sitdowns in the South, *New York Post,* March 28-April 3, 1960, incl.

Simpson, Atmore T.: From Sit-Ins to Sell-Outs (flyer), Atlanta: *The Black Voice of Freedom,* 1961.

Smith, Charles U., and Killian, Lewis M.: *Tallahassee, Florida: The Tallahassee Bus Protest.* New York: Anti-Defamation League, 1958.

The Southern Patriot, March, 1960-December, 1960 (monthly).

Southern Regional Council: *The Student Protest Movement.* Winter, 1960. Atlanta: SRC, 1960.

Southern Regional Council: *The Student Protest Movement, A Recapitulation.* Atlanta: SRC, September, 1961.

Southern Regional Council: *The Freedom Ride.* Atlanta: SRC, May, 1961.

The Student Voice. June, 1960-Feb. 1961 (approx. monthly), Atlanta, Ga.

Thompson, Charles H.: Editorial Comment, *J. Negro Ed.*, 29: 107-111, 1960.

United States National Student Association. *A Survey of the Southern Student Sit-In Movement and Nationwide Student Activity*. Philadelphia: USNSA, 1960.

Vander Zanden, James W.: The Nonviolent Resistance Movement Against Segregation, *Am. J. Sociol.*, 68:544-550, 1963.

Walzer, Michael: A Cup of Coffee and A Seat, *Dissent*, 7:111-120, 1960.

Walzer, Michael: The Politics of the New Negro, *Dissent*, 7:235-243, 1960.

Wakefield, Dan: Eye of the Storm. *The Nation*, May 7, 1960.

Westfeldt, Wallace: *Setting a Sit-In*. Nashville: Nashville Community Relations Conference, 1960.

Wilkins, Roy: *The Meaning of the Sit-Ins*. New York: NAACP, 1960.

Woodward, C. Vann: The Unreported Crisis in the Southern Colleges, *Harper's Magazine*, pp. 81-89, October, 1962.

Wright, Marion A.: Doughnuts and Democracy, *The Crisis*, 67:277-286, 1960.

Zinn, Howard: *Albany: A Study in National Responsibility*. Atlanta: Southern Regional Council, 1962.

Index

his book *SNCC*, xv
quoted, 21

TITLES IN THE SERIES

Martin Luther King, Jr.

and the

Civil Rights Movement

DAVID J. GARROW, EDITOR